YOU ARE NOT HERE:

Travels Through Countries that Don't Exist

ERIC CZULEGER

To Savannah, who has the fish.

Home is where I want to be.
But, I guess I'm already there.
-The Talking Heads

COVERING MY TUSH

I understood at the outset of writing this book that talking about unrecognized countries has the potential to make me more enemies than friends. One person's burgeoning nation state is oftentimes another's rogue den of terrorists. That was certainly the case when a group of violent revolutionaries met in secret to start what is now known as the United States of America. Ideology gives way to words, which catalyze action that leads to violence, and eventually another line is drawn on a very crowded map. I'm not here to endorse the existence of any nation over another. I am here to tell you about my experiences exploring some areas of the world which are vying for international recognition.

I lived in unrecognized countries to experience them rather than to dissect them into component parts and give you a dispassionate argument about whether they exist or not. However, names are important. Throughout this book I will refer to each area by the name used by the generally accepted international name. This is done for the sake of clarity and respect to those living in the area.

With this being said, I have used the terms Iraqi Kurdistan, or the Kurdistan Regional Government (KRG), to distinguish this region from the larger Kurdish area which exists between Turkey, Syria, Iraq and Iran. Kosovo is referred to as an independent nation which is separate from Serbia. Furthermore, I've opted to use the name *Transnistria* throughout for ease of further research. For the record, the country is also known as Prednistrovia or the Pridnestrovian Moldavian Republic. Its name is also typically written in Russian, which I do not know how to make my laptop do. Liberland is known as Liberland. Throughout this book I will call the autonomous northern area of Somalia, Somaliland.

Finally, this book is a work of nonfiction. All of the events you are about to read happened to me between July of 2017 and September of 2018. Some supplemental interviews were conducted in 2023 for additional accuracy and clarity. I did not have a tape recorder rolling for an entire year. I documented my adventure through personal journals, photographs, and emails. Some names have been altered, characters combined, and actions condensed for the sake of personal security and brevity. This is a travel book and a memoir. I employ the tools of a journalist, a historian, and a geopolitical analyst from time to time, but at its heart it is my story of getting lost while chasing, what I believe is an important question: What is a country?

I hope this book leads the reader to ask big questions about what it means to be a citizen of their own nation. It has been a privilege to travel to each of these places and know the people who call them home. I am aware that this is not a privilege afforded to everyone, particularly those without the passport, time, or financial means. I hope very much that I used all of these to tell a story which illuminates a bit more of the globe.

Foreword

Big answers to big questions are difficult game to hunt. They require you to go places you've never gone and do things you've never done. This was certainly the case for me in 2017 while I was briefly working as an open-source intelligence analyst. I was less interested in how the world was tearing itself apart through warfare, and more curious about the new ways that it was coming together.

I wanted to know what a country was. How do they come into existence? Why do we fight to the death for them? Is there a middle way to think of our respective nations between abject patriotism and apathetic cynicism? This kind of daydreaming made me a terrible intelligence analyst and an accidental travel writer. I want to summarize what I learned by living stateless for a year of my life. It's only fair to know what you are getting into. So here goes:

Countries are stories. They are illusions that lend necessary structure to the world. They connect our individual identities to something larger, and give us a place on an incomprehensible globe. Like all stories, they are not intrinsically good or bad. Like all stories, you can choose to believe some portion of them to the marrow of your bones, and dismiss other bits as absolute hogwash. Like all stories, they change over time.

We must understand and choose which stories we believe and determine why. By doing this we can see blind nationalism as the fever dream it is. Tales told by our individual nations are the invisible architecture of the world. We should admire the skyscrapers built by our collective ingenuity and dismantle fences installed by fearful ignorance. We are all a part of a singular legend. Lines are meant for maps, not hearts and minds.

PART 1 IRAQI KURDISTAN

HEADS WILL ROLL

I had watched the beheading 20 times and it wasn't even 6am.

I was in my Los Angeles apartment watching beheading videos so my boss wouldn't fire me. I was an intelligence analyst. Well, not really. I was a trainee. If I did well, I would become a full intelligence analyst with a fancy geopolitical forecasting company. But that depended on my ability to find critical information about warfare from publicly available sources. This is called *open source intelligence gathering*. It's like stalking your ex on social media, except your ex is terrorism. Doing this kind of work requires a knowledge of geopolitics, strong writing capabilities, and desensitization to the violence of the world.

The Islamic State video starts with their usual voiceover, except it's in Farsi rather than Arabic. It shows a line of prisoners in military uniforms on their knees in front of jihadists clad in black. The jihadists brandish their knives. Fingers in hair pull back heads. Knives go to throats. The camera pans across the faces until it focuses on one knife and one throat. The edge bites into the neck.

Blood.

I pause the video and look at the uniform of the man with the knife in his throat. It is my job to find out if the soldiers having their heads removed are Shia militiamen. It is not my job to care who the man is, or how he got on the other end of that knife. The soldiers wear the right uniforms, but that doesn't prove anything. I swallow hard and take a deep breath.

I play the video again.

Voiceover.

The knife digs in.

Off with the heads.

During our month of training in Texas, we were told to leave our emotions at the door and look dispassionately at each data point. The less I care, the better I will be at my job. This is difficult while watching people being dismantled. I play the video again. Soldiers. Jihadists. Panning shot. Speeches. Here comes the knife. There go the heads. My boss will chew me out for not knowing who those heads belong to.

I get a protein bar from the stash in my desk and hit play while tearing it open with my teeth. Our daily conference call is coming up, and I have no intelligence to analyze. Maybe the Islamic State is trying to send a message to Tehran, or maybe I just ruined my morning by watching gore videos.

I stare at my wall map.

I love looking at maps. Or at least I did. I used to see inexhaustible wonderment. Now I see a bloody chessboard. I thought being paid to learn about the world would be a dream job. Instead, I spend my time mumbling about the range of various missiles, World War I treaties, and of course, beheadings. I research riots in China, energy infrastructure in Belarus, and a guy exploding for seemingly no reason in Uzbekistan. By doing this work I have learned that I do not like doing this work. I also learned that sometimes people just explode and no one knows why.

I write a brief about the video and connect to the conference call. Cryptic voices sharing data crackle on the line as my eyes drift back to the map: Bhutan, Guyana, The Azores. I think about Mongolian nomads on the Eurasian steppe. I wonder what people are up to in Lichtenstein. I find myself along the coastline of Southern California huddled in a dark apartment watching nightmares.

I miss liking the world.

"Eric, what do you have?" my boss asks over the phone. I read my brief:

"The Islamic State released a video showing the beheadings of three soldiers. The insignia on their uniforms indicates that they are members of the Popular Mobilization Units or Shia Militias. We should care about this video because it has been released in Farsi and could indicate that The Islamic State is attempting to extend its sphere of influence into Iran. We should—"

"Next!" My boss says.

That means that my information is irrelevant. I watched the video for nothing. The next analyst begins speaking. I silence the conference call and open the news. In a couple of months the Kurdish region will be voting on independence from the Republic of Iraq. Attempts at creating a Kurdish state have been ongoing since before World War I. Maybe this time it will succeed. What is it like to see a country being born?

I search: *Jobs in Iraqi Kurdistan.*

I find: *The Kurdistan International School.*

I am fired a month later. Two weeks after that, I have a job in Iraqi Kurdistan and a plane ticket to its capital, Erbil.

I'm going to like the world again.

REALLY AFRAID TO BE HERE

I think that my girlfriend, Savannah, has been kidnapped. It is two in the morning at Erbil International Airport. Her flight arrived an hour before mine. She's nowhere to be seen from where I stand in the passport line. We've been dating for six months. Now, I'm convinced I lost Savannah in Iraq. Well, Iraqi Kurdistan. The line moves forward, and an official in the customs booth gestures for me to approach.

"Purpose of your visit?" asks the man.

"Teaching third grade," I say.

He stamps my passport. I pull up a picture of Savannah on my phone.

"Have you seen this person?" I say, trying to cap the growing desperation in my voice.

"I don't know, too many people here."

The airport is empty except for a woman pushing a mop around the luggage carousel.

"I just need to know if she landed. She was coming in from-"

"Go please sir," says the man in the booth.

The people behind me are getting impatient, and I don't want to seem like exactly what I am: a paranoid American in the Middle East. I go to baggage claim and sweat as the luggage carousel rotates. I am usually sweating for one reason or another, but this time I really mean it.

I am afraid of most things. I am afraid of serial killers, jihadists, and cults of all kinds. I am afraid of brain tumors, the Ebola Virus, AIDS, malaria, and guinea-worms (don't look those up). I am afraid of boredom, and success, and failure. I am afraid of karaoke. Mostly, I am afraid of irrelevance in the face of a world that grows bigger, louder, and more complex every day. This is why I travel. To be a little less afraid of everything.

My big red backpack spits into the luggage carousel. Everything I own weighs less than 30 kilograms. I throw it on and run-walk towards the arrival terminal. The sliding doors creak open. A breath of the desert air blows across my face. Relief replaces terror as I see Savannah smiling and waving. She is the only woman in an airport full of drowsy Iraqis and Kurds. We embrace as best we can, more slapping the sides of each other's backpacks than hugging.

"We're in Kurdistan." She is bright eyed in spite of early morning arrival. "You're sweaty,"

"I thought you were kidnapped," I say.

I look around the terminal, everyone is facing directly away from Savannah as if a glance at her would turn them to stone.

"I think that guy works for your school," she says, pointing to a young Kurdish man holding a sign that says:

Kurdistan International School
Mr. Eric

"Mr. Eric?"

He approaches with a megawatt smile, completely incongruous with the time of day. I nod and shake his hand and confirm that I am Mr. Eric. This is the first time I've been addressed by my new title. I feel that I should give him a sticker. The driver points us to the exit.

"You wait outside. One minute."

Savannah and I walk through the sliding glass doors into a place called Iraq by some, Kurdistan by others, and Iraqi Kurdistan by many more. The desert scrubland contained in the walls of the airport stretches hot and vast in front of us. Hours before sunrise it is over 90 degrees. In the distance the lights of Erbil twinkle and a military helicopter swings circles overhead. I wish I had wider eyes to capture it all.

A school bus pulls in front of us and the glass door folds open. Arabic pop music pours out. Savannah and I climb aboard. The driver slams his foot on the accelerator. We blast off into the early morning twilight. It's hard to remember what I was afraid of...

IT LOOKS LIKE
THE NEWS OUTSIDE

We arrive at my new apartment in the Ankawa neighborhood of Erbil. The rising sun turns the sky a pale indigo. A bleary-eyed Bangladeshi man unlocks the front door and helps us with our bags. He introduces himself as Yusef and gives me a skeptical once-over before taking us up to my new apartment.

Yusef flicks on the fluorescent lights. The apartment is slightly larger than a shoebox. A dusty couch sits next to a twin-sized bed with a single tiny window plugged into the wall. The bed is adorned with a fuzzy, tiger-striped comforter and two pillows wrapped in plastic. Savannah flops on the bed. I look out the window.

The early morning light bathes boxy sandstone buildings a water-color blue. Block after block stretches in front of me with signs written in Arabic, Syriac, and Kurdish. A street the likes of which I have only seen on CNN.

Northern Iraq. Kurdistan. The Kurdistan Regional Government. Whatever you choose to call it depends on your politics and a vote that will be cast a couple of months from now. Now, I live here.

"What does it look like?" Savannah asks.

"It looks like the news," I say.

NEW DUBAI

"The bus is here Mr. Eric."

Yusef calls from the hallway. I stagger down the stairs of the apartment building cursing myself for agreeing to begin training immediately. I am ushered onto another school bus and try out a Kurdish greeting on the driver. He gives me a polite nod and steps on the gas.

We fly through block after block of my new neighborhood. Supermarkets, churches, and liquor stores whizz by.
The streets are packed with stone houses and shops tied
together with a ramshackle latticework of intersecting
power lines. Shop owners spray down the sidewalk to
knock some of the dust out of the hot air, while head-
scarved women sip tea inside air conditioned coffee shops.
Above it all a billboard with a picture of a frosty Budweiser
announces that *Bud is the official Beer of Beer.* It's hard to tell
if this is an odd translation or an Iraqi Kurdistan-specific
targeted marketing campaign. Either way, I could use a
beer.

My new neighborhood, Ankawa, used to be its own
city before becoming a part of Erbil, the capital of Iraqi
Kurdistan. Ankawa is largely Christian Assyrian rather
than Arab or Kurdish Muslim, so crosses dangle from
rearview mirrors in cars, churches are full on Sundays,
and, presumably, they enjoy Budweiser, *the official Beer of
Beer*.

"Kurdistan good?" the driver asks without taking his
eyes off the road.

"Kurdistan good," I say watching the landscape roll by.
He gives me a thumbs up. I give him a thumbs up back. If
only the whole world could communicate like this.

We whip onto Massif Salahaddin Road, a super-
highway that reaches over desert hills towards the Iranian
border. The highway is flanked by communities of prefab
mini mansions with dystopian names like *Atconz, Family
Time,* and *Mass City*. A passing archway announces a new
development called *Future City,* but behind the gates there
are skeletons of buildings frozen in construction. Outside
every compound stands a guy with a machine gun who
looks either too young or too old to protect anyone from
anything.

In the most recent history, Erbil was hailed as a sort of new Dubai. During the US-led Global War on Terror, Iraq descended into sectarian conflict, but the autonomous Kurdish region emerged as a stable island in the middle of Iraq, Iran, and Turkey. The new Iraqi Constitution entitled the Kurds to a healthy chunk of oil profits and the valuable Turkish border crossing. While the rest of the country recovered from the war, billions in foreign investment poured into the region, which goes by the name of the Kurdistan Regional Government, or the KRG.

Aid agencies, construction firms, private security groups, and oil companies moved into Iraqi Kurdistan, betting on a stable and profitable future. Refugees returned from abroad, and Iraqi citizens moved from around the country to ride the wave of capital rolling into the Kurdish majority region. But then the Islamic State ruined the party by trying to start their own country.

In 2014, Islamic State fighters rolled across the border from Syria in a bid to capture Northern Iraq and make a new nation. The Islamic State declared its Caliphate in Mosul, about 45 minutes from where my bus is puttering along through Iraqi Kurdistan. Two nations on the threshold of statehood began duking it out for imaginary lines in a desert full of oil and ideology.

For four years, the US-backed Coalition Forces, along with the Kurdish Peshmerga, the Iraqi Army, and Shia Militias, beat back the Islamic State as they tried to build a country between Syria and Iraq. This scared off foreign businesses, leaving cranes frozen on every horizon. Each unfinished building and dusty scaffolding is a monument to the new Dubai that never materialized. That might change, however, as the KRG attempts to gain its independence a couple of months from now.

That's why I'm here.

Well, also to teach third grade.

DISORIENTATION

"These children have seen their parents tortured and murdered in front of them. How do we deal with this trauma?" Clare from the United States asks.

The orientation room falls silent after her question. The school director, a South African man named Mr. Johann, stands at the front of the room blinking. We were just listening to a lecture about positive reinforcement, namely the issue of high-fives. This is a very important topic for a third grade teacher. Then Clare brought up torture.

"Not many of our students have gone through anything like what you're describing," says Mr. Johann.

Clare scoffs in disbelief. She is a wiry, middle-aged woman wearing a satchel made out of rawhide with a preserved goat's hoof dangling from it. I have been sitting next to her for an hour, during which time she has been muttering about terrorism, just loud enough for me to hear. We have not been properly introduced yet, but I regret sitting next to Clare.

"Excuse me. No. These children have experienced horrifying things at the hands of the Islamic State. Many have seen their villages burned down or they have watched executions."

"What is your question, Clare?" asks Mr. Johann.

"How do we help these children?"

Clare turns to the Lebanese, Jamaican, English, and Syrian teachers gathered in the conference room. All avert their gaze. Personally, I would like to shift gears back to the topic of high-fives. Mr. Eric is a fan of high-fives. We are in a modern lecture hall with a digital whiteboard. Spa music plays on a constant loop in the school's reception area while the marble floor is polished by a team of janitors. The students that attend this school have private security details and legions of nannies. If any children in Iraqi Kurdistan need saving, it's not these children.

"Well, that's a good attitude to have. The children are our number one priority."

Johann moves on, clicking to the next slide of the PowerPoint. Clare goes back to muttering and the session concludes. The school is pro-high fives, in case you were wondering. We are sent to the cafeteria for lunch. I'm trying to make sense of the Iraqi Dinar in my wallet when Clare appears alongside me.

"Another American huh? What brings you to Iraq?" she asks in a conspiratorial whisper.

"Teaching third grade," I say in a reasonable cafeteria-line volume.

"Great. Me too. We'll be in the same department."

"Cool," I say, even though I do not think this is cool.

"Where are you living?"

"The Ankawa building? 6th floor."

She shakes her head and purses her lips.

"That's the worst place to be when the shit hits the fan. Don't worry. I'm working on an escape plan with some Special Forces guys I know in Erbil. Planes, trains and automobiles, you know what I mean?"

I have been in Erbil for less than 24 hours and known Clare for less than 5 minutes. She is planning an escape route with the Special Forces and I haven't unpacked my bags.

"I don't know, Erbil seems pretty safe to me."

"Don't kid yourself. This is one of the most dangerous places in the world. Every intelligence agency on the globe is working here right now." She looks around the middle school cafeteria, grabs a box of juice, and disappears into the recess yard.

TRIBES OF THE SCHOOL BUS

I'm comatose from jet lag on the bus ride home. All the teachers have sorted into groups of languages and nationalities. Lebanese teachers chat quietly in a mixture of Arabic, French, and English with their eyes drooping. Kurdish administrators in jewel-colored headscarves play games on their cellphones, while the Syrian teachers try to nap. Clare bellows her opinions over the rumble of the bus.

"You know what Iraq needs to do?" She sits in front of me talking with an Iraqi guy in his twenties. "They need to have a three-party state, with the Sunni controlling central Iraq, the Shia controlling the South, and the Kurds in the North. That's what Iraq needs to do."

I want to spontaneously combust as my fellow American lectures an Iraqi.

"We'll see what happens in the referendum," he says.

"It's tribalism. That's all it is. That's why Iraq has the problems that it does. It's just tribalism," says Clare.

I have noticed that people who use the word *tribalism* often believe that they're not in a tribe of their own. The whole world is in a tribe, except for their small group of like-minded, sensible, tribeless people who behave similarly. They're not in a tribe, you're in a tribe.

"This is the most dangerous place in the world," Clare says while she scans a passing KFC for enemy snipers.

"No, actually it's quite safe," he replies with a bright smile on his face and a slight English accent. Clare is having none of it.

The bus stops and lets her off at the market. I begrudgingly empathize with her. In the United States we're fed a steady diet of fear, until generalized paranoia feels like abject realism. Less than twenty-four hours earlier, I was convinced that Savannah was held captive by the Islamic State. All tribes worship something; some of my tribe, the American tribe, worship fear. Sometimes, your nationality is as inescapable as your shadow.

I introduce myself to the Iraqi teacher who Clare was haranguing.

"Astefano," he says. He is wearing hipster glasses, an untucked paisley shirt, and red Chuck Taylors.

"Cool name."

"My dad picked it because it was the first martyr that showed up in the Bible," he replies.

"I see you met Clare."

"She's seen too many movies. It's totally safe here."

The bus pulls up to a checkpoint. Soldiers with mirrors on sticks examine the undercarriage of the bus to ensure it's free of bombs. It is. I learn that Astefano moved back to Iraq in 2012 because his grandparents wanted to be in Mosul again.

"They hated it in the UK. Tea sucks in England. I didn't want to go, but Mosul is their home. We had to move back."

When Astefano moved back to Erbil he attended the Kurdistan International School for his last year of high school, a foreigner in his own country. Now he's the science teacher. The bus crosses under an overpass with a banner that says *Vote Yes on the Referendum!* In Kurdish and Arabic.

"Can you vote in the referendum?" I ask. He nods.

"Do you think it's going to work? Making a country?"

He thinks about it and then shrugs. "It's basically a country already."

"What's a country anyway?" I ask.

The question hangs in the air as the bus rumbles down the highway. I realize that it is a dumb question, but just because a question is dumb doesn't mean that it's not important. We all live in countries. The stories of our past are written in the nations our ancestors once called home. Millions upon millions of people have fought and died for their nations, but at this moment, on this bus in Iraqi Kurdistan, I have no idea what the definition of a country is.

"I'll check," Astefano takes out his phone. "Google says: A country is a nation with its own government occupying a particular territory."

"So, the KRG is a country?"

"According to that definition, yes," says Astefano.

Iraqi Kurdistan has a president, control over its territory, a language, shared history, a flag, an educational system, and even pop stars. Yet with all of the trappings of statehood, the KRG still has to petition for its independence from Federal Iraq. Is a country still a country if it's a part of another country? How do you gain independence in an interconnected world? What would it take to start my own country? Turns out, a lot of history is people fighting to answer these questions.

The bus stops at an intersection hung with portraits of the president of the KRG. A person photoshopped into a symbol that contains the highest hopes of a nation.

I rest my head against the window and sleep.

MARTIANS

At the center of Erbil there is an ancient citadel. Savannah and I are going to find it. If you ever find yourself in a foreign country and don't know what to do, I recommend orienting yourself by finding the oldest thing

27

in the city and looking at it. Then find the tallest thing and climb it. Sometimes the tallest thing and the oldest thing are the same thing. By that time you'll be hungry, so I encourage you to eat something unusual. Talk to strangers. Get lost. Get found. Rinse. Repeat. Everything else will work itself out. It doesn't matter if you get where you were going because you're probably already there; you are in the eternal right here and right now.

The sun has dropped behind the horizon, but the temperature still tops one hundred. A dry breeze kicks up while Savannah and I march against the wind, dodging taxis, and picking our way through broken sidewalks. Moving through Ankawa, we are like Martians arriving on Earth. Everything is new, unintelligible, and possibly dangerous. Neon signs light our way into the evening. The smell of shisha, tea, sweat, and diesel perfumes the air. As we pass by shops, people call out, waving us in for tea or just to ask us what we're doing. I can hear Savannah snapping photos while murmuring an astonished *wow* every couple of blocks.

"We're HERE." She wraps an arm around my waist. We stand agog at the streets of Erbil swirling around us like a kaleidoscope of the wild and excellent world.

"Do you hear that?" she asks.

Savannah scrambles across the busy road drawn by thumping bass and the wail of an Arabic song. I pick my way across the street to meet her in a park lit by a green neon sign where families sip tea around a speaker pumping *dabke* music with a techno beat.

"They're playing Omar Souleyman," she says.

A dance moves through her to the delight of the people who start clapping in time with the song. I'm used to Savannah running off to dance with strangers. I'm equally used to those strangers falling in love with her. This is because she glows. It is as if there is too much life inside of her small frame she must share it with everyone or spontaneously combust. I join hands with her and begin dancing.

Savannah and I met at the Last Bookstore in Los Angeles. I was giving a reading from a science fiction book I'd written, and she was one of the few audience members that wasn't a close friend or blood relative. It's hard to draw a crowd to listen to robot stories. When we first spoke I kept wondering *who are you and where have you been hiding in the billions of people on this planet?* The answer to that question was: she was everywhere doing everything.

She graduated high school early and moved herself to Vienna where she learned German and studied opera. She taught herself Russian because she loved the language too much not to sink it deep into her bones. As a child she would submerge herself in a pile of travel books at the local library and she cried on her first trip to Mexico to visit family because *the world didn't look like the books.* She became a photographer. They should have made 10 Savannahs for all the lives she has led and all she's capable of being. Fortunately, they only made one. And the one and only Savannah was in the same city as me for a brief moment while I was a struggling intelligence analyst.

"We've got to go to the citadel," I say, freshly doused in sweat, trying to pull Savannah away from the dance.

"I know, I know," she says, but then the song changes. "Oh man, I can't leave on THIS song."

Savannah knows every song in the world and loves them all. Except Taylor Swift, whom she abhors (sorry Taylor). Any attempt to drag her away from the circle of people dancing will be met with physical violence. For my own safety I stand back. The citadel has been there for a couple thousand years, and it's not going anywhere. We're right here, right now, and I should be dancing.

LAWN CHAIRS

"Let me see."

Savannah takes the camera from me as we stand on a street corner in Ankawa. She's teaching me how to take photos. She flicks the settings of my Cannon and snaps a clear photo of a passing motorcycle. I adjust the camera and try again. I produce a gray smudge. I realize simultaneously that taking quality photos is difficult and everything in the world moves fast.

"I think I'm going to take photos of things that stay still."

"Yeah, do that, you'll get it," she says. I take photos of plastic lawn chairs. Oddly, there are lawn chairs everywhere in Erbil. While French baguettes and Italian Vespas might be the hallmarks of their respective nations, the lawn chair must be the icon of Erbil.

They hide in alleyways. They spill into the street surrounding cafes. They peek from front yards waiting for someone to sit on them deep into dusty nights. They're occupied by old men drinking tea, women watching children play, and teenagers slamming down domino tiles. From what I can tell, when a lawn chair begins to give out, its owner places the failing one on top of a fresh one thus creating a reinforced super lawn chair made from a foundation of broken lawn chairs. This is a place that values sitting and talking.

"Where are you from?"

A guy in his 20s calls to us across a busy intersection. He sits outside of a shisha shop smoking in a circle of his friends, all of whom are riding lawn chairs in various stages of disrepair.

"USA," I yell back across the street.

"You smoke shisha?"

We dash across the street to join our new friend who introduces himself as Mo. A waiter appears with amber colored tea, a centimeter thick layer of sugar resting at the bottom of the tulip-shaped glass. I draw smoke from the hookah and sip the sugary brew.

"What are you doing here?".

"He's teaching third grade. I'm moving to Bulgaria. I'm just visiting," says Savannah.

I'm reminded that in a couple of weeks she'll be off on a Fulbright Scholarship, and I'll be left to drink tea, take pictures of lawn chairs, and see a country get made alone.

"I was living in the UK for six years, but I had to come back," Mo says.

"Why?"

"The referendum. Also, I missed all of this."

Mo gestures to his group of friends, and the shisha, and the side-street busy with motorbikes. The energy of the city is chaotic, but it's also big-hearted and electric. I can see why the well-ordered, well-mannered streets of London might seem lackluster.

"Do you know where the citadel is?" I ask.

"I do. It's really far away. You should take a taxi," he says, puffing on the hose.

"We're trying to see the city," says Savannah.

"You're going to see a lot of it if you walk. Good luck"

I finish my tea, slamming down the residue of melted sugar and leaves settled at the bottom. It is time to move. The distance and the heat mean nothing now. Savannah and I will run to the citadel.

"Just keep going and you'll see it," says Mo. We get up and try to pay for our tea. He makes me put my money back in my pocket. I will come to find out that attempting to pay in the Middle East is an open invitation for hand to hand combat. Generosity must be accepted unless you want a lawn chair broken over your head.

"Welcome to Kurdistan," he says.

WAIT, SO WHAT IS KURDISTAN, AND WHAT'S ERBIL GOT TO DO WITH IT, AND WHAT IS HAPPENING?

I'm glad you asked. I'll give you a couple thousand years of history while we try to find the citadel. There is no one singular, recognized Kurdistan. At least not at this point in history. Erbil is the epicenter of Iraqi Kurdistan, but it represents a small portion of the Kurdish world.

The Kurds are the largest stateless ethnic group in the world, and they are spread across modern day Iran, Syria, Iraq, and Turkey, with global diaspora communities. While here in Erbil, they speak a Kurdish dialect called *Sorani* and live under somewhat democratic institutions, there are other Kurdish dialects, cultural traditions, and political structures.

The Kurds were originally disparate nomadic groups, but they coalesced under Kurdish dynasties that emerged during the Middle Ages. The most famous of these dynasties, the Ayyubid, was led by Saladin the Great. As his name implies, he was pretty good. Specifically, he was pretty good at politics, warfare, diplomacy, and conquest. Saladin famously kicked the crusaders out of Jerusalem, united much of the ancient Islamic world, and became ruler of Egypt before he was 30. If one wants to feel accomplished in life it's best to refrain from comparison to Saladin the Great.

Saladin's Ayyubid Empire was followed by the Ottoman Empire, which spread throughout an impressive chunk of the world from the 1300s to 1918. This included the majority of the Kurdish world. At its height, the Ottoman Empire controlled everywhere from the southern tip of the Red Sea in modern day Yemen, to the Mediterranean, North Africa, and even Crimea. In those days if you were to throw a dart at a globe chances are good that you would hit somewhere in the Ottoman Empire. Also, you probably bought that globe and dart from the Ottoman Empire.

When history isn't heartbreaking, it is often ironic. In the case of the Kurds it's both. Saladin the Great is hailed as a Kurdish hero and a champion of the East who repelled crusaders and helped to unite the Middle East. But centuries later his people found themselves under Ottoman rule, then penned into separate nations when the empire came crashing down. While there is an unbroken band of Kurdish people spread through the Middle East, *Kurdistan* doesn't exist on any map.

Throughout history, the Kurdish people have fought for self-determination and recognition through alliances of convenience, momentary treaties, and violent revolution. The Kurds have found themselves victim to so many broken promises, geopolitical betrayals, and outright extinction campaigns that their common cultural phrase states they *have no friends but the mountains*. This is because the mountains have historically protected their people when surrounded by enemies and fair-weather friends. Still, nothing lasts forever and the churn of history gives humans chances to try and try again.

When the Ottoman Empire came to an end after duking it out with the Austro-Hungarian Empire in World War I, the victorious Western Allied Powers began dividing up the spoils of war in the Middle East. This was largely done by taking a ruler to a map and writing down who got what. Seriously, that's how it was done. Many of the countries that we know today got their shape during this period. For a brief moment towards the end of World War I, there was the possibility of an independent Kurdish state. The Treaty of Sevres in 1920 opened the door for a Kurdish region to vote on its borders, and therefore its future. This failed because the emerging Turkish empire was prepared to battle for better terms with the West.

Turkish leader Kemal Atatürk wasn't ready to settle into confining borders designed by the ruler-waving British and French. He kept fighting the war in Greece until the Treaty of Lausanne came along in 1923. To end the hostilities, Western European leaders were more than happy to trade the land and self-determination of the Kurds, for Turkish withdrawal from the West's darling, Greece. This pushed out Turkish borders and removed any mention of an independent Kurdish region.

At the end of World War I the French walked away with control over the areas of modern day Lebanon and Syria. The English claimed power over the newly created state of Iraq. Turkey emerged as a regional power center between East and West. And a Kurdish state was left unrealized because it didn't benefit the people who were drawing the borders. But the West's maneuvering didn't ·put a stop to the idea of achieving a Kurdish state, it just meant that they would have to continue the fight for recognition.

Kurdish movements attempted to carve out a homeland from inside the freshly minted nation-states in the Middle East. In 1922, the Kingdom of Kurdistan fought for sovereignty in Northern Iraq for only two years before it was snuffed out by British-mandated Iraqi leadership. The Republic of Ararat raised its red, white, and green flag with a shining sun at the center in 1927. It existed with marginal support from the United Kingdom until it was swallowed up by Turkey. The Kurdish Republic of Mahabad in Northwestern Iran lasted for less than a year after being founded in 1941 with the support of the Soviet Union. While all of these flags and borders were lost to history, the desire for a Kurdish land remained, shouting *I am here*, across the centuries.

Now, what we might know as Kurdistan is divided between Turkey, Iran, Syria, and Iraq. Mark Twain once said, 'History doesn't repeat itself, but it always rhymes,' and nowhere is this more true than right here in Erbil in 2017 as another stanza of Kurdish history is being written.

The Islamic State has been beaten back with the help of Kurdish fighters, turning the spotlight of the world towards the question of Kurdish self-determination. With temporary gratitude from the international community, the KRG is attempting to vote itself free of Iraq by referendum. This means there is a glimmer of a chance that a Kurdish state can gain recognition on a globe that has constantly told them that they do not exist. It is a thrilling time to walk through the streets of a place on the edge of history.

VERY DANGEROUS ROADS

"How do we cross this?"

Savannah's face is wrapped in a scarf to block out the dust. She looks like a post-apocalyptic freedom fighter. I am currently sweating through the third shirt of the day. I would like to tell you that this is a record for me. It is not.

"I have no idea," I call back over the din of the traffic.

We have come to an intersection at a highway called the Hundred Meter Road. It was named so because the speed limit is 100 kilometers an hour. This appears to be a suggestion since the off-white sedans rampaging through the street are going much faster than 100 kilometers an hour. Six lanes of metallic chaos roar between us and the other side of the street. Headlights mix with the dust from the road into an uninterrupted laser beam of white light and screaming metal. The traffic cop at the center of the mayhem seems to be entirely ornamental as none of the cars give the slightest indication of slowing.

I wave at the police officer. He waves back. More cars speed by. I think one of us misunderstands their job. My eyes are caked in the grit from the road and the sugar high from the tea has burned out of our system. We have come too far to go back now. We can only move forward.

"Maybe there's a crossing somewhere else," I say, but I'm too late.

"Now!"

Savannah darts into the street.

I chase after her, running full bore towards the other side. A big rig comes rumbling through the highway. We let it pass and then dash across the final three lanes. Huffing and puffing on the curb I take a moment to thank the U.S. for having infrastructure which allows pedestrians to cross the street without having their life flash before their eyes. There are many things that my home country does well. If you are blessed to live in a nation with good infrastructure, hug a stoplight when you get the chance.

"My eyes feel like they're made of dust," says Savannah.

"Mine too."

Then a police car flashes its lights in our direction. Two officers step out and wave us over. I reach into my pocket to check on my passport. It's back in the apartment. I have no idea if what we did was illegal. I have no idea how to say *sorry* in Arabic. We go to the police officers ready to throw ourselves at the mercy of the court. They have a spread of Coca-Cola and kebab sandwiches on their cruiser. Two American jaywalkers clearly ruined their dinner.

"Where are you going?" says one officer.

"Citadel?" I say and the police officer frowns.

"Too far," says the other.

"Which way is the center?" Savannah asks. The officer points down the street.

"Shokran," I say. *Thank you.*

This is one of the few Arabic phrases I know.

"Wait," the officer says.

The police officer then hands us kebabs and warm Cokes. Knowing better than to refuse hospitality in the Middle East, we continue our journey eating police-issued sandwiches.

In the distance, we can see the outline of ancient turrets rising out of the center.

EVERYTHING OLD IS NEW AGAIN

Streets become narrower as they get older. We wind through blind alleys and amble along broken sidewalks. Modern straightaways intersect medieval footpaths dotted with shops and the ever-present smell of tea, shisha, sweat, and diesel. Cats follow us through the dusty neon night, dancing between shadows as we pick our way along uncertain roads.

"No one has any idea where we are right now. It's only us out here," says Savannah. It's true and thrilling to be totally lost to everyone from back home. We stop in front of a mosque outlined in phosphorescent green lights and fall into complete silence. Not because there's nothing to say, just because no words would do it justice. We walk on, dusty, tired, and parched; neither one of us admitting that a taxi would have been a fantastic choice.

Erbil is big because it is ancient. Since the capital of Iraqi Kurdistan first rose out of the desert of Asia Minor it has been demolished, conquered, rebuilt, celebrated, and revered by anyone that happened through this particular part of the world. It's been home to the Assyrians, Seljuk Turks, Greeks, Romans, and Sassanids, to name a few. Both the Mongol Horde and Alexander the Great conquered their way to this nexus of the West, Middle East, and Central Asia. Each army marching their borders across the globe with the belief that one day they could call all of the known world home. Of course, all of them eventually crumbled into ruins as empires tend to do.

It is no accident that Erbil has remained a center of the world for so many. The city sits on a crosshair of valuable trade routes and important waterways. Outside of Erbil, the Zab River flows from Eastern Turkey into the Tigris River. Mountains rise in the distance, but Erbil is located on a flat plane, making it a perfect staging area for business, pleasure, and tea in between. If geography is destiny, then Erbil was meant for the history books.

We turn a corner from a twisting alley and there it is. Rising dark and ominous in front of us is the citadel. The structure is massive, perched atop a craggy mountain of rock and ancient debris. This is because the walls and turrets of the structure are built on thousands of years of things that came before it. Even though gods, languages, and cultures may change, real estate is forever.

"Is that it?" Savannah pulls down her dust-choked face scarf.

"I think so."

"Where's the front?"

"I have no clue."

We work our way around the outside of the citadel, quickly realizing that it is very large. If its purpose is to deter invaders, it is doing a great job. The citadel has stood in one way or another since the city began gathering names. The best guess anyone has is that *Erbil* originally comes from the Ancient Assyrian *Urbillium*, meaning *Four Gods*. The original citadel was a settlement with a temple dedicated to the worship of Ishtar, goddess of love, sex, power, and combat, which proves once and for all that polytheists have more fun.

In the Kurdish language spoken in Iraqi Kurdistan, Erbil is known as *Hawler*. It is common that an Arab will refer to the city as Erbil, while a Kurd will call it *Hawler*. However, at any given point in its history, the city was known as *Arbela*, *Arbaria*, and the impossible to pronounce *Arba'U ilU*. The upcoming referendum on independence will let us know what the city will be called next.

We hear music before the road spits us out into a courtyard lit with glowing multi-colored lights. Fountains mist the dust out of the air, dropping the temperature a couple thousand degrees. We are swallowed up by the Qaysari Bazaar. Hawkers sell everything from Turkish delight and olive oil soap to cell phone covers and knock-off Armani belts. Boys with samovars of tea attached to their backs pour steaming cups for people watching the night unfold. Old men play cards and puff hookah in centuries old tea shops. On the stairs leading up to the citadel, a *saz* player plucks out a sweet and dissonant tune.

We stand between the fountains misting water into the air. A sweet breeze blows across the open square sweeping the music of the *saz* over the ancient turrets and into the night sky. We are sweaty and dusty, but we made it. We made it to wherever we are. We decide to take a taxi back.

I have no idea how to tell the taxi driver where to go. I

39

have no idea where my apartment is. None of that matters for the moment, because we are standing in the middle of an ancient courtyard. We are at the crossroads of every country that ever existed. I decide that while I'm here I'm going to answer the question I asked Astefano:

What is a country?

A DICTATOR ADDRESSES HIS PEOPLE

"Aiham,"
"Here!"
"Anaa,"
"Yes sir!"
"Angela,"
"Present!"

I call roll on my first day of class. The room is full of side parts, pigtails, and gap-toothed smiles. It is indistinguishable from a first day of school in the United States, except for the fact that some of the students were dropped off in bullet-proof cars. Outside my classroom, a Kurdish supervisor prowls the hallways keeping peace and watching my every move to ensure that the Kurdistan International School System is followed. After two weeks of mock lessons, I have become a part of *the system*.

I am *the system*.

I close the register and look at my classroom. If you've never experienced it before, having 35 eight-year-olds stare at you is horrifying. It's like being in front of a firing squad, but instead of firing bullets they fire tears. As a teacher, I am simultaneously responsible for my students and terrified of the mayhem that they can cause. Any small emergency can turn a docile class into a maximum-security prison riot in seconds. The only power a teacher has is to create and maintain the illusion of control.

In this way, being a third grade teacher is a good deal like being the dictator of a small, internally divided, and violent country. A leader creates ironclad rules. They reward adherence and punish rebellion. When a student listens and works they get stars next to their name. When they speak out of turn and hit other kids, their parents get a phone call. A classroom is a government on a small scale, and Mr. Eric is a benevolent despot. I prepare to give my first address as dictator of this new country.

"Hello everyone. My name is Mr. Eric!"

The entire classroom responds:

"HELLO MR. ERIC!"

I look at the seating chart and make a mental note of their reactions. Sara in the back is hiding behind her hands, she'll need some extra encouragement to speak up. Raad in the front row is a screamer. He wants attention. To my left, Meer is distracted by his erasers. Those must be taken.

"Today I'm going to go over the rules, and then we're going to start reading our book. Mr. Eric only has three rules."

A good dictator makes his demands easy to follow. He is quick to reward and slow to punish, for it is better to be loved than to be feared.

"Rule number one is we respect everybody. What is rule number one?" I ask.

"Respect everybody!" The children call back.

"Who can tell me something that is respectful?"

A small hand pops up. Neatly organized desk in the back. Overachiever.

"Yes." I call on a young girl with coke-bottle glasses.

"It's respectful to listen to the teacher."

"Very good!" I come in for a high-five. She swings and connects.

"Rule number two is we are kind to everybody," I dictate. "What is rule number two?"

"We are kind to everybody!" All of the children respond except for Meer, who is busy playing with his erasers.

"Meer! Can you help us all remember what rule number two is?"

He looks shocked that he is still visible to me while playing with his erasers. Mr. Eric is all-knowing; dissent will be crushed.

"What is rule number two?" he says.

"Can we help Meer remember rule number two everybody?"

"We are kind to everybody!"

The class shouts as I remove the offending erasers from his desk. You will not play with your erasers in Mr. Eric's classroom. Only those loyal to Mr. Eric shall have erasers.

"Very good everybody!" I say. "Rule number three is we are safe..."

"We are safe," say the children.

"What is not safe?" I ask this of a shy boy in the back who was not raising his hand.

"If, maybe, we hit another student. That is not safe," he says before ducking behind his hands.

"Good answer. Hitting another student is never safe."

I frown, to demonstrate Mr. Eric's feelings about hitting.

"You get a star."

I take out a marker and put one next to the student's name. He smiles. The supervisor is gone from the window. I sit back down on my desk. Even though Mr. Eric is the leader of the classroom, Mr. Eric is not the leader of the school. Everyone lives under a certain kind of tyranny, even tyrants. Even third grade teachers.

"Can I have everybody take out their books please?"

The children take out their reading books and put them on their desks. They move as one now.

"Today, we are going to start reading Cinderella."

I will become a river to my people. I will become a flood if they dare disrespect my power. Mr. Eric has arrived.

ALL THE DISTANCE IN BETWEEN

Savannah is getting frisked by security guards in a booth at the Erbil International Airport. I'm patted down while a soldier checks the underside of the cab with a mirror on a stick. He waves us on after confirming the cab is bomb-free. We get out at another ring of security and walk through metal detectors. Somehow, I wish this process would take longer so that Savannah and I could spend a couple more moments together before she leaves Iraq. Kurdistan. Iraqi Kurdistan. Wherever we are right now.

"I'll see you in Istanbul next month," she says.

"And then Bulgaria for Christmas," I continue.

This is a plan we've repeated to one another no less than a hundred times since stitching it together over the last couple of weeks. We hope that somehow we will not lose one another in the vast world between Bulgaria and Iraqi Kurdistan. Believing in something makes it exist.

"Go find out what a country is," she says

"You go teach Bulgarian kids how to speak English."

"They're going to speak so much English when I'm done with them," she says.

We hug, my arms unable to reach around her backpack.

"See you in Turkey."
She turns and heads into the airport.

ROOFTOP NETWORKING OPPORTUNITIES

3 ½ weeks to the referendum…

I am at a rooftop party for war correspondents and aid workers. I don't know anyone on this rooftop and it occurs to me that outside of work, I don't know anyone on this continent. I decide to drink until I change that.

11:30 p.m.

I have a paper cup of warm vodka. Enrique Iglesias croons through an ancient PA system. Sunburnt journalists and aid workers greet each other with cheek kisses and big hugs. The party stumbles into a night lit by strands of Christmas lights that twinkle until a power cut knocks the city block into darkness. The music still plays, so no one seems to notice or care. I hear snatches of conversations in English, Arabic, French, Italian, and Sorani. Drunk reporters and oil prospectors mingle while Kurdish fixers spread through the crowd looking for clients to bring to the front line.

I know the Peshmerga at the border.

If you want to go to Mosul it's not a problem.

You need someone with a connection to Asayish?
(Kurdish secret police)

I sip my vodka and eavesdrop. It reminds me of a Los Angeles party where everyone knows everyone and they're all far more important than you. People speak in acronyms and move on quickly when they realize there is no money to be made out of a conversation. Everyone has enough friends, but nobody has enough business.

I know someone who works for the DOD, I can connect you.

Oxfam is hiring someone right now.

I work in M and E for a WaSH program with UNHCR, but I think I might go over to IRC. How about you?

I've come 7,000 miles to a networking event.

12:10 a.m.

Someone cranks the volume on the sound system. Top 40 hits, sprinkled in between Middle Eastern house music, pump out of the speakers. People straddle the rooftop with bottles of wine in both hands and cigarettes hanging off of their lips. I slip into a group of aid workers. A French film-maker is lamenting that the parties used to be crazier back in 2014 when the Islamic State was still gaining ground.

"Those parties were great. I miss those parties," I hear her say as she lights a cigarette.

"The night is still early," replies an Italian aid worker. He turns to me. "What do you do here?"

"I'm a third grade teacher," I say.

"You mean an American spy?" says the French lady.

I chuckle. They do not. I sip my drink. I'm not sure if I should deny being a spy. That's probably what a spy would do.

. . .

2:00 a.m.

I take a shot with two security contractors from the UK. They haven't said they are security contractors, but the fact that they are both covered in tattoos and built like refrigerators made of muscle is a clear indicator.

While listening to two soldiers talk about their jobs, I limit my responses to single words. *Huh. Whoa. Interesting.* Pretending to know anything about their point of view would be like expecting them to understand the importance of handwriting books to my students. Different strokes.

They live near me in Ankawa. One is a sniper and the other disarms bombs. They commute to the active war zone in Mosul every day.

They carpool.

The demolitions guy tells me that the Islamic State loves to leave backpacks full of plastic explosives in grammar schools as they retreat from the city. The sniper watches his back while he disarms the bombs so that the children of Mosul can come back to school when this is all a strange memory.

The sniper tells me that he liked his previous work in Afghanistan because everyone he knows in his Welsh hometown has a heroin problem. When he killed opium farmers he felt like he was taking the needle out of the arm of one of his neighbors. Somehow, all stories are connected.

The soldiers put in their eight-hour workday, turn around and carpool home. They tell me that the money is good, too good to turn down. They tell me that after they finished their service in the British military it was hard to go back to normal life. They tell me that they love what they do.

"Huh," I say.

"Whoa," I say.

"Interesting," I say.

2:45 a.m.

"I love Fox News!" Bawar yells at me over the music. "They paid me $900 a day to bring their journalists to the front line. $900 cash!" Bawar is a pudgy Iranian Kurd in his mid-twenties. He speaks English with an Irish accent from his time in Dublin. He drapes his arm across my shoulder and pours me some more vodka. It's clear that Bawar thinks that I am a freelance journalist with the money for a fixer.

"I get CNN, MSNBC and Fox News because I market myself." He takes out his phone and opens his website. It shows a professional headshot and a list of the news outlets he has worked with. If I'm being pitched, it's working. At least it would be if I had any money.

"Who are you working for?" he asks.

"I work for the Kurdistan International School!" I yell over the music too. "I teach third grade."

He looks confused for a second, mutters *sorry* and walks away. It's just like a Los Angeles party. I see Bawar opening his website up for a journalist on the other side of the rooftop.

"I love Fox News!" he says.

3:00 a.m.

I am sitting on the ledge of the roof. The city glitters behind a veil of dust. Frozen cranes and skeletons of skyscrapers. Oil derricks sit dormant. Bulldozers and back-hoes left with loads of bricks to be laid. It's as if the city is holding its breath. People prefer to talk about the war at the party because the war is ending and the Kurds helped win it. When Kurds talk about the referendum they mention it in hushed tones with cautious optimism, as if wanting independence too badly will stop it from happening

The electricity cuts out. The song changes.

The whole roof cheers when a Yemeni hip-hop song comes on. Europeans, Americans, Kurds, Arabs, and everyone in between form a circle and dance, whistling, clapping, and shouting. I put down my vodka and link pinkies with a Kurdish fixer on one side and an aid worker on the other.

We dance to the music on the darkened roof.

OLD GUYS AND SEEDS

Two weeks to the referendum

My bank account is dwindling and the school won't pay me for another week. After I finish grading papers, I walk around and look at stuff. I recommend that you try this when low on funds. There's always stuff to look at and it's free.

I walk the dusty boulevard towards the center of Ankawa. The roasted smell of *baklava* and *knafeh* rolls out of sweet shops as bakers wheel trays onto the streets. Radiant gold chains glow in the windows of jewelry stores. The guys at the Shisha bar paint a Kurdish flag on the wall of their shop to ensure that it is on the right side of history.

The market road pours me out into a place called *Darga,* Kurdish for *doorway.* It's a roundabout surrounded by snack shops and bubbling samovars of tea. Motorbikes and trucks rumble around the circle leaving only a vague sense of which way traffic is supposed to go. *Darga* is like a battery pulsing life to every streetlight in Ankawa. Since the Islamic State moved into Mosul, Christians were driven out of the surrounding Assyrian villages and the population of Darga exploded. This filled the center with stores, cars, and new lawn chairs. Everyone waits for the fighting to die down so they can rebuild their homes.

"Want some tea?"

A bald, middle aged guy calls out to me. I turn to see a group of old men clustered around a large bag of sunflower seeds. The answer to this question is always yes. As I approach, two of the old men jump up placing hands on their hearts and pushing lawn chairs towards me. I place my hand over my heart and shake my head. We circle the seat in a polite mixture of musical chairs and Russian Roulette everyone shaking their heads and pantomiming:

No, you take the chair.

No, YOU take the chair.

Nobody takes the chair.

"Just sit down. They're not going to let you stand," says the man who called me over.

I sit.

Tea and more chairs appear. Everyone resumes their position and continues eating without giving me a second thought. I take a couple of seeds out of the bag. I notice that we're in front of a shop that sells colorful birds. We eat seeds, the birds eat seeds. I want to comment on how we're all eating seeds, but I don't speak Arabic, Kurdish, or bird.

The man's name is Ian. He's a Kurdish security guard for a local NGO. He's originally from Dohuk, a big city on the border between Turkey and Iraqi Kurdistan. There, billions of dollars in trade flow from Turkey into Iraq. While federal Iraq and Turkey don't like the idea of an independent Kurdistan, the region has grown wealthy by facilitating trade. In the '90s, when Saddam Hussein waged his extinction on the Kurds of Northern Iraq, refugees flocked to the Turkish border outside of Dohuk. Eventually, the United States instituted a no-fly zone and began offering aid to the Kurds during Operation Provide Comfort. This had the effect of giving the Kurdish region de facto defense and the makings of a viable economy. Atrocity sowed the seeds of the burgeoning nation state. I ask Ian how he ended up in front of this bird shop in Darga.

"I was in the Iraqi army for a while. I was good at English, so I became like a translator for the Americans in Baghdad. But at the time in the war they started killing translators. I have a wife and two daughters. I'm not going to get myself killed over this," says Ian, ash growing long on his cigarette.

"My friend, he is working as a driver here in Erbil. He asks me if I want to learn how to do security, like, you know, car security. Driving. Sounds good. Now, I work with some Norwegian aid people. We go out with the cars and help refugees. Bring them where they need to go."

Ian pulls out his phone and shows me a picture of his two girls. Pigtails, and big smiles, they might as well be my students.

"My daughters. They speak English better than I do. I bought them a cable box. English TV. Cartoons."

Ian opens YouTube on his phone.

"They love this one." he says, playing a video of the children's show *Peppa Pig. Peppa Pig Meets Mr. Hedgehog.*

"This is our international school."

We watch *Peppa Pig* sitting in our lawn chairs for a moment. Ian's daughters in Iraqi Kurdistan will grow up watching the same cartoons as kids in the United States, Europe, and all over the world.

We watch Peppa Pig. We drink our tea. We eat our seeds. The birds chirp

VOTE YES

One week before the referendum...

The flags appear overnight on Massif Salahaddin Road. I've been teaching at the Kurdistan International School for one month and every bus ride has been the same until this one. A rustle of chatter goes through the teachers as they notice the flags.

They are brand new, with creases still visible from where they were folded. It's hard to imagine the manpower it would take to place thousands of flags along the central divider of a superhighway in a single evening, but there they are, flapping in the breeze and letting everyone know that the referendum is in one week.

The short story of the referendum is this: Kurdish president Masoud Barzani wants Iraqi Kurdistan to be independent from the Republic of Iraq. But he also wants to take the oil-producing region of Kirkuk with him. This would make an independent Kurdistan a wealthy and fairly powerful state. The problem is that none of its international partners or regional neighbors wants Iraqi Kurdistan to become independent.

Turkish, Iranian, Syrian, and Iraqi governments have all condemned the referendum for their own reasons. Turkey believes a Kurdish state will encourage the Kurdish Workers Party (PKK) to fight harder for independence from Turkey. Iraq doesn't want to give up the valuable oil or trade routes contained within Kurdish territory. Iran doesn't like the idea of a Kurdish state loyal to the U.S. along its Northwestern border. In spite of repeated condemnation, threats of civil war, and UN negotiations,

Iraqi Kurdistan is moving forward with the vote, someone worked really hard to put all these flags up.

Astefano sits next to me on the bus playing a game on his cellphone while I look out at the waving flags of an independent Kurdistan. When I ask him what he thinks will happen. He does the mental math around the election like he's sizing up a World Cup matchup.

"Erbil and Dohuk will definitely vote yes. They're Barzani territory. Sulaymaniyah is a big city near Iran. I don't know if they'll vote yes."

"Do you think there will be any violence?" I ask.

"Man, It's Iraq. So maybe."

While I was a trainee intelligence analyst, I learned that the most important question in geopolitics is not *will they?* But *can they?* Will they vote yes on the creation of a Kurdish state? Probably. Can they create a Kurdish state? Not without international backing, air power, bloodshed, supply lines through hostile countries, and most importantly, of course, money. Is Iraq ready to give up revenue from the oil contracts in the KRG? Is Turkey willing to trade with a Kurdish country while suppressing their Kurdish minority? Can they make a state if no one wants them to? I have no idea. I'm a third-grade teacher.

Unfinished buildings draped in Kurdish flags line the road as the bus crawls towards school. Smeared across every banner and painted on every underpass is the same phrase.

"Vote yes!"

Vote yes on the referendum.

Vote yes on creating a Kurdish state, because this country has borne genocides at the hands of its regional neighbors and been used as pawn by international superpowers. *Vote yes* because of the smiling child on this poster. *Vote yes* because of the Anfal Campaign where Saddam

Hussein eradicated 100,000 Kurds with gas and helicopters. *Vote yes,* because when the United States enforced a no-fly zone over Kurdish territory, Saddam sent tanks, since tanks don't fly. *Vote yes* because the United Nations is more than happy to reduce Kurdistan into a geopolitical word problem, rather than a country of five million people hoping to determine their own future with a word.

Yes. Vote, yes.

How could you vote no?

FISHING FOR JOURNALISTS

Three days before the referendum...

I pass through the metal detectors at the Ankawa Royal Hotel. The security guards check my backpack for weapons and send me through. I order tea from the waiter because I cannot afford a beer at the opulent Western hotel. On the border of every conflict zone is a hotel exactly like this one expensive but safe. When foreign dignitaries, aid workers, or journalists come to the KRG they foot the hefty price tag for additional security, imported beers, and, in the case of the Ankawa Royal, a weekly seafood buffet.

I grab a table on the patio, open my laptop, plug earphones in, and pretend that I am busy. Really, I am waiting until I hear someone speaking English because I'm fishing for journalists. With the vote two days away, I want to tag along with a crew of reporters who are covering the event. I don't have the backing of a newspaper or any contacts, so I'm trying to use someone else's. I don't know if this makes me into a horrible writer or a brilliant one.

In front of me a table of Arab businessmen smoke cigarettes and drink tea. Behind me, waiters buff smudges out of glasses. Next to me, two middle-aged guys sip

German beers, which means they have money to spend. Their dust-free boots tell me they probably just arrived before the vote which means they're likely journalists. One is tall and blonde, and the other has a slight frame and dark hair. I pretend to be deeply engrossed in my laptop while straining my ears to hear what they are saying.

They are speaking English but I can't place their accents. French and German maybe. I overhear one of them asking for the WiFi code. The waiter gives it to them on a small card, and I decide that it's time to make some new friends.

"Excuse me. Do you know the wireless code here?" I ask them.

"Sure," says the blond guy as he passes along the card the waiter handed to him.

"Thanks. What brings you to Erbil?"

"We're working on a documentary," says the other guy. *Journalists you say? How interesting.*

"Why are you here?"

"I got a job as a third-grade teacher here because I'm trying to figure out what a country is."

Both of them nod and sip their beers as if what I just said was perfectly reasonable.

"Want to join us?"

INTRODUCING LIBERLAND

I am now drinking a German beer with Roel the blonde guy, and Marcel, his skinny, dark-haired friend. They are Dutch filmmakers who filmed in Syria at the beginning of the war, Louisiana during the hurricane, and Washington during the elections.

"Were you ever in Aleppo?" asks Roel as if inquiring about whether I'd seen The Grand Canyon.

"No, I've never been to Syria," I say, as if wanting to finally make that trip to The Grand Canyon.

"We're going to Kirkuk after the vote if you want to come," offers Marcel.

I wish I could go to the disputed territory between Federal Iraq and the KRG, but my kids need to catch up on their handwriting books and I have a spelling test to mark. I tell them none of this. Instead I say:

"I can't make it then, but would it be okay if I linked up with you for the rallies?" I ask.

Roel and Marcel say something in Dutch to one another. They both nod.

"No problem."

Roel stands up to pay the bill. I reach for my wallet but he waves me away. Dutch journalists. Great people. They give me their cards and turn to head up to their hotel rooms. Before he leaves Marcel turns to me and says:

"If you're interested in other countries that don't exist, you should check out Liberland. I did a documentary about them. It's a new country on an island in the Danube River. I can give you the president's contact information if you want."

I've never been offered the details of a head of state before, so I accept. He writes *Vit Jedlicka, President of Liberland*, on a piece of paper and slides it over to me and I jam it in my pocket.

Only one day to go before the referendum.

THE TALLEST PERSON IN THE ROOM

2 days before the referendum...

My students return sweaty and red-faced from recess. They get a long weekend for the vote and they're on the verge of pandemonium. They yammer about video games and YouTube stars. They scream for no reason. They tug on my pant leg as I write on the board, telling me that someone hurt them. Throughout my reign as third-grade dictator I have realized that my students look at me as an authority figure because I am taller than them, and therefore, in charge. I participate in the charade because someone has to be in charge.

The kids fight. They form alliances, they make deals, they break truces, they stab each other in the back and save one another from ruin. Ibrahim wept every day because he was forced to sit next to his sworn enemy, Mahmoud. Soon, Ibrahim realized that Mahmoud could draw *Dragon Ball Z* characters. Mahmoud discovered that Ibrahim loved *Minecraft* as much as he did. A new alliance formed from a common goal: ignoring Mr. Eric entirely. Third grade is the United Nations without the suits and salaries.

It's the last class before a long weekend. We won't get anything done today. Helen stomps to her desk crying and pressing her hand to an angry black welt under her eye. I drop my dry-erase marker and guide her out of the room. One crying child can turn into thirty crying children in a heartbeat. It's important to isolate the source of the tears before they spread.

I hear Helen's story through heaving sobs. Hawar was taking off his backpack. A bungee cord hanging off of it snagged on a table and whipped her under the eye. It was an accident, but it still hurt. Once she stops crying I examine the wound. It's not bad, but she was scared. I ask Hawar to come into the hallway.

Hawar apologizes to Helen, and goes back to his desk.

Helen goes to the nurse.

Mr. Eric takes a brief moment of blessed silence in the hallway before re-entering the classroom.

"We have to say we're sorry if we hurt someone. Even

if it was an accident." I say this to the whole class. They say it back to me. I use the word *we* because no one is above the law, even tall foreign people who become teachers. The second bell rings and I have two empty chairs. I go to investigate as more chaos arrives.

Siva comes storming down the hall, tears of rage spilling out of his eyes. I stop him before he gets into the classroom because one angry student can turn into 30 angry students. Mohammed runs up behind Siva to get in front of the lies that Siva is probably telling Mr. Eric. Mohammed's face is bruised and also streaked with tears. The boys begin yelling and crying at one another. I separate the children. *Mohammed please go stand on that side of the hallway. Siva, stay here and talk to me.* I tell him that I just want to know what happened. His small chest heaves.

Mohammed allegedly told the class that Siva liked a girl. Siva reportedly said *fuck you* to Mohammed. Mohammed and Siva came to blows because their egos were too damaged to discount words as just words. The boys swung fists and lunch boxes. They kicked and bloodied one another. They fought under the stairs while some students watched, some went to tell teachers, and others were too absorbed in the thought of the long weekend to care. This is how conflict works in the world. This is how conflict really works.

The boys point fingers. They say *he did it. He did it.* Crying, scraped, and bleeding, they learned the valuable lesson that violence humiliates us all.

I am losing ten minutes of class time.

> *Yes, I did say he liked a girl.*
> *Yes, I did say fuck you.*
> *Yes, I punched him.*
> *Yes, I kicked him.*

I can't do much. I've got 30 other students who haven't beaten the snot out of one another. I have to be the tallest person in class for them too. I punish both of the boys for fighting. No lunch recess. Same rules for everyone. I tell them to wash their faces and come back to class when they are ready.

Meanwhile, Helen has returned from the nurse with a frozen water bottle on her eye. I reenter the class and tell my students to take out their books. The kids are too keyed up on the fighting to focus on spelling and sentence structure, but we might as well look at our books to say we did. Hassan does not get his book. I ask him why with my patience fraying. It is three days before the referendum and no one in the entire school can sit still and focus on their work. The patience of the country is fraying.

"Mr. Eric, I can't get my book because I can't stand up," says Hassan.

"Why can't you stand up Hassan?"

"I'm tied to my chair," he says.

I walk to the back of the classroom to inspect how Hassan became tied to his chair. His shoelace is stuck in his desk and it's wrapped around his foot in a way that makes it impossible to remove the offending shoe. I pull at the shoelace. It does not give. I give it another pull. Nothing. The shoelace will have to be cut. Hassan is right, he cannot stand up. He is tied to his chair.

He will have to wait until the supervisor can bring scissors and free him from his chair. Until then, the class must go on with two children bruised and bleeding, one with a frozen water bottle pressed to her eye, and another tied to his chair. The class has to move on because the class is more important than any one student.

Iraqi Kurdistan is voting in three days. There has been talk of economic sanctions and civil war. Five days ago,

Turkish forces bombed Northern Kurdistan for the first time in two years. The Iraqi army is beginning to crackdown on border checkpoints. Iran has shuttered their border. Military helicopters are flying over the desert. Russia has just cut a deal for Kurdish oil. The United States is sitting back and watching it all play out.

We will soon find out who the tallest person in the room is.

"Everyone open your books please," I say.

LIKE A DOG CHASING CARS

One day before the referendum.

I can't get ahold of the Dutch guys, so I decide to chase cars. It is the day before the referendum. Erbil is made of noise. Celebrations pour onto every block. Streamers of red, white, green, and gold fly from every vehicle. SUVs speed past blaring their horns. Teenagers hang out of windows with flags tied around their faces. Two fingers in the air. V for victory. Erbil is electric in a way that makes me wonder if this is what it feels like when history is happening. Somewhere in the city the President of Iraqi Kurdistan is speaking to thousands. I run after anything that looks like it might be going to the party.

A Star of David whipping on a sedan catches my eye. I snap a picture. Israel claimed support of Kurdish independence months before, and homemade Israeli flags have been popping up around the city. Maybe Israel believes in the cause of a free and independent Kurdistan. Maybe they just want to put a thumb in the eye of Iran. Regardless, the population of Iraqi Kurdistan needs international friends to help draw their line on the map, and their biggest ally is missing in action. Days before, a U.S. delegation flew into Erbil to try and stop the vote.

An SUV pulls past me and into a parking lot. I follow it inside. After chasing cars for most of the morning I do this mostly out of habit. I'm met with a gathering of old Kurdish men dressed in traditional clothes. Baggy gray pants, starched jackets, worn with a headscarf and a wide cloth belt. I don't know if I am allowed here, so I just look dumb and lost. This is easy because I am. A guy in his early twenties wearing traditional dress steps out of the car that I've been chasing.

"Journalist?" he asks.

"Kind of," I respond.

"Where are you from?" The guy speaks American-accented English with a surprising southern twang. He extends his hand to me.

"The U.S.," I say, shaking his hand.

"We love America around here. Thank you!"

"I love Kurdistan," I say. It feels strange to say *you're welcome* when I am thanked for being born in my country.

"Hold on, I'll tell everyone you're here."

I don't know who everyone is, but my new Kurdish friend goes to a group of old men. *Ameriki* I hear him say. The old men look in my direction. They scowl at me and give me a round of thumbs-ups. I scowl at them and a thumbs-up. They nod. I nod. We have established diplomatic ties.

"Come over here! They want you to take a picture."

I do as I am told. Twenty men gather around in a half circle and allow me to snap a photo. They clutch fists and look into my camera with steely resolve. Their shoulders are draped with patriotic scarves. They look like they've been through a century of fighting for Kurdish independence. I chased the right car.

"Come on. We have got to go," says my new Kurdish friend.

"Where are we going?"
"To see Barzani speak."

NOTHING COULD POSSIBLY GO WRONG

"Here you go," Arez says.

He puts a scarf with the green, white, gold, and red colors of the KRG flag around my neck. I feel any impartiality I once had melting away. I wanted to be non-political while in Kurdistan, but I am realizing that being a fly on the wall is political because I chose to be a fly on this particular wall.

Real politics don't happen in voting booths or at debates. Real politics happen at the market, picking up a couple extra bags of rice because the price of food is going up. Real politics happens when you can't sleep because you're angry at people in charge, but you need to get to sleep because you have work tomorrow. Real politics happen when you put on a scarf or a hat or a button. Real politics happen when you choose to not wear a scarf or a hat or a button. I keep the scarf.

We walk onto the street and join the river of people traveling towards the stadium.

"I was living in Tennessee. Nashville," he says. "I grew up there for the most part, but my family moved us back here so that I could go to Kurdish university."

"Did you like Nashville?" I ask.

"Nashville is like Erbil. Kurds everywhere."

Looking up and down the dusty boulevard filled with cheering people holding flags, I find it hard to believe that Erbil is just like Nashville. Then again, I've never been to Nashville.

A cheer ripples through the crowd

"I study farming out here, industrial soil science."

"Cool," I say.

"There's really good land here and my professor says that they're going to need people that know how to farm it when we become independent."

Arez says *when we become independent* as if it's a foregone conclusion.

"Do you think it's going to happen?" I ask.

"Everyone I know is voting to leave Iraq."

I'm being carried along in a river of humanity that stretches as far as my eye can see in any direction. If you and everyone you know decide to start a country, what's to stop you? What is a country? I try to ask Arez but he doesn't hear me as we come up against a clot of people singing patriotic songs.

"Come on, let's get around this group."

Arez grabs my hand and pulls me through the crowd, the question forgotten somewhere behind us. We run around the group of singers and turn a corner to find ourselves in front of the Franso Hariri Stadium. It is being swarmed by people from all directions.

The crowd pushes and pulls. It is a deluge of humanity and noise. Plastic horns blast, people scream, and sing, and chant. I'm no longer moving with the crowd, I am a part of it. My boots barely touch the ground as I'm pulled through the muck of discarded cigarette butts, plastic water bottles, exploded firecrackers, and half-eaten pastries collecting on the ground.

I look up at the walls of the stadium and see soldiers. They grip the stocks of their rifles with fingers on triggers. What if something happens? What if a bomb goes off? What if there is an attack? What will these soldiers do? In a crowd like this it would be so easy to take the lives of hundreds. A cold sweat greases the back of my neck.

The crowd pushes forward. A firework goes off. I flinch.

"Don't worry, you're fine," says my Arez.

"There are a lot of people here!"

I raise my voice to be heard over the swelling crowd. My pulse jackhammers as the people pull towards the dark entryway under the stadium. Humans crash against one another, shoving and fighting to get inside. Women try to leave with children clutched in their arms, but they're forced back into the crowd. The people are going one direction: forward. I stop against the flow and tug at Arez's hand.

"We have to get inside the stadium to see Kak Barzani."

"I know! It's just a lot of people and—" I try to think of any reason I can give for not going into that dark doorway full of people other than *I'm afraid*, but I can't. Excuses are political. Leaving is political. Staying is political. Fear is political.

Behind Arez an enormous Kurdish flag held aloft by hundreds of people comes barreling through the crowd. Hands grab on and it's held high. Bits of the green, red, white, and gold are torn, but hundreds push and pull it forward.

"Do you want to go in?" he yells.

I do want to see the president talk. I don't want to get crushed to death. I came here to stop being so afraid.

We grab hold of the Kurdish flag. My fist is twisted in white fabric. I clasp my friend's hand, pulling, pushing, and cheering as we enter the darkness under the stadium. In the concrete hallway voices are echoing into a cacophony. I can't see any light at the exit, just a tattered Kurdish flag traveling through the darkness. There is screaming. I realize that I am screaming too. My boots are slipping and

I am trying to find purchase on the ground. I can't fall. It's not my flag, but I can't fall while carrying it.

Mistakes are political.

Someone drops to the floor and I am body checked sideways into a concrete wall. I feel people trip against me. I lose Arez's hand in the mass of humanity as more bodies crash upon me. I'm sucking at breath in the sweaty, hot air trying to pull the flag through the never ending dark. I can see the light in back of me diminishing. Another person crushes me against the concrete.

I want to push forward.

Fear snags.

Panic rises.

I can't breathe.

I feel as if my collar bones might break under the weight of the people against me. Panic rises. A firework goes off outside the tunnel. I try to catch my breath. The flag moves onward. More bodies fall against me. I let go of the fabric and turn to fight my way back to the light at the beginning of the tunnel, gasping for air.

Cowardice is political.

CRASHING THE PARTY

I catch my breath standing in a pile of plastic bottles, broken horns, and cigarette butts. The punishing sun is cutting orange rays across the people in front of the stadium. I wait for my pulse to settle. More people pack into the darkness of the tunnel grabbing onto the flag while I curse myself for letting go. I watch the rest of it disappear inside without me.

I think about finding the nearest air conditioning and watching the rally on television. I'll write about the rally from the comfort of my apartment. No. That's wrong. I didn't come half way around the world to watch a nation be created on television.

History is a series of parties, and I've never been invited before. I'm too young to have seen the first moon landing and the fall of the Berlin Wall; I'm too old to colonize Mars. For this short span of time, I have a beating heart, working legs, and a reckless disregard for my own personal safety. I owe it to myself to crash the party.

I am going to find a way into this rally.

A REAL FAKE JOURNALIST

I spot two foreign journalists walking through the crowd. I know they are journalists because they are carrying large, expensive cameras. I know that they are foreign because they are clearly Japanese. The men are surrounded by fixers and armed security ushering them through the mass of people towards a gate marked *Press*.

I take my camera and school ID from my bag and hang them around my neck. The ID states that I am a teacher of the Kurdistan International School, but at first glance it could look like a press pass. I follow close behind the Japanese journalists and push into their security cordon. The guards don't notice, which means either I should be a spy, or they're bad security guards. It's likely the second bit.

I mimic everything the journalists do.

They walk up to a checkpoint. I walk up to a checkpoint.

They raise their hands to be patted down. I raise my hands to be patted down.

They put their bags of camera equipment on a table to be X-Rayed. I put my backpack on a table to be X-Rayed.

They lean in to whisper to one another. I listen and

nod as if I understand Japanese. Security moves us into the press area.

"You're a journalist?" I hear a police officer ask.

I grab my school ID, hold up my camera, and point to the two Japanese journalists. The officer waves me through the final checkpoint. We are met on the other side by men in full-body armor, with clean rifles and shined boots. These aren't rent-a-cops with rusted kalashnikovs. These are presidential security. We stop in front of the soldiers and I bury my head in my bag as if I am looking for something important. I'm surrounded by soldiers and credentialed journalists. Armored SUVs block off the street and there is nowhere to retreat. Security begins inspecting bags and equipment. I twist my hand around my school ID. The lanyard is soaked with my sweat.

The Japanese journalists have noticed me. I smile. One gives me the slightest nod. They say something to one another in Japanese and look back at me.

"Hi. I'm Eric," I say.

"Are you a journalist?" says one.

"Sometimes. Where are you guys from?" I ask hoping that they won't alert the authorities.

"Tokyo."

"Cool, always wanted to go there."

Big smile. Big, desperate, *please don't tell on me*, smile. The same kind of smile I've seen my students give to one another when they don't want their neighbor to tell Mr. Eric that they spilled glue all over their desk. Nothing changes, but when you get taller the stakes get higher.

"You are a freelancer?" asks one of the journalists.

Just then the soldiers open the doors to the stadium and wave us in.

"I think we're moving now," I say as we're rushed into the rally.

It looks like I'm getting into the party.

ONE VERY BIG VOICE

We pass through the guts of the stadium. Under the rows of seats I hear stomping and the cheering of one giant voice. It's equal parts terrifying and thrilling. Inviting and destructive. Something you want to be a part of. Something you want to run from. The power of thousands.

We're spat out of the into the center of the stadium. The nuclear-bright sun blinds me and in this moment nothing exists except orange-white sunlight and the hurricane of voices. The green, red, gold, and white of the Kurdish flag bleeds back into my vision as I see thousands upon thousands of faces screaming, singing, and cheering. People stand on guardrails and hang off fences. They ride each other's shoulders and dance in circles. The grass in the field is invisible because of the thousands upon thousands of people who have gathered. They are like one living breathing, singing, fighting, dancing soul. I look down and I realize that the Kurdish scarf that Arez gave me is still around my shoulders. Wearing the same colors, I am indistinguishable from the crowd.

A Kurdish security guard shouts over the din of the crowd.

"The President is about to speak."

The journalists nod and pull out their cameras. I lift my camera trying to find him on the dias. I hear the chant begin from the football pitch. Soon it is echoing through the stadium. One voice. A sound that vibrates my ribs.

Kaka! kaka!

Big brother.

There are too many people, and flags, and raised hands

to get a shot, so I let the camera fall by my side and I stand on tip-toe hoping to catch a glimpse. The chant rocks the air around me.

Kaka!

I catch a brief glimpse of his face and I call out.

"Kaka!"

The word jumps out of my mouth. I realize that I am chanting along with the people.

Kaka! Kaka! Big Brother!

I am wearing the same colors, chanting the same words, and listening to the same speech. This is not my country— in fact it's no one's country yet— but I am cheering at the top of my lungs when he speaks words I don't understand. It doesn't matter. I am a part of the singular voice rising from the stadium and it feels good. When the line between *us* and *them* is drawn you want to be on the side of *us*. You want to be on the side of the noise and the dancing and the celebration. When a large voice shouts, you want to shout with it and not against it.

It is an illusion, but it is a powerful one that moves the world.

Sometimes, it's easy to forget what you are shouting for.

VOTING DAY

9 a.m.

A bus waits outside my apartment building. We've been told that it will take us to the airport in case of violence. I go to the roof and look across the city. The streets are doomsday empty. For the first time in months Erbil is pin-drop quiet. It's like someone turned down the volume so that Baghdad wouldn't hear the KRG voting itself free.

As a teacher, I don't trust the quiet. Quiet is when a

flying pencil hits someone in the eye. Quiet is when Siada starts crying because someone passes her a note stating that, in no uncertain terms, she smells. Quiet is the sound right before chaos. I decide to walk through the city.

Doors shuttered. Lawn chairs stacked next to tea shops. The sound of honking traffic, slapping dominoes, and bubbling water pipes has been replaced by the hushed drone of the Kurdish news playing on the TV in every house and a helicopter hovering somewhere. Maybe this is what the first day in a new country looks like. Quiet streets and closed doors.

Outside municipal buildings are lines of people dressed in traditional clothing. Voters holding prayer beads while they wait their turn to say *yes* or *no*. An armed guard ushers them inside. Moments later they emerge with an ink-blackened fingertip to prove they have had their say. Nothing to do but walk home, close the door, and wait.

11 a.m.

I have two cups of tea, one coffee, and a plate full of fruit. I'm sitting with the gardener of a local park. I met him one weekend on a walk downtown. For some reason he wanted me to take pictures of his pigeon coop. I obliged. Since then, tea with the gardener next to his pigeon coop has become a weekly ritual. He either thinks that I speak Arabic, or he doesn't care that I don't.

We sit in a small office next to his birds. He is agitated today and keeps bringing me food. He paces back and forth in front of an ancient television. He brings me an orange and some dates. He paces. He eyeballs the news. He brings me a bowl of nuts. He stops with his hands on his hips and stares into oblivion. He brings me a knife. He mutters to himself. I sit there watching the news in Kurdish. I try to drink all the tea he's given me. I can't

69

understand any of the words that he's saying except for one.

Mushkila

It can mean a problem or mistake. It was one of the first words I learned in Arabic. He hands me a cigarette. He hands me a cookie. He hands me a napkin.

Mushkila he says, shaking his head.

Mushkila I say, nodding mine.

He sits next to me and shows me his ink-darkened finger. I nod my head. The news plays in the background. I have a lap full of sweets, and there are problems on the television.

Mushkila.

3 p.m.

I hear an engine roar in the distance while walking along the Hundred Meter Road. A school bus speeds by followed by Humvees and Jeeps. Have I missed an evacuation? I aim my camera at the approaching vehicles. The bus is full of men in black balaclavas and shouldered rifles. They speed towards the airport.

I think it's best to get back to my apartment.

YES, AND NOW WHAT

It passed. It passed with 92 percent of the country voting itself free of the Republic of Iraq.

But Iraq doesn't accept the decision. The hallways are tense the week after the referendum. Emergency negotiations begin. Foreign teachers pack their bags and leave the country without a word. Baghdad threatens military action. School buses are late because of increased bomb inspections. Embassies threaten border closures. My students begin asking loaded questions like:

Mr. Eric, is California its own country?

No one knows what's next, but I have tickets to Istanbul in a week. I'll see Savannah for a couple of days in a country which very much exists.

SOMETHING IS
HAPPENING SOMEWHERE, MAYBE

"You cannot go to Turkey. Baghdad says the airport must close."

San, my grocer, stands on tiptoe poking a roll of paper towels on the top shelf with a broomstick. Every grocery store in Erbil has a similar inventory management broomstick. I do not know how he gets the paper towels onto the top shelf in the first place, or how this system works with jars of pickles. However, I have more important questions:

"What does that mean?"

"Baghdad says no airplanes." The roll of paper towels falls off the shelf into his hands.

"But I'm going to Istanbul." I say this to him as if he has a direct line to the Iraqi Parliament behind the counter.

"There is a bus. Erbil to Istanbul. Maybe 30 hours, if Turkey does not close the border. Maybe it's better that you stay here. Too many *mushkila* right now."

"Yes," I say. Lots of *mushkila.*

"Maybe two weeks and the airport will open. Too much money comes through the airport. It is all about money, you will see. Barzani gets paid from the airport and Baghdad gets paid from the airport. Maybe two weeks *inshallah*," he says.

"Inshallah," I say.

In the Middle East, *inshallah* or *if God wills it*, can translate anywhere between *that might occur* to *there's no way this is happening.* San gives me my paper towels, and I go into

71

detective mode. My neighborhood operates on an economy of rumors. If you listen to enough of them it's possible to crowdsource a reliable version of the truth. Let's take the example of three rumors circulating after an explosion heard right before the referendum. Can you spot the facts?

That explosion at the Peshmerga base last week? That was weapons from the Islamic State that they were storing incorrectly. That's what my friend Ahmed said, and he is Peshmerga.

But actually, those weapons exploded because Baghdad was trying to secretly disarm Kurdish troops so they couldn't fight back if Iraq wanted to take over the KRG. My wife's sister knows someone with the government.

No, the explosion was Americans mining for gold inside their base. They've been stealing our gold for years and taking it on secret flights back to Washington D.C. My aunt cooks for the soldiers there.

What do all of these rumors tell us? In this case, all we know is that an explosion happened and everyone has extended family. That's all. The truth is a slippery thing, but everyone seems to have a relative who knows a guy that saw it one time. I seek out my finest informants to find out more about the airport.

Mahr, my vegetable guy, grumbles that the airport will open soon. He adds that I am American and can do whatever I want.

The Nepalese waiter at the Turkish restaurant says he doesn't know anything about an airport, but he asks if I can help him get a visa to Europe.

I question a drunk war correspondent who tells me not to take the bus because a friend of his just got locked up by the Turks.

I text Astefano, the one source of absolute truth in trying times.

Eric: Hey everyone says that the airport is closed. Is that true?

Astefano: Yeah. Sucks.

Eric: I'm visiting Savannah in Istanbul soon.

Astefano: You could take a bus if Turkey doesn't close down the border. You might not be able to get back in though.

Eric: Hopefully Baghdad will be cool about it.

Astefano: They're never cool about anything.

The evening news makes it official. Baghdad is forcing the KRG to hand over its airports. Until they do, all flights are grounded. This raises more questions. Is the Iraqi government extorting the Kurdish region as punishment for a referendum? Are they planning on starting a civil war by rolling tanks into the KRG?

One thing is certain. I will not see Savannah in Istanbul.

I go up to the roof of my apartment.

It's dusk and the sky looks like an oppressive lid. Between Baghdad, the United States, Turkey, Iran, and Russia, Kurdistan feels like an ant farm and everyone is tapping the glass. Military helicopters hang in the air over the base in the distance. Large black birds with heavy bellies travel in slow lines across the sky.

BLAME IT ON BAGHDAD

"So I'm not seeing you in Istanbul?" says Savannah over the phone. I never thought that Baghdad would inter-fere in my love life, but here we find ourselves. I've been pacing in my apartment, trying to find a solution but coming up empty.

"I'm locked down in Kurdistan for the next couple

months. I might be able to get out for Christmas if I take the bus. That's only if they don't close the border."

The words land into a pool of silence on the other end of the line.

"That... really sucks."

She's right. It really sucks. I look out the window to the street below. Motor bikes have gathered around the burning coals of a shawarma grill. The airspace is closed and my relationship is on the rocks, but life goes on and people need shawarma.

"What happens then?" she asks.

"I don't know if I can get out of Erbil. If I leave, I don't know if I can come back. Things are more complicated, and I don't know if you're okay with that," I say, fatigue and agitation leaking into my voice.

"I am if you are. Are you?" she asks.

The shawarma chef cleans up metal plates. Customers hop on their bikes and putter down the road. I wonder if Savannah is looking out her window in Bulgaria at some small piece of life passing by. Across the globe, she has been teaching teenagers and making a life. Her voice at the end of the day has become a separate peace away from the madness of school and the uncertainties of borders.

"Of course," I say. "We'll just see each other at Christmas."

"Christmas in Bulgaria. Got it. Sorry you're locked in Kurdistan Eczu."

I smile. We stay on the phone chatting about the trials and joys of our days. A loud class. A joke with a neighbor. A free bag of dates thrown in with groceries. We say goodnight and somehow it feels like the map between Bulgaria and Iraqi Kurdistan has been folded so that two points, thousands of miles away, are touching.

I turn off the lights and stare at the ceiling. A helicopter floats by in the distance. A taxi honks and some motorcycles race down the street. My mind paces out each of my anxieties for the next day, month, year, and the rest of my life. Sleep is something for other people. I grab my jacket to get my phone and a small piece of paper falls out. The contact information of the President of Liberland, Vit Jedlicka.

I've never had the contact information of a President before. I think it would be a shame if I didn't reach out. I open my phone and begin typing a message.

Dear President Jedlicka. I'm interested in unrecognized nations...

WAR TOURISM FOR DUMMIES

My cell phone pings while I'm grading papers in the teachers lounge. It is not the President of Liberland. It is the Kurdish news: fighting has begun in Kirkuk. Some say that the Peshmerga shot first and held the line. Others say that the Iraqi Government has allowed the Shiite Militias, the Popular Mobilization Units, to repel the Peshmerga. Reuters and the AP are also reporting which means that it's serious.

"I went to Kirkuk yesterday," Clare announces without prompting.

Our red pens go down. All eyes go to Clare for a bit more detail as to why she thought it was a good idea to do some sightseeing ahead of a firefight for oil.

"I considered dressing myself as a man to blend in..."

A brief image of Claire dressed like a Kurdish man flashes in my mind. This image will always haunt me.

"Instead, I got a hijab and paid a cab driver a couple hundred dollars to take me there."

My colleague Henrietta from Zimbabwe clucks her tongue.

"Clare, you could have gotten yourself killed," she says.

"I know. I got out of the cab and talked to one person, but they told me to get right back in the cab and come back so I did."

She beams a grin around the table. Clare, as it turns out, is a war tourist. She believes that wandering through active conflict zones will somehow give her meaning. This explains the constant mumbling about the Islamic State and her fetishization of industrial-scale violence. In a rare moment of telepathy, Henrietta says what all of the teachers in the room are thinking:

"Clare, when you get kidnapped or killed, you understand that we will have to teach your classes."

She gives Clare a look which I would call *third-grade death eyes*. Clare's smile disappears. We continue grading, mentally resigning ourselves to teaching Clare's classes when she's inevitably detonated.

Kirkuk is a flashpoint because it is a major oil-producing region. Back in the day the area was largely Kurdish, but Saddam Hussein decided they had too much power sitting on millions of barrels of black gold, so he decided to *Arabize* the area. That's the term, *Arabize*. It's as if he had a laser which he could fire at the region to make everyone Arab. In practice, it's much worse.

Using some classic moves from the Dictator's Handbook: he targeted the language and institutions of minority populations and created laws against them. Eventually, Kurds were forced out of their homes and replaced with Arabs who were incentivized to move to Kirkuk. For some reason, authoritarians always believe that they can legislate offending cultures out of existence. As a rule, this ends badly.

Then the United States rolled in and kicked Saddam out.

In a characteristically clumsy, outwardly well-intentioned, and ultimately destructive gesture, the United States made matters in Kirkuk worse. After taking over the area, the coalition forces allowed Kurds to return to their previously *Arabized* homes. This meant that Kurdish families showed up to their old houses with furniture strapped to the top of their cars ready to move back in.

If the history of the Middle East could be distilled into a single moment, it might look like this: an argument between two people speaking different languages explaining that the other is living in their house, while foreign soldiers look around trying to figure out why they are there.

Since then, the region has become a checkerboard of Kurdish, Arab, Turkmen, and Assyrian populations. As the referendum approached, Kirkuk decided to cast its lot with the rest of the KRG and vote itself free of Federal Iraq. But in the immortal words of The Notorious B.I.G *the more money we come across, the more problems we see.* Since there's a lot of oil in Kirkuk, there's a lot of problems.

Baghdad doesn't want that money to go to a newly independent Kurdish state. They decided to fight. No one really wants to go to war, but bullets and blood are cheaper than losing barrels of crude and the economic engine for an entire country. That's why it's a bad idea to go to Kirkuk right now.

Gathered in the teachers lounge, we grade our papers wondering what will happen next. Or maybe just trying to imagine Clare walking through Kirkuk wearing a fake mustache.

ILL-ADVISED TRIPS

We lose another teacher. This time the teacher left the

Kurdistan International School in Sulaymaniyah, the second biggest city in the KRG. The teacher made the journey across the Turkish border, leaving all his things and a hundred children without a science teacher.

Mr. Johann talks Astefano into transferring to Sulaymaniyah until they can find a replacement. I plan to visit, but the week after he gets settled in, fighting spills over the road that connects Erbil and Sulaymaniyah. To ensure my safety, I ask my soothsaying grocers if I can travel.

San tells me that it isn't safe and that I should wait until fighting dies down. I ask him when the fighting will die down. *Inshallah,* soon, he tells me. Mahr says I can do whatever I want because I'm an American. The Nepalese waiter asks if we can become Facebook friends. Finally, I text Astefano:

Eric: Hey, do you think it's safe for me to come up to Suli this weekend?

Astefano: Yeah. Just don't take the main road.

Eric: How do I tell them not to take the main road?

Astefano: No one will be taking the main road because it's not safe.

Eric: Cool. I'm coming.

THE SPICE MUST FLOW

Well this was a mistake.

I think this to myself as my taxi pulls alongside a column of soldiers. I am in a shared car headed towards Sulaymaniyah when we come upon a column of soldiers. Hundreds of troops clean rifles, smoke cigarettes, and drink tea alongside a caravan of Humvees. We left Erbil an hour ago and the only vehicles that we've seen have been military.

The system of mass transit in Iraqi Kurdistan is a shared taxi. Sitting behind me in the beige Mercedes are two Kurdish guys with their hair coiffed into perfect pompadours. A Turkmen woman fiddles with prayer beads as our cab slows to a crawl alongside the soldiers. The driver and three other passengers begin speaking to one another in rapid-fire Arabic. I try to pick out a few words but only understand five:

Jaysh: Army
Kurdi: Kurdish
Hashid Shabi: Shiite Militia
Mushkila: Problem
Kirkuk: Kirkuk

From this I understand: *Kurdish forces and the Popular Mobilization Units (Shiite Forces) something something something in Kirkuk something something something, problem.* I wish I had studied more Arabic. Our cab passes the detachment of troops and we give a collective sigh. Just past the horizon is Kirkuk, oil, and a lot of guns. I begin listening to an audiobook of Dune to calm myself while I look out at the passing desert scrubland. It does not help.

If you've never read Dune, let me give you the summary: it's about a desert planet called Arrakis. This is the only planet in the galaxy where *spice* can be mined. Spice lets you live forever, makes intergalactic travel possible, and gives people telepathic powers. Since it's the most valuable substance in the universe, it's also used as money. Needless to say, everyone wants to control the flow of spice. Shockingly, people are willing to go to war in a desert to control a valuable resource. Did I mention that it was written in the '60s?

Anyway, the galactic emperor, a guy named Shaddam IV, worries that the House of Atreides wants to take over the galactic empire, and he can't have that. He assigns control of Arrakis and all of the spice production in the galaxy to the House of Atreides over their sworn enemies. This tips off a centuries long feud with another house called the Harkonnen. Playing one side against the other is a classic move by those in power that want to keep it that way. Basically, Atreides: good; Harkonnen: bad. But really there is no good and bad, there is only who controls what and the side you're on.

Both sides go to war. Meanwhile, caught in the middle of this are people who actually live on the planet, a rough and tumble group of nomads called the Fremen. The Fremen just want everyone to get the hell off their planet and stop taking their natural resources so they can ride sandworms in peace. Naturally, no one cares what the Fremen have to say because they barely have an army and they have some crazy religious beliefs. There are big sandworms and some cool knife fights.

We drive through the parched foothills. The desert stretches on to infinity in front of us. Our dusty Mercedes chugs along towards Sulaymaniyah. Out there in the desert there is money and resources and men with guns wearing slightly different uniforms. Somewhere men in slightly different suits made a choice that put them there.

The spice must flow.

STILL NOT A SPY

Security stops our cab outside of Sulaymaniyah and takes me in for questioning. Surprise interviews like this are becoming kind of fun. It's like being on a first date with someone carrying an AK-47. The Peshmerga outside of Sulaymaniyah wear different uniforms than those in Erbil. The two sides are both united under the banner of Iraqi Kurdistan, but they don't really get along. This means that anyone, especially foreigners, coming up from Erbil are suspect. I sit in a wobbly chair, where I wait for my speed date with the Peshmerga of Sulaymaniyah.

While Erbil has been under the rule of the Barzani clan since time immemorial, Sulaymaniyah, situated to the southeast, was governed by a guy named Jalal Talibani before his death (he is in no way related to the Taliban of Afghanistan and Pakistan).

Talabani and Barzani both had a different point of view on the future of Iraqi Kurdistan. While Barzani envisioned Iraqi Kurdistan as an independent state, Talibani advocated for a unified Iraq with an autonomous, Kurdish-controlled region. In 1994 the KRG exploded into civil war, which left thousands dead on both sides and an uneasy peace between Sulaymaniyah and the rest of Iraqi Kurdistan.

A soldier sits down across from me. I hand him my passport, my Kurdish work papers, and my international school identification card. He looks through the cards and eyes me up and down. I smile at him, simple, dumb-looking, the kind of person that you wouldn't want to detain.

"Why are you here?"

"English teacher."

"Are you a spy?"

"No. I'm an English Teacher."

"Where are you from?"

"USA."

"Are you a spy?"

"No, still an English teacher."

The soldier hands me my passport, my Kurdish work papers, and school ID.

He waves me back to my cab.

I wonder how many spies he has caught.

REFUGE

Sulaymaniyah is a crush of traffic. Furniture, televisions, and suitcases, are tied to the roofs of cars pressing into the city. I hop out of the cab when it becomes clear that I'm better off on foot. Families from Kirkuk fill the streets shopping for supplies, bargaining for hotels, or wandering towards the center with their lives packed in suitcases.

I climb the stairs of a tea shop above the river of human beings. It stretches in every direction, trickling through the gridwork of stalled cars, flowing along sidewalks, and pooling around mosques. The shop is packed with people charging phones and laptops while puffing on pipes of Al-Fakhr double-apple shisha. I stand by the window watching the city absorb another population. I can't help but think of the rally in Erbil. Millions of people voting for independence forces thousands of people from their homes while hundreds of soldiers carry out the orders of a couple of political leaders.

It's as inconceivable to witness as it is to realize that it will continue to happen over and over again.

ASTEFANO AND SULI

We walk through the heart of Suli as it's known for short. The center of the city cleared up as the sun set. Now only a few men remain smoking cigarettes at plastic tables or sweeping the sidewalk in front of their stores.

The city feels like the artsy cousin to Erbil. Instead of being a tangle of dusty highways under a knot of power lines, it's a sloping landscape with open air markets and artisanal shops in underground walkways. Minarets and modest skyscrapers are framed by the Zagros Mountains.

Instead of passionate bursts of Arabic stitching together the Kurdish, Assyrian, and Arab communities, you mostly hear lyrical Sorani, Kurmanji, and Farsi. It sits on the Iranian border, but the Kurdish population spills across the imaginary line, making Suli a waypoint for smuggling vices into the Islamic Republic. If Erbil is rock and roll, then Sulaymaniyah is jazz.

Astefano and I stop into a hip bar which would look at home in Los Angeles. People talk quietly over beers sitting at tables made of repurposed wood. A movie plays silently, projected onto a canvas screen while a waiter delivers artisanal cocktails. I fill Astefano in on all the school gossip, including Clare's trip to Kirkuk.

"If she had stayed she would have been one of the people walking into the city today."

He chuckles and cleans his glasses. During the entire time I have known Astefano, I have never once seen him show the slightest bit of concern. He accepts everything from hours of additional classes and stacks of grading to border closures and Islamic State advancements with the quiet calm of a buddha statue.

"You always seem…unflappable. I mean that in a good way," I say, knocking back the dregs of my cocktail.

"That's most of us. Unless something is blowing up right in front of us, we're pretty much just wondering about who we're drinking tea with later on." He raises his hand for the waiter.

Paranoia is practiced as a way of life in the United States. While many of us have never experienced violence, we are dead certain that it is lurking around every corner. With every *NEWS ALERT!* and *BREAKING STORY!* we're reminded of some horror lurking out there. It's in darkened parking garages or long hallways with flickering lights. It's coming across our borders for our children. We arm ourselves, not just with weapons, but with staunch individualism, knee-jerk cynicism, and adherence to one of our two political allies, all in the hopes that when violence comes to our country, it will be the other guy who gets it. When Astefano tells me this I realize how scared I have been all day. When I realize how afraid I am I realize how American I also am.

We order another round of drinks.

ISLAMIC STATE JOKES

Astefano tells me a joke. It goes like this:

"A Christian man is driving into Mosul with his family. He gets stopped by one of the Islamic State fighters at a checkpoint. As the fighters approach the Christian man, he takes the crucifix off of his rear view mirror before they can see it. His wife and children are nervous because they have heard what the Islamic State does to Christians. The man seems quite calm though. When the fighter walks up to his car he greets the man.

'Asalaam u laykum!' says the Islamic State fighter.

'Waa alaykum salaam,' says the Christian man.

'Are you a Muslim?' asks the fighter.

'I am!' says the Christian man, much to the surprise of his family.

'That's wonderful to hear,' says the Islamic State fighter, 'Could you kindly recite a chapter from the Quran for me?'

At this point, the Christian man's wife and daughter are terrified, but he clears his throat and begins reciting a passage from the Bible. A moment passes and the Islamic State fighter claps the man on the shoulder and exclaims,

'Beautiful! Have a pleasant journey'

The Christian man starts his car and drives off. As he is

putting his crucifix back on his rearview mirror his wife slaps him on the shoulder.

'You recited the Bible to that man, we could have been killed! You've never read the Quran in your life!'

The man smiles and calms his wife saying:

'Don't worry! No one in the Islamic State has ever read it either.'"

The table is full of cocktail glasses. We're both hammered enough to share our favorite Islamic State jokes. Astefano was living three miles away from Mosul where the leader of the Islamic State, Abu Bakr Al Baghdadi, made his speech declaring that IS would be the world's newest country. At the time he was on the roof of his family home adjusting his satellite dish so that he could watch a World Cup qualifying match in high definition.

"For the most part I didn't really care," says Astefano. "The Peshmerga came and said that something was going on in Mosul, but that they would stay there. I just cared about the World Cup. I mean, unless the Islamic State had a team in the World Cup, I didn't mind and my family didn't either."

Astefano's family lived in the Christian village of Bartola. His father was a professor at the University of Mosul. He went to teach class every single day, regardless of the new Caliphate waging a constant grinding war against everyone who stood in their way. Then the Islamic State took over Bartola, and Astefano and his parents joined the many Christian refugees in Erbil.

"My dad called one day and said that we couldn't go back to our house, that the Islamic State had taken it."

"Weren't you...mad?" I ask, hoping that Astefano has experienced anger about something at some point.

"Yes, but only because they took my Xbox."

"ISIS stole your Xbox?" the image of Islamic State

fighters sitting cross legged on Astefano's floor playing *Fifa* in their black balaclavas crosses my mind.

"ISIS stole my Xbox," he confirms, finishing his drink.

"Those motherfuckers."

QUIET ROADS, TAKE ME HOME

The roads are clear on the way back to Erbil. In the distance, ever-present military helicopters hover like lazy flies on a hot day, but in front of our dusty Mercedes there is nothing but sun-baked asphalt and desert foothills. The momentary storm of soldiers and refugees had moved on, at least from this road. Baghdad swallowed up Kirkuk and clamped a lock on the airspace. The KRG tried to demand its freedom through a democratic process, but Baghdad had the only vote that mattered. Even though the referendum passed, it wasn't accepted, because declaring independence and gaining recognition are two very different things.

At its height, the Islamic State was able to take a landmass roughly the same size as the United Kingdom. It took the end of World War I and the threat of more fighting to dig the borders of the modern Middle East away from the Ottoman Empire. Meanwhile, Iraqi Kurdistan tried to vote itself free, only to be met with deadly force and more control. Maybe a country is just a violent revolution frozen in time by those who benefit from it.

The next month drags by. In the background is the low simmer of conflict on the borders of Iraqi Kurdistan. The teachers are no longer able to leave Erbil for fear that we won't be able to return. One day Mr. Johann pulls me aside and asks if I would consider staying during the holiday break for double my salary.

I tell him that I will think about it.

PROFESSIONAL WRESTLING
IS AN INFINITE GAME

I tell Mr. Johann that I can't stay, so I'm grading the last packet of papers before I leave for the holidays. It feels like everything is coming apart. The coffee shop I'm sitting at rattles with a low panic as journalists, aid workers, and locals try to determine what the failed referendum and the subsequent swell of violence means for their near future. Meanwhile, the BBC drones from a television in the cafe, and the news is bad everywhere.

At any moment it seems that Turkey could close its borders with Iraq, or Baghdad could reclaim the Kurdish area by force. Combined with the closed airspace, this would make leaving Iraqi Kurdistan incredibly difficult, and returning almost impossible. Between drags on bubbling hookahs and endless tulip cups of black tea, it seems that everyone in this coffee shop is trying to answer the same question famously asked by The Clash all those years ago: *should I stay or should I go?*

If I leave, I don't know if I will be able to come back and I'll also lose my job. If I stay, I will likely lose Savannah due to distance and the frayed nerves of being locked next door to international conflict. Everything sucks in a very specific way right now. Suddenly, the essays that I am grading feel a lot less important. I put down my red pen and allow myself to be absorbed into the comfortable panic of watching an endless parade of atrocity on the television.

Then the channel changes to show a man in spandex leaping through the air onto another man in spandex. A crowd cheers. Apparently, one of the employees prefers professional wrestling over the news. Frankly, I welcome the change. It's been a long time since I have watched professional wrestling, and it appears that none of the spirit of the institution has changed. Large men and large women beat the tar out of one another for the honor of wearing a large belt. For some reason they can't solve their disagreements about who should wear the belt through conventional means, and acrobatic violence is the only answer.

"I can't stay here any longer."

I hear an aid worker muttering to a Kurdish colleague. There is an apology in her voice and a long silence afterwards. There's nothing to say because there is nothing either of them can do about the situation. They sip their tea. The crowd on television cheers.

In professional wrestling there's a bad guy that everyone loves to hate and a good guy that everyone loves to love. The moral lines between good and bad are so mercifully clear that everyone can sit back and enjoy the chaos of finding out who gets the belt. Because the belt isn't made to be won. It's meant to be lost again and again in an unbroken chain of thrilling ownership. Professional wrestling and politics are infinite games. There's no actual end. Winners get to keep playing, losers get thrown through a table.

"The billing department hasn't paid me in six weeks. I'm trying to get my uncle across into Turkey with me," says a Kurdish journalist over a Skype call, head in her hands.

I realize that I am lucky enough to be able to try and cross the border. I have a passport that lets me travel through Turkey and into Europe if I want. I have someone waiting for me on the other side. What am I doing here if everyone else is trying to get out? Am I a war tourist like Clare?

A bell dings. The referee slams his hand on the mat

three times while one glistening wrestler pins the other. The men in spandex are separated. The wrestler on top claims the belt and the other limps out of the ring. The camera whips across the audience. Screaming and cheering, a stadium of thousands is moved to chaotic ecstasy over what they know is orchestrated violence.

The story has taken a hold. The fight is no longer in the ring, it's in the audience. It's in their hearts, because when their guy wins, they win; when their guy loses they lose. It's not about the belt. It's not about the flag. It's not about the borders. It's about identity. This is when wrestling is at its best; this is when politics is at its worst.

This is when anything can happen.

"Hey, sorry can you turn it back to the news," an American journalist calls out to the waiter.

The waiter gives him a tight-lipped smile and flips the channel back to the Kurdish news service. All eyes go to the television. Everyone waits for what will happen next.

I take out my packet of tests and begin marking again.

I'm not a journalist or an aid worker.

I'm not a diplomat or a soldier.

If there is more violence here there is nothing I can do to help and school will be canceled anyway.

I am a third-grade teacher.

I decide to leave Erbil and hope that I can make it back by next semester.

THIS IS NO TIME FOR PIGEON RACING

"Why do you have a bird shop?"

I have been going to Ian's bird shop for months, and I never thought to ask. Now, the night before I leave Kurdistan, it occurs to me how many questions I've left unanswered. He translates to the men sitting around the bag of seeds. The birds stop tweeting for a moment as if they can understand us.

"We're pigeon racers," translates Ian.

"How does that work?" I ask.

Ian asks them on my behalf and they fall all over themselves to explain the ins and outs of pigeon racing at the same time. The old men who were once grumbling to one another about the state of the world now leap up in a cacophony, waving their hands to demonstrate flight patterns, and pointing to cages of chirping birds.

Even if I could understand what they were saying, I don't think Ian could translate fast enough. He raises his hand and the men sit back into their seats.

"They love talking about the birds. Keeps them away from talking about politics. We train the birds, so they always fly back here to the shop. Then, we drive them a couple hundred kilometers away. Start the timer, and they fly back here. We see who wins," says Ian, smiling.

"Can I go to your next pigeon race?" I ask Ian. He looks surprised and then taps ash off his cigarette.

"We don't know if we can do it now," he says.

"Why?"

"We don't know if it's okay to cross the borders. We usually drive the birds all the way down to Basra and let them go from there, but now? I don't know. Maybe it's not the time."

Ian stubs out his cigarette and rises from his chair to examine one of his birds. With slow practiced hands he withdraws a gray cooing pigeon from a cage and eyes it carefully.

Militias have surrounded the KRG. President Barzani has disappeared from public life, and the borders of Kurdistan are suddenly a lot smaller. Ian and his friends used to be able to drive 900 kilometers south to race the birds. Now they don't have 900 kilometers of country.

"Here."

He hands me the bird. Its light frame vibrates softly as it murmurs to itself. I hold the bird like a football, unsure of what I'm supposed to do with it.

Ian lights another cigarette and begins an animated argument with the man next to him. I can tell the subject is birds. I look at the one in my hands, wide-eyed and twitching, as if it is constantly wondering if it left the stove on.

"*Hallas*, that's enough."

Ian gently takes the bird from my hands and holds him up to his friend. The man eyes the bird. The man then wipes both of his hands together and raises them in the air in a universal sign I've come to know as *I don't think you're right, but I want to end this conversation.*

"What are you talking about?" I ask.

"He does not think this bird is pregnant. I think that it will lay an egg soon."

Ian puts the bird back in the cage.

"You can tell just by looking at them?" I ask.

"Of course," Ian comes back and settles into his chair. "You'll find out who was right when you get back."

He winks at me and grabs a handful of sunflower seeds. I hope I can come back to find out if that pigeon lays an egg. I say my goodbyes and head home to pack my bags.

As I take my final walk to my apartment, I think about what it must look like to a bird as it flies home. Maybe they see the foundations of Assyrian ziggurats, the char of a spent battlefield, or oil derricks owned by multinational organizations pumping crude.

Maybe they catch updrafts along the Zagros mountains

and dive into a stream of cool air above the Euphrates river. Maybe they're bored of the endless horizon.

Never once do they see the borders that enclose Ian and his friends.

SKETCHY AS FUCK

"I'm going to take a bus from Erbil to Şırnak across the Turkish border. Then I'll fly to Bulgaria. After the new year, I'll return to Turkey, take the bus from Diyarbakır to Erbil and be here in time for the next semester. It will be easy."

As I finish saying this, I realize that this will not be easy at all.

Astefano and I stand in front of the Erbil international bus station wrapped in large coats to cut against the icy desert wind. It's impossible to believe that when I first arrived in Kurdistan the weather was well into the hundreds. As usual, the minutes and hours dragged and the weeks and months flew. I look to Astefano for reassurance before I get on the bus.

"That sounds sketchy as fuck," he says.

In the four months that I've know Astefano I have never heard him tell a half truth, exaggerate, or swear. If anything, he downplays the volatility of situations. This is inconvenient for me, because I would really prefer that Astefano told me that my trip would be safe, easy, and comfortable. A good friend will tell you when something sounds sketchy as fuck. I am sad to be leaving my good friend.

"It does," I admit, as I watch the bus driver loading baggage.

He gestures for my backpack. Almost time to go again.

I don't know what to say to Astefano. I don't want to say goodbye for fear that I will mean it.

"I'll be back right after the new year," I say, handing over my bag.

"I mean, if you can't come back here you can always go to Liberland," he says.

I laugh and make a mental note that I should continue my online harassment of Liberland. The driver waits for me to climb aboard. I give Astefano a hug. I can't think of much else to say to him, so I leave him with one final thought:

"It really sucks that the Islamic State stole your Xbox."

"Yeah, it does," he says.

A VERY LONG TRIP TO THE MIDDLE OF EVERYWHERE

No one wants to read about 48 hours of traveling from Kurdistan to Bulgaria, so I am not going to write about it in excruciating detail. You should know that it was incredibly uncomfortable and generally unpleasant. It's like listening to one of your most boring friends tell you about their dream while looking at the horizon in Kansas and having to pee for two days straight.

That's it. That's the chapter.

AROUND THE WORLD TO SIT ON THE SAME COUCH

I limp my bag through the streets of Sofia, Bulgaria. I feel like I was in a rock tumbler during the last two days of travel. They passed like a hallucination of standing in lines and trying to force myself to sleep in buses, planes, and taxis. Now, with a couple of blocks left to go before reaching Savannah's apartment, I feel the ache of a thousand miles.

Even though I've traveled through Bulgaria before, it feels foreign. The language, smells, and architecture of the Middle East carries in swirls, turquoise, and sandstone arabesque. Eastern Europe is right angles, gray slabs, pipe smoke, and boiling stews. The volume has been turned down from a vibrant turmeric yellow to a cool sapphire blue, and Erbil feels like a dream that I am trying to keep hold of.

I see the park Savannah described in her email, hitch my backpack and pick up my pace in spite of my aching spine. We haven't seen one another since she left Erbil. I hope the spark we kindled is still alive in spite of time, distance, and the million things of daily life. I see her front door.

I hike up her front stairs. During my time in Erbil I spent every second wondering why I was there. In fact, I couldn't think of a second of my life in which I wasn't wondering why I was doing what I was doing in the first place. But I never once questioned Savannah. She was a new kind of gravity in my life since we met. Impossible to refuse. Someone worth years of uncomfortable buses, trains, and planes.

There are billions of people on the planet. There is only one that I have met who glows with a radiance that my life is intolerable without. There is a single woman who happens to live in this Bulgarian apartment complex who is so beguiling that I was more than willing to cross through a demilitarized zone to sit on a couch and eat snacks next to her. It is absurd how inconvenient it is to love someone.

The tiny Soviet-era elevator lets me into the hallway outside of her apartment. I knock on the door. The old hinges squeak as it opens. Before she can say anything, gravity pulls me into her arms like a meteor falling to earth. The months and miles and laughter and fights are all gone. I am home.

HOME FOR A BIT

Savannah and I spend Christmas together. I get her a Middle Eastern stringed instrument called a *saz* and a bar of soap from the bazaar called *virginity soap*. I am unclear if it is meant to restore virginity or if it makes one smell like their virginity is still intact, Either way, it is a funny bar of soap. Savannah has made me a shirt that says *The Spice Must Flow* due to the fact that I had been reading *Dune* for a month and never once shut up about it.

We make dinner. We watch horror movies on the couch. We browse through bookstores and drink coffee. We buy a small chess set and have tiny battles over cocktails across the city. For a moment our relationship is normal. This is strange, but welcome.

After Christmas in Sofia, Savannah and I decide to spend the remaining days traveling through Turkey. I've got to head back to Kurdistan through Turkey anyway, so we pack our bags and get tickets on the night train from Sofia to Istanbul. We fall asleep in a private car as the train chugs towards Turkey.

I can think of nowhere I would rather be.

THINGS GO SIDEWAYS

Border guards pound on the side of our sleeper car, jarring us awake at 3:00am. After hours of dreaming we've hit the Turkish border. We stand puffing breath into the December night outside the border checkpoint. Icy indigo darkness stretches out in every direction with only the control booth cradled in light.

We flip our passports open to the Turkish visas and hand them over to a guard in the booth. I wait for him to slam down his stamp so that we can officially cross this invisible line and get some shut-eye.

"Americans?" asks the man in the box as two additional officers wearing street clothes join him.

We smile in a way that insinuates that we're the cool Americans that you totally want in your country, rather than the lame Americans who overstay their welcome and blow stuff up. The box man confers with the two new guys.

"You can't come in."

All three border guards grin which makes it seem like they are kidding. Suddenly, I am not so sleepy and cold. I am agitated and sweaty. I watch as my passport is swapped between the men like it's a new toy.

"Where do you live?" one of the border guards asks Savannah.

"I live in Bulgaria," she says.

Though I don't know it right now, I am about to royally mess up my life by saying a single word. I am going to ruin this vacation and I'm going to get both Savannah and myself elbows deep in trouble. The border guard looks at me so that I can inform him about where I live. Without thinking about it, I say the one thing that you should never say to a Turkish official.

"Kurdistan."

"Kurdistan?"

Heads go up. A round of shark smiles cross the faces of the guards. At this exact moment I do not realize what a titanic mistake I've made. At this moment I still think I'm going into Turkey and back to Erbil. Yet, with these three syllables and my announcement that I live in a place that doesn't appear on any map, I seal a very strange fate for myself.

INTERROGATION ROOM TANGO

The interrogation room does not have a mirror like in the movies. I find this disappointing. I wonder what Savannah's interrogation room looks like and how mad she is going to be at me for getting us in this situation. I realize after my first hour of being interrogated that really any room is an interrogation room if you're being interrogated in it. The officer spreads my personal effects across the table.

My work papers for *Iraqi* Kurdistan, passport, and school ID lay in front of me. My backpack sits on the floor next to him. My interrogator is a guy about my age who looks like a Turkish version of Seth Rogan. We seem to go back and forth between getting along like old chums and him accusing me of being a spy. He is both the good cop and bad cop simultaneously, which makes him a confusing and unnerving cop.

"You are PKK?" he asks for the third time.

"I promise, I'm not. I'm a third-grade teacher in Erbil."

I push my school lanyard towards him. He glances down at my ID and then back to me, unimpressed. I sit back in the chair and cross my leg because we're all buddies here.

"Sit up straight."

He swats my knee. Bad cop rising. I do as he says. He dips a hand into my backpack and removes my camera. A cold sweat creeps across my shoulders as I realize that the last time I used that camera was at the rally. It's going to be very hard to convince this man that I am not squarely on the side of Kurdish independence as soon as he takes a gander at those photos. The screen glows to life. I grit my teeth and stare at my hands, sitting ramrod straight. He breathes a sub-audible *hmm* as he is treated to a montage of hyper-nationalistic Kurdish imagery.

While I am being run down by a big rig full of my own poor choices and genuine ignorance, I'll give you a brief refresher as to why there is no love lost between Turkey and the Kurdish people. At the end of World War I, the Ottoman Empire shrunk to the borders of the modern nation of Turkey. With no Kurdish state on the emerging map, the Kurds living in Turkey were given a choice by the new government: they could call themselves Turks, or they would become persona non-grata.

Actually, that's an understatement. The Kurds were and are actively policed out of their history, culture, and language. Kurds in Turkey are unable to maintain institutions in their own language. Some say the Turks are afraid the Kurds will take over the rest of the country if they begin to gain power. Others say that they just want the Kurds to assimilate, and that they can practice their culture and traditions privately. Regardless of the window dressing, when you try to use force to change someone's identity they fight back.

Kurdish resistance movements like the PKK, the Kurdish Workers Party, sprung up to defend their people, and this morphs into the usual game of *revolutionary or terrorist?* To the man sitting across the table from me, my camera full of flags and my apartment in Erbil might mean that I'm helping to blow up Turkish police stations, or it might just mean that I'm sympathetic to the Kurdish cause. Either way, it looks really bad. I decline to tell him that a couple weeks ago I was in a stadium crying out for President Barzani. He puts the camera down on the table and looks at me. I sit up straighter. He stares at me while he determines if I will enter Turkey as a tourist, or I won't be able to leave Turkey because I'm a prisoner.

He looks at me for a very long time.

A VERY COLD BORDER CROSSING

We are told to walk back to Bulgaria. It is past four in the morning, near freezing and there are 17 kilometers between us and the nearest Bulgarian town, Svilengrad. Savannah and I show the Bulgarian border guard the papers that we have just been issued. They state in very clear terms that we have been banned from entering Turkey. The border guard takes pity on us and says that she can call us a cab but it will cost 60 euro.

"Well, maybe we could walk it," says Savannah, a smile on her face even after an interrogation.

I'm ashamed and frustrated. I am tired and cold. I am pissed at the U.S. government and the Turkish government. Mostly I'm pissed at myself, but it's always easier to be mad at governments because they don't care about you. I do not want to be the reason that we have to walk through the freezing night at four in the morning. I do not want to pay 60 euro for a cab from the middle of nowhere to the middle of nowhere, but I don't see another option. I look at the cold, silent road in front of us.

"I think they kind of liked us," Savannah says, her breath visible in the freezing night.

"I do too, actually. My interrogator was cool sometimes."

"What do you want to do?" Savannah asks, nudging her backpack into mine.

"I want to go to Turkey."

"They just kicked us out."

It's too cold to walk. I dig in my pocket, hoping to find 60 euro worth of Bulgarian money.

As we turn to the border guard, a car pulls up from the Turkish side. *Royal Hotel* is printed on the side of a black sedan. The guard leans down to talk with the driver and points in our direction. The driver looks at us. We wave. After everything that has happened, I assume that the driver will step on the accelerator and leave us to the foggy road stretching in front of us.

Instead, the driver waves, unlocks his door, and brings us in from the cold.

SAINT DIMITAR OF SVILENGRAD

"The Turks have a lot of problems," says Dimitar, our savior.

We're warming up in the backseat of his cab. *Thank yous* in English and Bulgarian punctuating every other sentence. We watch while kilometer after kilometer of freezing pavement passes by. Traveling teaches a lot of things if you're willing to learn. One of the most important lessons is gratitude for what you get, even if it isn't what you wanted. It's easy to feel defeated by being kicked out of a country, but at least Dimitar had a warm cab and a big enough heart to let us ride for free.

"We have all kinds of hotels in Svilengrad. It's like a little Las Vegas. What kind of hotel you want? Nice one?" he asks.

"The cheapest," we say in near unison.

He nods.

When we arrive at the cheapest hotel in Svilengrad, Bulgaria, a cockroach greets us as we flip on our room's punishing fluorescent lights. It skitters under the door and we push the two cardboard twin beds together. We look up at the ceiling unable to sleep, wondering where in the world to go next. For right now, at this moment, we can only stare at the ceiling in the cheapest hotel in Svilengrad, Bulgaria and wait for sleep to come.

Savannah and I wake up in our tiny beds very far from anywhere that could be considered home. The light filtering in from outside is Balkan gray: heavy as lead, wet, and cold as day-old snow.

"Bus station?" asks Savannah.

"Yup," I say.

We emerge from our hotel to gaze upon the glory of Svilengrad. Chunky buildings crouch along crumbling streets next to neon-drenched casinos named things like *Pegasus, Macau,* and *Star Princess.* A scattering of Bulgarians appears out of the fog, pacing down the street with their faces downcast in a way which could mean either that they are having the best day of their life or that their dog just committed suicide. Several street signs have fallen over, suggesting that they just gave up on being a sign.

The town has all of the charm of a cinder block.

NEW YEAR, NEW COUNTRY

It's New Years and we were supposed to be in Istanbul. Instead, I stay up coughing for half the night, and spend the other half having fever dreams about being late for class in Erbil. My brain wants to go home again. I look at Savannah and I know I am home, so I am divided against myself. One part of me is hungry for the adventure I set out on, the other half wants to embrace the reason, safety, and the company of someone I love. I think about the Kurdish flag entering the tunnel and the disgrace of turning my back. I think of how I found another way forward. I think how little I know about what a country is.

101

My fever surges. Savannah wakes me at midnight to ring in the New Year on her balcony in Sofia. We light sparklers and wave them back and forth while fireworks flourish across the sky. I love being here, but I have to find a way back to my life in Erbil. The next day, I call the American consulate in Turkey and explain my situation.

"Is there anything I can do?" I ask between coughs. I hear the foreign service officer sigh on the other end of the line.

"I am not speaking as an official of the American government right now, but as a person. I would advise you to never cross the border into Turkey again. We already have a citizen in Turkish prison for the last ten months for doing the same thing. There is nothing the consulate can do for you if you're taken prisoner. Count yourself as lucky that you were just banned."

I thank her, hang up, and join Savannah on the couch.

"The American consulate said that we are lucky that they didn't arrest us."

"So those officers at the border did like us?" says Savannah.

We laugh. She hugs me. I let out a round of hacking coughs. I lost my job, my apartment, all of my clothes, and I got banned from a country in the last 72 hours.

"Where to now?" she asks, knowing that I have to leave.

"I don't know."

I cough and cough and cough.

ANOTHER NATION IN THE GRAYZONE

I shiver and sweat on a five-hour minibus ride from Sofia, Bulgaria to Skopje, the capital of Northern Macedonia, another place trying to write its story for the world to read. I go for a bowl of soup in the Skopje bus station and review my hastily constructed plan for the next year like a house of cards I'm planning to use as a step stool.

If I can't spend the rest of the year living in Iraqi Kurdistan to find out what a country is, then I will travel to other places that exist somewhere in between the lines of the map. A quick search reveals there are a lot. In fact, here is a non-exhaustive list of regions vying for independence and recognition in the world:

- Tibet
- Palestine
- Taiwan
- Mapuche
- Tuareg
- Catalonia
- Sahrawi Arab Democratic Republic
- The Republic of South Ossetia
- Abkhazia
- The Republic of Artsakh
- Chiapas State
- Cascadia
- Jefferson
- Texas (Whenever there is a Democratic President)
- California (Whenever there is a Republican President)

A lifetime could be spent exploring the places between borders, but for the sake of finances and sanity, I'm constraining myself to a year. My journey will end in Somaliland, a chunk of the Horn of Africa fighting for independence from the federal government in Mogadishu. Before that I will go to Transnistria, a small slip of land between Moldova and Ukraine, which goes by the unsavory name *The Black Hole of Europe*. Meanwhile, I will keep bothering the President of Liberland for an invite to his libertarian paradise. But first, I have to go back to the place that inspired me to look at nations differently in the first place. I pay for my soup and throw my backpack around my shoulders.

Time to go to...

PART 2 KOSOVO

SERBIA

MITROVICA

NEWBORN
PRISHTINA

ALBANIA

NORTH
MACEDONIA

MOTHER TONGUE

I squeeze into a freezing bus between men wearing round felt caps and women in white headscarves. I hear a language I understand—Shqip (Albanian)—and it's like tuning a radio dial to a familiar song.

Aside from English, it is the only language that I can passably speak due to my Peace Corps service in northern Albania. It is also the mother tongue of the majority of the population of Kosovo. In the 1990s, fighting over this language and its people turned centuries of conflict into ethnic cleansing as Yugoslavia rattled apart, leaving Kosovo a partially recognized nation.

An old woman sits down next to me and casts a skeptical side eye.

"*Përshëndetje, si jeni?* Hello, how are you?" I say slipping into Shqip like a suit I haven't worn in awhile.

Her ancient face breaks into a glowing smile.

"*Shumë mirë! Nga jeni?* I'm very good! Where are you from?" She asks, chuffed and a little confused at the foreigner speaking her language.

"I'm from the United States," I reply. She kisses her fingers and raises them up to the heavens.

"Thank God for the U.S." she says.

I smile. As you might imagine, few places in the world thank God for the U.S. due to our tendency to blow stuff up and leave the locals to put it back together. But here we are in another bus, so it's time for some history:

Kosovo used to be part of Yugoslavia, until the nation broke apart into six distinct countries in the 1990s. Yugoslavia translates to *land of the southern Slavs,* so the ethnic majority was (shockingly) Slavic. *Slav* likely comes from an antonym which means *word*, an indicator that the Slavic people could be broadly defined by sharing a similar language family and, typically, Christian beliefs.

Granted, this is a wide umbrella which also includes Muslim and animist populations. In fact, a whole book could be written about what exactly makes a Slav a Slav. This is not that book. But language and religion are catalyzing forces in cobbling together a single nation from different identities. In spite of the vast array of cultures spread through the Balkan Peninsula, the pan-Slavic identity united millions in separate republics operating as a single nation.

The first iteration of Yugoslavia appeared following the end of World War I when the Ottoman Empire fell and the Allied Powers debated who got what. This process left the Kurds stateless while giving rise to the Kingdom of Serbs, Croats, and Slovenes which eventually became the Kingdom of Yugoslavia. In the 1940s a Socialist Revolution left the monarchy in the rearview mirror and The Socialist Federal Republic of Yugoslavia was born. But there was a problem: within the Serbian Republic there was an area called Kosovo. This was a place that the non-Slavic, largely Muslim, ethnically Albanian population called home.

The next part of the history is a point of fierce debate between Serbs and Kosovar Albanians. Since I am on my way to Kosovo I will tell you their point of view. Albanians see themselves as the indigenous people of the Southern Balkan Peninsula. Albanians descend from the Illyrian Tribes of antiquity and in Kosovo many trace their lineage to the Kingdom of Dardani, which goes all the way back to the 3rd century BC. The commonly held archeological record places Slavic migration into the Balkan Peninsula around the 6th century AD. For Serbs, Kosovo is important because it was the seat of original Kingdom of Serbia and the site of an important battle, which I will get to later.

From the Albanian Kosovar point of view, Serbian settlements are an intrusion on indigenous land. From the Serbian perspective, Kosovo is their spiritual and cultural heartland which was settled before any organized Albanian state. You can probably see where this is all going. At the intersection between language, religion, culture, and geography lies the fuel for centuries of conflict. Unfortunately, this is a story told time and time again in the Balkans.

The modern borders of the Balkans are a patchwork quilt stitched together from the remnants of ancient cultures enveloped into empires that crumbled. This leaves the people with two maps: one appears on the modern globe, the other is held in the heart. A Bulgarian will claim that Northern Macedonia is truly their country. An Albanian will describe the outline of their actual homeland stretching into modern Greece, up to Montenegro, encompassing a chunk of Northern Macedonia, and even parts of modern Serbia. Everyone will claim Alexander the Great as their ancestor. With thousands of years of unsettled history, a battle fought with swords and horses can reignite with machine guns and fighter jets. And that's what happened in the 1990s.

In Yugoslavia, Albanian Kosovars demonstrated for the right to provide their own infrastructure catering to communal needs in the Albanian language. This system made a tenuous but separate peace between them and the Serbian-speaking Slavic majority. In fact, Albanians and their mostly Serb neighbors lived, worked, and socialized together during this time. Still, powerful countries usually can't tolerate a massive diversity of identity for too long.

Minorities become scapegoats of convenience when things get hard. If you don't believe me I encourage you to look at all history ever.

Cue Serbian nationalist leader Slobadan Milošević's rise to power in 1989. As Yugoslavia began to collapse, the strongman attempted to rally control around Serbian-led Slavic nationalism while crushing independence movements across Yugoslavia. Like a despotic DJ he played the hits of totalitarianism: ethnic isolation, hypernationalism, whataboutism, and rewriting history on the fly.

The problem with Yugoslavia was not flagging economics, the fall of the Soviet Union, or the end of the Cold War. No, it was the Catholic Croats, the Muslim Bosniaks, and of course, those non-Slavic, Albanian-speaking Muslims. Suddenly, the Albanians were not an independently operating marginalized community, they were the problem. A brief sidebar: for those of you reading this who might want to grow up to be a dictator some day, don't try to police a culture out of existence. That's exactly how you get an insurgency and a civil war.

And that's what Milošević got.

In Kosovo, Albanian-speaking schools and hospitals were closed. The population resorted to peaceful protests and a network of homeschools to provide services and education. Demonstrations were met with violence as Milošević's police force turned into a military occupation. Albanian insurgent groups took up arms as Yugoslavia began to crumble.

Independence movements in Slovenia, Croatia, and Bosnia and Herzegovina surged as Milošević tried to write a singular story of their nation with bullets and mass ethnic cleansing. Like the Kurds in Iraq, the Albanians in Yugoslavia were a problem to be solved by politics, brutality, or both. From February of 1998 to June of 1999 Serbian security forces locked bloody horns with Albanian paramilitaries and the next chapter of war in Europe had begun. Some 700,000 refugees poured out of Kosovo, mostly crossing the border into Northern Macedonia or Albania. That's when the international community stepped in.

War brought an opportunity for regional influence. NATO (The North Atlantic Treaty Organization) stepped into the conflict and according to the Kosovar Albanians, God was on their side. Political pressure from NATO could only go so far, and the U.S. led a bombing campaign against Serbian armed forces. With the sky dominated and craters left in the capital of Belgrade, Milošević's multi-front war failed and he was forced to the negotiating table. UN Security Resolution 1244 was signed in 1999 and a UN-administered interim government was placed in Kosovo, while Serbia, Croatia, North Macedonia, Slovenia, Montenegro, and Bosnia and Herzegovina carved their borders out from the body of what was once Yugoslavia.

As of this writing, the Serbian government claims that Kosovo is Serbia. Belgrade maintains the rubble of the bombed buildings as a monument to NATO aggression. In Kosovo's capital Prishtina, there is a statue of Bill Clinton who instigated the bombing. While the old woman in the bus next to me might thank God for the United States, another old woman on another bus in Serbia bus might curse us as the devil.

"Why are you coming to Prishtina?" she asks.

"I'm going for Independence Day," I say.

"*Shume bukur,*" she says.

Very beautiful.

PRISHTINA'S PAST LIVES

Upon arriving at the bus station in Prishtina, Kosovo, I'm reminded that I have no job. Albanians usually think about problems like this by going on a long slow walk around the town. This is called a *xhiro* (gee-row) in the standard *Tosk* Albanian, or a *shetitje* (she-tEEt-ya) in the *Gheg* Albanian dialect spoken in Kosovo. After years of living in Albania, I know how to *xhiro/shetit* with the best of them. I begin my walk from the bus station towards the snow-lined heart of Prishtina.

An endless chatter of crows greets me as I pass by a statue of Bill Clinton forever holding a disproportionately large hand in the air. I've asked several Kosovars why his hand is so big and no one seems to know but everyone notices it. It looks like he has a tennis racquet on the end of his wrist.

I climb a slush-lined hill behind President Clinton and survey the city. Prishtina doesn't look like the capital of a country; it looks like the foundation of one. Pallets of paving stones and building projects sit at the intersection of new construction and historical preservation. The Mother Theresa Cathedral is festooned with scaffolding near The National Library of Kosovo, sometimes called *the ugliest building in Europe* (look it up and you decide). In the distance a collection of mosques sing the call to prayer from the cobblestone streets of the old town. A Serbian Orthodox church sits abandoned and lifeless in the city's heart. Gray smog hangs over the tiny metropolis caught in the bowl of foothills.

As I descend into the measured chaos of Prishtina, I realize that I feel at home. My first walk through Erbil was a potentially disastrous game of traffic hopscotch and cultural faux pas', but in Prishtina, I know how to read the signs, cross the street, and hopefully find a job. For the moment, the world seems legible and kind.

The city center is a sleepy improvisation of traffic-crammed streets and just-laid boulevards. Skeletons of brutalist Yugoslav architecture are filled with a mix of sumptuous cafes, garish neon bars, and smoke-thick restaurants playing the jangling chords of Northern Albanian folk music. Coffee shops are full at all hours with young people in puffer jackets nursing espresso while they watch old men with prayer beads walk the same route they've traveled since before Kosovo gained its partial recognition.

On every corner is evidence of the city's past lives. Serbian street names are blacked out with spray paint, photos of freedom fighters and folk heroes gaze from portraits draped across buildings, a United Nations security base crouches behind high fences guarded by foreign peacekeepers. I pass by city workers clearing snow drifts off the road under blue and gold banners shouting *10 years of Independence*.

LEARNING TO WALK

One benefit of being unemployed is having the time to stare at things on the street. After all, I have no where better to be. I stop outside the National Palace of Youth and Sports and find large concrete letters spelling the word NEWBORN. When I first came to Kosovo for its five-year anniversary in 2012 it was painted bright yellow. It glowed as a kind of declaration: *We've been here for five years and we're not going anywhere.* It was as if the Kosovar people were born again with all the hope and optimism that comes from a new life.

Now, Newborn is covered with handwritten messages and the B has been replaced with a 1 making it into

NEW1ORN. After experiencing the failed referendum in Erbil, I wonder if I've misunderstood the statue. Newborns are vulnerable, they rely on others to hold their hand as they take their first steps. Is Kosovo *newly born...* or is it *a newborn?*

Since I can't spend all day looking at statues, I begin my quest for employment. While looking for a local English school I notice a storefront sign reading *Kosovo 2.0.* A quick search reveals that it's a culture magazine written in English, Albanian, and Serbian. I press the buzzer on the intercom. A voice speaking Albanian comes on the line.

"*Përshëndetje,* Hello?"

"Hello," I say.

At this point I realize that I have no idea how to introduce myself. Am I an exiled English teacher on the run after being banned from Turkey? Am I a lost American returning to the last place that felt like home to regain a lost sense of self? Am I a part-time journalist attempting to answer a single pointless question? The truth is I am all of these, but I probably shouldn't say any of them. Instead, I say:

"I'm a writer and I speak a little Albanian. I was wondering if you needed anyone to work here?"

I wish that I had had a couple more days of practicing my Albanian before unleashing that parade of words. Silence on the intercom.

The lock clicks open and a voice tells me to come up.

COMMON LANGUAGE

Kosovo 2.0 was founded on the philosophy that shared narrative can bridge a cultural divide. Humanity is something we all share and the currency of humanity is story.

Unfortunately, humanity doesn't pay very well, at least that's what my new editor Jack tells me.

"We can't pay you anything, but we'd be happy to have you work with us."

We stand in the freezing office kitchen sipping mugs of tea surrounded by magazines organized around a universal theme which defies being crammed into borders like family, sex, and tradition.

"Sounds good," I say, even though this sounds just okay.

"Great, I'll show you to your desk."

We walk down the hallway to a small office where I meet my new colleagues. Atdhe, a tall photo journalist with red hair nods at me while editing images. Leonora, a writer with a dark bob cut and glasses waves while talking on the phone and jotting notes. Eraldin, stands up from his desk to greet me. As I shake his hand and introduce myself I notice the cornea of one of his eyes has gone white from an injury. I take note but don't ask.

Jack shows me to an empty desk by the window. I take a seat in my new chair. It's been a month since I left Iraqi Kurdistan, a week since I got banned from Turkey, and an hour since I got my new job in Prishtina. I take a spin in my office chair and look at my new colleagues.

Home again for now.

A GOOD WAY TO LOOK LIKE
YOU'RE DOING SOMETHING

A story comes across my desk the next day. Apparently, Prishtina is one of the most polluted cities in the world and the people are fed up. So, they're organizing a march.

This is weird since the tiny nation has no major indus-trial manufacturing, a shrinking population, and the largest city can be walked across in a brisk 45 minutes. However, since arriving in Prishtina my lungs have felt like I've been smoking a carton of Marlboro Reds daily. Leonora tells me that she is going to the protest, so I grab my camera and follow her. The air is cold but murky with gray smog. She strides towards the main drag filling me in on the situation.

"Too much building, too many cars, and the power plants. They're just making things for political reasons not because we need it."

She shoulders a camera bag. She's like every great journalist I've worked with: too smart, too busy, and underpaid. The kind of reporter that is able to snake charm high ranking government officials and then barbecue them in print.

"Every successive government promoted the idea of building bigger power plants to sell electricity outside of Kosovo but people aren't connected to the grid here. They heat their houses with wood burning stoves. On top of that, they're building roads we don't need."

"Why?" I ask.

"Corruption, money laundering. Everyone gets paid while they're building and it looks like the government is doing something."

We hear the protest from down the street. A PA system squeals as a microphone is plugged in, we hear marching footsteps on the boulevard, and excited conversation from a crowd of hundreds. Atdhe whizzes by us puffing on a cigarette as he adjusts his focus and takes aim. People wear surgical masks and re-breathers. School children hold hands with grandparents and students march alongside businessmen in suits. A chant starts among them as they fill the street.

We want to breathe.

I begin interviewing. Young mothers with children

squirming in their arms worry about them growing up in clouds of smog. Old men talk about suspicious cancers and friends that made it through the war only to be killed by the air. Young professionals lament having to leave Kosovo because the opportunity to quite literally breath free is somewhere else. I meet an engineer working at the power plants. He takes off a face mask to talk with me:

"The margins on electricity are better than cocaine."

I am unsure of how he is calculating a cocaine-to-electricity ratio, but I'll take his word for it.

"They think that if we sell electricity to the rest of the region that maybe no one will start fighting again. Capitalist peace theory." His voice drips with cynicism.

The idea is that if you can entangle two economies in a mutually beneficial way then countries will have more incentive to collaborate than to fight. This is sometimes called the *McDonalds Peace Theory*, which says that no two countries with a McDonalds would ever go to war. Seriously, this is a real theory. This theory was obliterated when Russia went to war with the Republic of Georgia resulting in the creation of South Ossetia, another unrecognized nation. While the rest of former Yugoslavia might need Kosovar electricity, it's difficult to believe that would be enough to build a foundation of lasting peace. After all, neither Kosovo nor Serbia has a McDonalds.

The man I'm speaking to adjusts his mask.

"But making these oversized power plants ruins our air right now, so that *maybe* we can sell electricity in the future. It's foolish."

"Are the plants making jobs for people?" I ask.

"Maybe, but that doesn't help much when everyone wants to leave. Some government officials and Western European companies will benefit, but they don't care what happens to us. The people who benefit from this policy don't live here. We do."

The protest goes as most protests usually do. Everyone stands around and chants. Rousing speeches are followed by lip service promises from politicians. In this case, they stop allowing cars entering the city center to momentarily scrub the air. It seems that politics in Kosovo are similar to many places. It's more important to seem effective rather than to be effective. It occurs to me that this is not about pollution, it's about having a right to a future tense.

What do you do with a country once you have it?

DECLARING INDEPENDENCE
AND YOU CAN TOO

No one makes a country on their own. Countries are made with a soldier's blood and a politician's ink. But, between the end of fighting and the signing of a treaty, conflict settles into tense ambiguity with the constant threat of violence. This is what happened in Kosovo. The war ended in 1999 but it was not declared an independent nation until February of 2008. Nine years of uncertainty. This is where making a country gets confusing, because declaring independence and gaining recognition are two different things. You can declare yourself a country right now if you want. Write it down on a piece of paper, make a flag, yell it across the coffee shop you're sitting in. See? Nothing happened.

That's because if you want to make a country, you need to declare yourself a nation and then gain recognition from the rest of the world. The second part is way harder. Ideally, every nation in the world agrees on your existence. But, getting every country on earth to agree on anything never happens. While Kosovar sovereignty was recognized by over 100 nations it was rejected by many more.

At this point we get into what I call *Kosovo's weird venn diagram of transnational bodies and international relations (or the KWVDTNBIR)*. The EU and UN officially recognize Kosovar independence and NATO fought for it; the United Nations, European Union and the North Atlantic Treaty Organization don't speak for their constituent parts. That means that five European Union countries and a slew of other nations don't recognize Kosovo. This might be because of a close relationship with Serbia or fear of igniting internal separatist movements. After all, Spain would look pretty silly supporting a sovereign Kosovo while suppressing Catalonian independence. According to the countries that don't recognize Kosovo, in February of 2008, nothing important happened and there was no new nation in Europe. Kosovo? Never heard of them.

A nation that isn't universally recognized turns their place on the globe into an island. When new passports were issued for Kosovo they came with heavy restrictions. To live and work around the world, Kosovars need to navigate a complex system designed to keep them isolated rather than integrated. Want to leave Kosovo? You'll pay a hefty application fee and wait six months to a year for an interview while you risk being rejected anyway. Ironically, both Serbia and Kosovo continue to lobby the European Union for entrance, but their outstanding conflict means that no one gets in. The people of Kosovo are left with new passports and very few places to use them.

THE TWO DAFINAS

The next day I'm invited to attend a media conference. Given that I've been working for Kosovo 2.0 for less than a week, I hope that no one asks me any questions. Fortunately, at lunch I am seated across from two women, both named Dafina, who have collectively drunk six glasses of white wine, so they're doing most of the talking.

"Why are you here?" asks Dafina One.

"I got banned from Turkey while trying to find out what a country is, so I came to Kosovo."

"Weird," she says.

"I know. So, what is it like to build a country?" I ask.

Dafina Two, does a tight-lipped downward frown that says, *you don't really want to know.*

"After the fighting, the treaty, all of it, that's when the real struggle begins," she says, refreshing my glass of wine.

"We should tell him about the evacuation," says Dafina One.

To my surprise they both start laughing. Evacuating ahead of an ethnic cleansing doesn't seem like comedy gold to me. When they pull themselves together the first Dafina looks at me from across the table and begins the story:

"This was in Ferizaj, where we are from." She points between herself and the other Dafina.

"It's close to Prishtina. Maybe 30 minutes. Fighting was starting. It's not like an army coming into the city. Serbs were our neighbors. Albanians are all trying to get onto the train to leave." Dafina One drinks her wine and Dafina Two takes over:

"But we don't know how long the train will keep going. I remember the adults just pulling us along to the train station. We just had what we were wearing."

"Where was the train going?" I ask.

"Skopje." They both answer at the same time.

The capital of North Macedonia was one of the safer

places for Kosovar refugees because of the sympathetic Albanian population there and the direct rail connection.

"We are running towards the train platform. The whole town is there. We can hear guns," says the first Dafina.

"The doors of the train open and everyone goes into one cabin. But it's too many people, it's too hot inside. No one can breathe. We feel like we're dying. We just want the train to go. It's not going. The adults are pushing and fighting. People we have known all our lives. They are like animals because this is the crisis mentality. Animal mentality."

"There is one guy with a bottle of water," interjects Dafina Two, with acid in her voice. "And he will not give it to anyone. He says, 'No, this is my water, you should have brought some.' And I think that they're going to kill this guy even though he is Albanian."

"Because that's the mentality. Like animals. You can't imagine," choruses Dafina One.

"But then the train moves. We're hot, and thirsty, and scared and we don't know what will happen when we get to the border. And this guy is just drinking his water while everyone wants to kill him."

Then the Dafinas laugh, unable to continue.

"Wait. What's funny about this story?" I ask, wondering if I've missed the punchline.

"When we got off the train," Dafina One says, "we realized that the other train cars were empty and they had bottles of water in them. We all just jumped in the same car and almost killed that guy because we were scared."

"Animal mentality," I say.

"Yes, you can't imagine," the Dafinas say.

They're right.

I can't imagine.

GRAVEYARD ON THE BORDER

I meet Shaban at a sun-drenched coffee shop over-looking Prishtina. The mechanical engineering professor looks exactly like whatever mechanical engineering professor you're imagining. He has a shock of wild white hair, a neat beard, and he has the ability to make the most complicated topic understandable. This might be why, during the war, he became the head of the Reuters bureau in Prishtina.

"What do you want to know?" he asks as tea arrives.

We start from the beginning. Shaban tells me that he went to an English language School in the United Kingdom for a short term in the 1970s when Kosovo was firmly a part of Yugoslavia.

"I remember, I introduced myself to the group and I said 'I am an Albanian from Yugoslavia.' Now, there was another Serbian guy there too. He comes up to me after-wards and says 'why don't you just say that you're from Yugoslavia?' And I told him that it's important to say I'm Albanian because this is who I am. We got along after that though."

"But this was when Yugoslavia was under Tito. Was he a bit better for the Albanian population?" I ask. Josip Broz Tito was the first Communist leader of Yugoslavia.

He stirs his tea and looks up at me.

"No, this is a misunderstanding. He was deporting Albanians. Making them change their names, this kind of thing. It became something different with Milošević. More killing. You can't imagine what Prishtina looked like. Origi-nally, we set up the Reuters office in the Grand Hotel, but it was too dangerous so we moved."

"Where did you go when the fighting started?" I ask, trying to imagine this quiet city crumbling in war.

"I was in Prishtina, but when NATO bombing started I moved my family to an apartment in Skopje. It was a frightening time because my wife was pregnant and I had two daughters, eight and four years old. My son was born in Macedonia, but we had to use a hospital in Tetovo. His birth in Skopje was not welcomed as a Kosovar Albanian."

"And then you came back?"

"Of course, I had to. And you, why are you here?" he asks.

"I began this trip in Iraqi Kurdistan because I wanted to see a country being made. But that didn't happen. Now I don't know what a country actually is."

Shaban nods.

"When we were covering the Peace Agreement in Rambouillet in 1999, some Kurdish guys came too. Protesting, asking why they didn't have an agreement for a state as well."

The Rambouillet Agreement in 1999 was aimed at establishing a self-administered Kosovo. It's hard to imagine Kurdish activists attempting to gain recognition for their state while a tentative line was being drawn around Kosovo. Just like at the end of World War I, the West was ready to fight for Europe and let the Middle East fend for itself. Just like at the end of World War I treaties were backed by the threat of violence. When Serbia did not accept the Rambouillet Agreement, the bombing campaign began.

"When you moved your family back to Prishtina, was it a happy time?"

"We had to start over. Everything was broken or taken because the Serbs moved into our apartment. The things I would see and hear once we got back, it would be hard for you to imagine. Like all Albanians, we were still under

123

repression by the Serbian forces, and this was during 78 days of bombing."

"Was there ever that moment of euphoria? Like when the peace agreement is signed, or maybe when Kosovo became a state? Did you ever feel like you won?"

He shakes his head and finishes the last bit of his tea.

"No." Shaban pauses me to greet some passing neighbors. Just a couple of middle-aged people enjoying a quiet, normal day, kissing one another on the cheek and exchanging platitudes. *It's a lovely day out isn't it. Yes it is.*

Shaban takes his seat again and looks at me.

"Like I was saying. No, there's no moment of euphoria. We just keep going."

"When does the fight to actually make a country end?"

He purses his lips and looks across the city.

"There's a graveyard on the border of Albania and Kosovo. I think that's where it ends. At that point, you have no other responsibilities. You've done everything you can."

"What about the Serbs still living here?"

"I can't speak for them. You should find out though."

GHOSTS AND MONUMENTS

"This is where the battle happened." My cab driver points out the window at a stone tower in the distance.

We're cruising along the modern super-highway following plumes of smoke from the power plants. They're huge tumors of machinery cradled in a nest of roads and foothills. My driver, Ishak, glances back at me in the rearview mirror. He sports some Morpheus sunglasses and slicked back hair. Metallica blares in the car as we speed down the road.

"Sorry, which battle?" I ask, realizing that this is a very broad question in the Balkans.

He yells over the music, "The Battle of Kosovo. Gazimestan. See? The Serbs have it fenced off."

I look out the window. The collection of gas stations, furniture stores and a go-kart track give no indication that this was the site of a major historical event. Ishak pulls off the highway. Barbed wire and security cameras seal off the grounds from the outside world. It looks like a military installation instead of a monument.

"You want me to wait for you?"

"No, I'll find my own way back." I hand him a couple Euros.

"Okay, good luck."

He speeds off as I enter the gates. There, a Serb guard takes my passport and searches my bag. Another guard peeks out from the top of the tower. I try not to do anything suspicious. Gazimestan represents a critical moment in the Serbian story of Kosovo. But, the Battle of Kosovo didn't take place in the 1990s and they weren't fighting Albanian paramilitaries. History lasts a long time and whoever protects it gets to keep their version alive.

In 1389 the Ottoman Empire was on a path of conquest through the Balkans that led right through Gazimestan. This broad swath of land is currently the intersection of two highways and that's more or less what it was for a medieval army on a warpath. Sultan Murad I rallied his army to overtake the Balkans and plunge into the heart of Europe. Medieval armies aren't so great at climbing mountains, so this wide flat plain flanked by rivers made for a perfect onramp. However, similar to today, people don't much like being conquered. Serbian Prince Lazar Hrebeljanovic cobbled together an allied force which included Serbs, Bulgars, Macedonians, Greeks, Bosnians, and yes, even Albanians.

Differences in culture, language and history could be

set aside in the face of conquest. While the blow-by-blow of the Battle of Kosovo is not clear, the outcome is. It ended with the death of both Prince Lazar and Sultan Murad I. The Serbian-aligned forces were too weak to mount their defense against the Ottomans, and eventually much of the Balkan peninsula surrendered. Now all that's left is a strip mall next to a monument.

I climb to the top of the tower passing another guard in the stairwell. He follows me to the viewing deck. There, I find a plaque that shows the Ottoman battle positions indicated by the crescent moon. Opposing them is the Serbian-led position. I try to imagine medieval soldiers preparing themselves to crash into one another and wonder what might be going through each of their minds. Was Prince Lazar able to make them forget their separate languages, cultures, and beliefs for this one battle? Were they thinking about the glory of reviving the Serbian Empire or just wishing they could be back home doing whatever it is people did in the Middle Ages.

The guard leaves, content that I won't steal the plaque.

I stand looking at the power plants chugging smog into the air like the smokestack on a train to nowhere. The world has come a long way since 1389, but within these fences the memory of the Battle of Kosovo is frozen in time. If I were the ghost of a soldier that fought and fell here, aside from marveling at the go-kart track in the distance, I would probably notice the mosques dotting the landscape. I'd see the crescent moon everywhere around me and conclude that we didn't win. At this point I don't think I would care about nationality.

Even though the Battle of Kosovo was a loss it became more profound as it passed from the heartache of defeat, to anger at conquest, before finally settling into a rallying cry for Serbian sovereignty over Kosovo. The story paints

Serbia as not only a protector of Christendom in the Balkans, but the faithful in Europe. This is what led Slobodon Milošević to give his famous *Gazimestan Speech* in 1989 on the 600th anniversary of the Battle of Kosovo. On this field, in front of millions, he spoke in the thinly veiled parlance of a dictator tip-toeing towards atrocity masked as liberation.

He promised that Serbian leadership, regardless of national or religious affiliation, was the only way towards prosperity.

He cited disunity as the reason for the loss of the battle of Kosovo, while reminding the millions gathered that the fight had not truly ended.

He mentioned that the battles the Serbian people were facing were not armed. He hinted that they could be soon. It's hard to imagine a million people in this field stirred to nationalist fervor while the Albanian population looked on, wondering when words would turn to bullets.

But Gazemistan is empty now. Except for the two guards and a dog sleeping by the entrance, I'm the only one here.

According to the over 100 countries that recognize Kosovo, this holy site is no longer in Serbia. It is as if Gettysburg was suddenly a part of Cuba. But from the Serb point of view, high on this tower looking out into Kosovo, the battle may have been lost, but the war was far from over.

I wonder if that's true for the Serbs still living in Kosovo. I collect my passport from the guard, pass through the barbed wire fences, and continue down a street lined with Albanian homes.

It's a very long walk back to Prishtina. I should have had the cab wait for me. I just thought there would be more to see.

ANOTHER DIMENSION

A billboard with the Serbian president greets me as I enter Gračanica. I'm surprised to see him only a couple miles from the center of Prishtina in the Serbian enclave. It's like being dropped off in an alternate reality where Kosovo never cleaved itself from Serbia.

I close my coat against the frosty wind and walk through the center of town. An old man sells cabbages from the front of his grocery store, cafes blast Balkan techno-folk, dogs nip each other in an unfinished building. It looks like any other small town in Kosovo but everything is written in Serbian. Fifteen minutes in the opposite direction is a capital preparing to celebrate an independence day that, it seems, never happened here.

This is the strange voodoo of new borders. When the war ended, some Serb communities were left in Kosovo, while some Albanian communities remained in Serbia. A line drawn in the court of compromise means that the people of Gračanica are now citizens of a country they never wanted to be a part of. But leaving is difficult, because to them, they are stewards of the heartland which will eventually be reclaimed. Their ancestors fought for Gračanica for hundreds of years, so why would they stop now?

I follow an Orthodox priest with a long beard and black robes to an ornate monastery protected by thick stone walls, barbed wire, and more security cameras. The entrance welcomes visitors into the ancient building made of pale stone topped with crosses. The church and monastery in Gračanica have stood in some way since the 1300s, but its foundations go back to Byzantium. It has been defended against everyone from the horse-mounted janissaries of the Ottoman Empire to the bombs of NATO.

In the courtyard, feather-light snow filters down from a gray sky. Women in heavy coats light beeswax prayer candles and stand in silent contemplation in an outdoor chapel. From what I understand the candles lit on the top rack are for the living, and those on the bottom are for the dead. I wonder who the women are praying for.

I pass by nuns' quarters, a small garden, and a grave-yard of marble crosses where lacquered pictures of monks gaze out into eternity. A small pile of ashes catches my eye. It is a half-burned Serbian flag. I find this odd since the monastery wouldn't want to burn their own flag. I enter the church to see if I can find an answer.

When I push through the heavy wooden door I'm greeted with the smell of incense and paintings of bearded saints under shimmering halos. Jesus Christ peers down at me from the domed ceiling and I am suddenly aware that I haven't been to confession in over 20 years. I cross myself for good measure. I turn to see a painting of the final judgment framing the entrance.

On one side, sinners are tortured by demons next to a blood-red river. For some reason none of them are wearing pants. On the other side Saint Peter holds the keys to Heaven in front of a gate guarded by an angel with flaming swords. Within the walls of Heaven the prophets Abraham, Moses, and Jesus hold the faithful, all of whom are wearing pants, in their arms. But there is an additional figure that I don't recognize.

"You are from where?" Startled, I turn to see a docent entering from the chapel. He's in his sixties wearing a cropped beard and gray hair pulled back into a neat ponytail.

"The United States," I say.

He gives me a curt nod and turns to leave.

"Who is this other person?" I ask, hoping to find some common ground.

"Do you know your Bible?"

He approaches the fresco. I shrug hoping that I can call upon my Catholic school education. He points towards the figure standing next to Jesus.

"The thief that died at the side of Christ."

"Saint Dismas," I say, knowing this because my friend, Dave, took it as his confirmation name. The man raises his eyebrows, impressed with my fun Bible fact. He introduces himself. Trojan is a Serbian living in Kosovo who volunteers to share the story of the monastery. I ask him about the burned flag.

"We found it outside of the monastery, maybe some of our neighbors lit it on fire to send a message. We told the police. What else can we do?"

I nod. I don't know what they can do.

We stand in front of the last judgment as we try to navigate a difficult conversation about Kosovo and Serbia.

JUDGEMENT DAY

"Let me show you something."

He guides me to a corner of the church and points out a brick that is brighter than the rest. Its edges are crumbling with a pile of dust collected underneath.

"This is a new brick. It's maybe 30 years old and already breaking. The rest are maybe 300 years old, but they don't break." He places a hand on the ancient stone work. "We think that we are so smart because we have computers. But why is this brick breaking when the rest are strong? We have forgotten something."

"What do you think that is?" I ask.

"The truth," he says.

"And the truth for you is that Kosovo is Serbia?" I ask.

He nods and begins walking me through the alternate history hovering over this land.

"Serbia is one of the first Christian nations. We have the documents protected in Greece and Istanbul that show Serbian churches with land and communities for centuries. But Albania is…"

I can see him try to parse his words.

"Albania is a western invention from 1913. Even the word, *Kosovo*, it means nothing in Albanian, but in Serbian it means *field of crows*. They destroyed our churches, which for us is worse than killing a person."

As he speaks there's an emotional rattle in his voice and the corners of his eyes redden. He wipes his hands together and raises them to the sky.

"But this is all a political thing," he says.

"Do you think that this area will eventually be returned to Serbia?" I ask. He nods and puts a hand to his heart.

"Of course. This is like… half time, in the football match. It is not over. The truth will always win."

The thought of more violence spilling across this place chills my blood.

Does Trojan think this will be the last independence day before Serbia comes to reclaim its land?

Does he want that?

I don't ask because he begins moving me towards the exit. He points out that we are walking under the painting of Judgement Day. I am very aware of this fact.

"This is a good lesson to take into the world. You always have two choices. Which side will you be on?"

Trojan and I part ways in the church yard and his words ring in my head.

BIG GLASS PENIS
FULL OF BOOZE

Snow falls in thick sheets and it doesn't look like I'll be able to get a ride back to Prishtina any time soon. After speaking with Trojan I find myself doubting reality, history, and even bricks. Is he right? Is this brief moment of relative peace and recognition just an intermission before a bloody second act? Are there really documents in foreign monasteries which prove that Kosovo is indeed the heartland of the Serbs? What do they do once that brick crumbles entirely? It must be important if they put it there.

Two competing stories battle, pushing an invisible line to the north and to the south. But what I think doesn't matter because it's not my country, I don't have an army, and I am not an ambassador. I am not penned into these narrow borders awaiting a diplomatic resolution, or a bloody revolution. What do you do with a country once you have it? What happens if your fellow citizens don't believe the same thing you do?

I have wandered into a coffee shop, and I am staring out of the window at snow falling in the street with a cold espresso in front of me.

"Where you from?" asks a guy about my age from behind the bar. He has a short beard and the high and tight buzz cut favored by the gentlemen of the Balkans.

"Los Angeles," I say hoping that he doesn't want to talk about politics or history or genocide or churches or bricks.

"L.A. Big city," he says, reaching under the bar. He retrieves a big glass penis filled with clear liquid. He balances the bottle on its testicles and raises his eyebrows.

"You know what this is?" he asks me.

"It looks like a big glass penis." I reply.

"Correct," he says."It's full of rakija. You tried rakija?"

He removes a cork from the phallus and pours shots. Rakija is a flammable moonshine enjoyed all over the Balkans. This will not be my first rodeo with rakija.

"Yup, just never quite like that," I say as he approaches my table.

"I'm Aleksandar. It means, defender," he says, putting a shot in front of me and setting the big glass dick full of booze between us.

"I'm Eric, and I have no idea what my name means."

We knock back our shots.

PEACE, RECONCILIATION, AND ALIENS

"I never saw an alien, but I think they are out there," says Aleksandar. "The universe, it's big. We cannot be alone."

We've already drained the head and the shaft of the bottle and we're working our way towards the balls. Somewhere between the first and second shot Aleksandar and I decided to solve the Kosovo conflict together. By the third or fourth we decided that it was better to stop talking about politics, and we got onto aliens.

"An alien invasion is the only way that we get all of humanity working together," I reply.

"But then we have aliens to worry about."

"That's true."

"It's like the Will Smith movie," says Aleksandar behind a veil of cigarette smoke.

"*Independence Day*. Totally. Humanity worked together. Maybe we need the aliens," I say, realizing that I sound as drunk as I am.

"Yeah, but it was propaganda."

"*Independence Day*?"

"They came together because of America. The whole

movie is like, the *American* president making speeches and the *American* military blowing shit up. Then the *American* scientist finds out how to kill the aliens. It's all America. It's propaganda. It's even called *Independence Day*."

"Other countries have independence days," I say before catching myself. Aleksandar gives me a cold glare and then breaks into a grin.

"It's fine. Prishtina can have its celebration. It's not my independence day," says Aleksandar as we sip our shots.

"What do you think a country is?" I ask.

"Do you ask that to everybody?" He stubs his cigarette out.

"Pretty much."

"I don't give a shit man. I just want to live. To work. Have a family, whatever. Same as the Albanians. They can call themselves whatever they want. I'm gonna call myself whatever I want." Aleksandar grabs the bottle and shows it to me. "We're all drinking from the same dick."

He sloshes the liquor from head to balls. I contemplate his words like a zen riddle. The snow has stopped falling. Aleksandar offers me a ride back to Prishtina. He's drunk enough to offer and I'm drunk enough to accept. We put up the chairs, turn off the lights, and leave the penis mostly empty. We hop into his old Peugeot and putter through the snow.

"You should go to Mitrovica. You're gonna see real Kosovo there," he says as I jump out of his car in Prishtina.

"I will, and thanks for everything." Aleksandar nods his head, lights a cigarette and leans out of his window.

"Remember man. We all drink from the same dick."

He rolls up the window and drives off through the slush-lined streets. I stagger through the snow towards my apartment. If people could just live and work and make a future for themselves, would it matter what their passport said or what they called themselves? Can you separate a country from its wealth and military? It seems that half a penis full of rakija is enough to turn me into a libertarian.

That's when I remember Liberland. I drunkenly pull out my phone in the middle of the street and decide to message the president.

Dear President Jedlicka! This is Eric...

THOMAS THE NATIONALISM ENGINE

I sit in the newsroom of Kosovo 2.0 nursing a hang-over. I feel like I got drunk and had a one-night stand as a Serbian nationalist. I remember the city that Aleksandar mentioned, *Mitrovica*. I've heard the name before when I was working as a fledgling intelligence analyst.

Mitrovica is a town in northern Kosovo where the Albanian and Serbian populations are divided by a river. In 2004, while diplomats negotiated the borders of Kosovo, the region plunged into chaos once again when a Serbian teenager was wounded in a drive-by shooting. The next day three Albanian children drown in the river dividing Mitrovica, allegedly because they were chased by Serbians.

These events unleashed the collective anger and resent-ment between Serbs and Albanians left simmering after the war. While foreign peacekeepers tried to maintain order, riots erupted throughout the country, leaving almost 30 people dead, and countless homes and Orthodox churches destroyed. Years later, Mitrovica is still a keg of dynamite, because no country or city can hold two stories at the same time. Reality only works if we all agree on it.

While I was an analyst, I reported on the Serbian government sending a train painted with the words *Kosovo is Serbia*, in multiple world languages to Mitrovica. The

Serbian government was dedicated to keeping their narrative alive and in this case, the fight took the form of a commuter train carrying symbols of Serbian nationalism.

The Albanian population was furious and Kosovo's limited armed forces deployed along Europe's newest border. Meanwhile, the Serbian population residing in the country cheered for its arrival. International powers urged calm as the train made its way towards Mitrovica. It looked like a passenger train painted with the words *Kosovo is Serbia* might be the spark to set the conflict burning once again.

Then the train stopped and returned to Belgrade. The purpose of this was never to reestablish commuter service, it was to deliver a message. Blind nationalism is a poison that can be hidden anywhere, a hat, a song, or in this case, a train. If you ever find yourself unreasonably angry or filled with pride because of a political symbol, it's best to wonder who wants you to feel like that.

"Hey Leonora, is it safe to go to Mitrovica?" I ask across the office.

"You can. Maybe don't cross the bridge," she says and goes back to typing.

GOD AND COUNTRY

The highway connecting Prishtina and Mitrovica is a mixture of the 1980s and the 1380s. Concrete houses sit half built alongside medieval cottages surrounded farmland. New BMWs cruise alongside mule-drawn carriages. This is a place evolving and crumbling at equal speeds locking it into a strange twilight. A light patter of rain falls from the steel gray sky clamped over Kosovo.

My bus stops to let a woman in a wheelchair and her mother aboard. With practiced motion, the woman lifts herself into the seat next to me. Her mother folds the chair and stows it behind the driver. After the usual *who are you, what are you doing here, and why do you speak Albanian?* She tells me that she's coming back from a physical therapy appointment in the city, since they have no doctors that can treat her in Mitrovica. The bus chugs along and we drift into silence watching rain speckle the windshield. Her mother nods off to sleep.

"What is your faith?" she asks.

This is a fairly common question in Kosovo which can read as invasive to foreigners. Other such examples of this include: *How much money do you make? Are you married? Why aren't you married? And You're a little bit fat aren't you?* I tell her that I am a Catholic for lack of a better spiritual description. She searches my eyes as if trying to determine my faith in God.

"I'm Muslim. God keeps me safe," she says, patting her legs. She goes on to tell me that during fighting in Mitrovica a bullet hit her in the spine.

"I was laying in the street. A lot of blood around me. I thought I was going to die that day," she says as a simple matter of fact. "I was very lucky God wanted me to live. He will keep you safe too" She points to the roof of the bus, above which God is certainly watching.

"Do you ever think about leaving Mitrovica? Maybe just to be closer to your doctor?" I ask. She clucks her tongue at me which is Albanian for *of course not.*

"No. It's my home. I can't leave my home."

THIS IS A DIVIDED CITY

Mitrovica feels like it has been pulled inside out. Cities usually direct you towards their center. A historic core, marketplace, or tower that guides newcomers to the beating heart of a place. This is not the case in Mitrovica. Its heart is split in two.

The weather has turned to a constant freezing dribble. I walk through crowded streets of people out for their daily walk. Bursts of conversations leap from raucous coffee shops, teenagers smoke at bus stops, and market customers examine produce with a jeweler's eye. As I approach the center of Mitrovica voices recede. Nothing but quiet and a distant river.

I know that I am in the center when I see no one on the street except for a United Nations vehicle with old bullet holes plugged into the windshield. The main street extends onto a bridge that divides the Serbian North Mitrovica from the Albanian South. I walk along to the sound of my solitary footsteps and the early rain until I hear a helicopter hovering. The ever-watchful eye of the United Nations.

I come upon a statue gazing towards the Serbian side of the city wearing a traditional rounded felt cap. He holds an Albanian flag and wears a revolver around his waist, forever ready to fire at anything that might come his way. Isa Boletini, a Northern Albanian folk hero who spent his life fighting for the independence of his people against the Ottoman Empire, now stands at the flashpoint between Albanian and Serbian Kosovo staring across the river.

I want to know what he is looking at.

OVER TROUBLED WATER

I approach a couple of *carabinieri*s (Italian peacekeepers) drinking espresso by the bridge and ask them if I can cross. They shrug. This is not a ringing endorsement for my safety. If I cross this bridge am I asking for trouble like Clare dressing up in drag to run around Kirkuk? If I don't go, am I letting fear pen me into comfortable under-standing and easily held beliefs? As usual, I'm afraid but I'm doing it anyway.

I walk towards the bridge. I hear the rushing water and the occasional *thup thup thup* of the helicopter. There isn't a person in sight, but I feel like both sides are watching when I stop at the dead center. To the south sit empty Albanian coffee shops and restaurants; to the north, Serbian flags and concrete roadblocks. Below me, water rushes from the mountains of Montenegro to the Black Sea.

I cross through the barricades and onto the paved walking street where I assume Serbs have a nice *xhiro* or whatever they call it. A statue appears and there he is: Prince Lazar pointing what feels like an accusatory finger in my direction. He must know that I'm not from around here. Even though I can't see him, I can feel the Isa Bole-tini statue staring down Prince Lazar from across the river.

Boletini lived 500 years after the death of Lazar, but surprisingly, they lived their lives and died their deaths in similar ways. Both rebelled against the rule of the Ottoman Empire as it began swallowing up the Balkan Peninsula. Both collaborated across ethnic and religious lines because domination by a larger power was enough incentive to put aside differences. Both died violent deaths, and became statues.

I find myself wondering how they would feel about their standoff in Mitrovica. Maybe they would be thrilled to hear that the Ottoman Empire no longer appears on maps. They might be enraged that the borders of Albania and Serbia have shrunk. Once they were caught up on the whole Kosovo situation I assume they would high five about beating the Ottomans and then go back to fighting for Kosovo.

Two different stories can't live in the same place at the same time.

THIS IS A JAZZ CITY

I order rakija and a pack of cigarettes to blend in at a bar called Bebop Cafe behind Prince Lazar. A drowsy jazz standard plays on an old jukebox, black and white photos of Herbie Hancock, Wynton Marsalis, and Miles Davis line the walls. A couple of locals eyeball me but everyone keeps to themselves. I feel radioactive, like I am an island of *them* in an ocean of *us*. Aleksandar told me that I would understand Kosovo by coming up here and maybe this is what he meant.

"You a Balkan guy?" asks a voice from the end of the bar. I turn to find a man with a salt and pepper beard nursing a shot of espresso.

"Why do you ask?" I rotate my stool towards him.

"Well, you drink like a Russian, smoke like a Turk, and look like a Jew. So, I can only assume that you are Balkan," he smiles, seemingly pleased at one of the most brutal and accurate descriptions of me ever delivered.

"I'm from the U.S.," I tell him.

"Well, then I cannot sit with you!" he says, pretending to storm off before chuckling and taking his seat again. The man introduces himself to me as Ertan, an architect for the North City of Mitrovica.

"Can I buy you a drink," I ask.

"No, I'm Muslim, but I'll have a coffee." He scootches to the seat next to me.

"You're a Muslim Serb?"

"Well, no. I'm a Bosniak. We are here too, you know?"

I'd heard there were Bosniak communities in Kosovo, but never thought they would be in a Serbian stronghold like North Mitrovica. When Yugoslavia broke apart, Milošević's bloody campaign didn't just reach down into Kosovo, but first tore a hole in Bosnia and Hertzegovina's Muslim community. The Srebrenica Massacre was the most poignant manifestation of Milošević's policy of elimination: over 7,000 men and boys were systematically murdered in the span of a few days with the goal of crushing their resistance to Serbian dominance. And yet here was Ertan, sipping an espresso and designing infrastructure for Mitrovica.

"I know, it's confusing. But this is a Jazz City. We're all just making it up as we go along." he says gesturing at the pictures of jazz greats lining the walls of the BeBop Cafe.

"Mitrovica is a Jazz City?"

"They used to have one of the best jazz bands in Yugoslavia. Serbs, Albanians, whoever, all playing together. There's still a festival every year, but not so many Albanians come across the river. Maybe in the future. Who knows. Maybe music can bring us together."

"Do you ever go across the bridge?"

"No. I don't like crossing the bridge so much. They're not bad people, it's just a different culture. Sure, we're both Muslim, I even speak their language, but they're not-"

"Slavic? That can't be it," I say.

"You're not a Balkan guy after all. You would understand if you were. Look, I'm a Bosnian because my father says I'm a Bosnian. I'm a Muslim like Albanians but I know I'm not them. Just like I'm not Serb or Croat."

"So, you know what you *are* by what you're *not*?"

"Something like this. Besides, the Serbs treat us well now. I was in Istanbul with my family during the war. We have to let the past be past," he says, sipping his espresso.

I think about Trojan hoping that the past will come roaring back to reclaim Gračanica. I think about Shaban, the Dafinas, and everyone in Prishtina trying to move on from the past in the face of daily reminders. Simply letting go of it rattles me because so many people are killing or dying to keep it alive.

"Hey, do you want to see how condolences are offered to a Muslim family in a Serb city?" asks Ertan, tearing open two packets of sugar and dumping them into his coffee.

"Like, go to a funeral?" I ask.

"Something like this. Come tomorrow."

"Who died?"

"My mother."

BACK TO THE USSR...
KIND OF

"Ivalyo broke his arm," says Savannah over the phone.

I'm laying on a tiny bed in a creepy hotel in South Mitrovica. The entire place is empty except for a moth fluttering around the single buzzing fluorescent light at the center of the room.

"Wait, Ivalyo who throws chairs?" I ask.

"Yeah, chair-throwing Ivalyo. I don't want to say I'm glad he broke his arm, because I'm not. I'm just happy that I haven't had to dodge another flying chair."

I imagine Savannah leaping out of the path of a seat launched by one of her Bulgarian sixth graders. Strangely it makes me miss my students in Erbil.

"How much longer are you in Kosovo?"

"I'll leave next week after Independence Day. Then back to the Soviet Union, well, Transnistria."

"Theee Sovieeeet Uniooooon," says Savannah in a Russian accent. "Comrade Eczu, do you want me to meet you in Transnistria for Easter celebrations?"

"Da, comrade, I need your Russian language skills," I say, imagining Savannah and me in large Cossack hats in the middle of Red Square.

Transnistria is a strange vortex where the Soviet Union still exists. I look around my empty hotel room in Mitrovica and wonder if I will ever stop getting myself lost in strange vortexes.

"Very good. I will meet you in Tiraspol. There we will dance to celebrate Easter comrade."

"Looking forward to it, comrade. Hey, really quick, what do you bring to a Bosnian funeral?"

"Why?"

BAKED GOODS
FOR A FUNERAL

I buy a box of baklava from an Albanian bakery. I don't know if the Albanian writing on the box will offend anyone but you should never show up to a wake empty handed. Ertan had sent me a picture of a chair in an alley with some coordinates and told me to meet him there. This is a common way of giving directions in the Balkans where addresses are more ornamental than actual. I cross the bridge without a second thought. Maybe it's because the sun is shining and I have a box of baked goods, or maybe it's just because I know someone on the other side.

When I find the chair in the alley Ertan is sitting in it.

"You came," he says as I hand him the box of sweets.

"Come on, we'll go meet everybody." I follow him into a hospital-clean home with the name of Allah written in Arabic over the door frame. I remove my shoes and enter a sitting room where I'm greeted by a circle of bearded men. Every man stands up and places their hands over their heart simultaneously. I do the same and then work my way around the circle greeting everyone before taking a seat. A young boy brings me a glass of Coca-Cola, then the men with beards and I look at one another. I also have a beard, so I don't look as out of place as I feel. Eventually one of the men clears his throat and speaks up.

"So, what are you doing here?" he asks me. This is a fair question, and one which I don't know the answer to.

"I met Ertan and I wanted to extend my condolences to his family."

The men accept this answer and then go back to chatting quietly among themselves while I sip my soda. Ertan returns, helping an old man by the arm. Everyone stands and places their hands over their hearts. I do the same.

"This is my father."

Ertan guides him around the circle to each man who shakes his hand. Eventually he comes to me. I take his hand and tell him that I am sorry for his loss as Ertan translates. His father squeezes my hand, nods his head, and sits. He's physically with us, but I can tell from his gaze that he is far away on a distant island of grief. We all sit with the man in silence. All of us are unable to do anything but hold space where it's offered.

"Come on, let's go smoke," says Ertan after a few moments. I stand up, say goodbye to each of the men and follow Ertan outside into the alleyway.

"Thanks for coming. It will be like this all day. We have family and friends coming from all over the world to pay their respects."

Ertan shakes a cigarette out of his pack. He was a livewire in the bar the night before, now he seems distant to the point of becoming transparent.

"From all over... Yugoslavia?" I ask, trying to choose my words.

"Everyone is coming from everywhere. Let me show you what she looked like."

Ertan directs me to a telephone pole where a piece of paper has been stapled. A box of green ink surrounds the portrait of an older woman who has eyes just like Ertan. He touches the paper, smoothing some of its wrinkles.

"It's in green to say that we're Muslim, but otherwise, all of these death notices are the same. Same for the Albanians, same for the Serbs, same for everyone."

More cars begin to arrive and Ertan goes to meet each guest while I stand looking at the portrait of his mother. I think about what Shaban said about the graveyard between Kosovo and Albania.

At a certain point it really doesn't matter. The dead don't care about their nationality. At a certain point maybe all that matters is who shows up for you when you're gone.

"Sorry," he says, returning to where I'm standing.

"It's fine. I should go soon."

"Okay, thanks for the sweets," he says, before trailing off into silence.

I don't want to leave him in the middle of an alley surrounded by his grief, but I don't really know what to say.

"Hey, do you want to hear a joke I heard in Iraq?" I ask.

"Sure."

"So there's this Christian guy driving with his family outside of Mosul and the Islamic State stops him…"

When I get to the punchline of the joke that Astefano told me, I get a laugh out of Ertan. He flicks his cigarette into the alley.

"That's good. That's a good one."

TEN YEARS OF INDEPENDENCE

I can hear the drums from my bedroom. The syncopated beat rings out from every street corner in Prishtina. I go to the balcony and see a group of young men in red vests, white pants, and felt caps playing instruments and dancing down the street towards the center. Independence day is here, so I grab my camera and hit the street.

When I leave my front door, I'm caught up in the flow of people pushing towards the center. Joy, rapturous joy, is in every window. People are dressed in traditional costumes, military uniforms, or their finest clothes, with patriotic scarves draped across their shoulders. Songs shout from every corner as I'm pushed alongside the crowd. The smells of roasted chestnuts, fireworks, and popcorn make the street feel like a carnival.

At the center, parade floats cruise through the crowd waving flags of Kosovo, Albania, the United States, and the European Union. A couple weeks prior, the same street was filled with people in masks and protest signs criticizing the new nation's leadership. Now they're celebrating its existence. When people want to make a point they walk slowly in the same direction declaring that they are here.

A circle of dancers breaks open at the center of the parade and cheers go up into the sky. Strangers link hands as musicians join in with the *Valle Kosovare:*

unë mendoj bashkë t'jetojmë
ma rembeve shpirtin tim
një jetë e re plot dashuri
sot kalon kjo beqari

I join hands with the dancers feeling the counter rhythm thump of the calf skin drum. A man takes the center with his arms spread wide imitating the flight of an eagle. Cheers and laughter.

ne do t'vallë zojmë, në kë t' rini
dhe dolli krushqit t'i ngrejnë
je sikur zanë, na ka zili
se martohemi ne të dy

We whirl together, suddenly not individuals but an infinite circle of celebration. Linked by sweating palms and welded together by the beat of the drum and the sonorous wail of a clarinet. Another man enters the circle, falling onto one knee and clapping the back of his hand into an open palm.

valle valle kosovare
t'paska hije, yll dashurije

Someone grabs me around the neck with rough friendship and pushes a bottle of rakija into my hand. I take a burning shot of the liquor and he asks me where I am from. I yell over the music that I am from the United States. He kisses my cheek and thanks me. I tell him that I am happy to be here and we continue arm-in-arm down the street.
We did it...
I think.
We did it.
But then I take a break from the dance and find a quiet corner to look at my photos. *We* didn't do anything. I'm not from here. In fact, I don't have the same exuberant nationalism for my own country. I couldn't sing the National Anthem if you put a gun to my head because I only know the *land of the free and the home of the brave* bit. I'm certainly

not dressing up in traditional American costumes and dancing to celebrate our independence from the British on July 4th.

I realize, in that quiet moment watching the parade go by, how easy it was to get caught up in the excitement of Kosovar Independence, because I didn't have to do anything to make it happen. I don't have to face an uncertain future of building this country or healing the still fresh wounds. I don't have to make the tough decision to immigrate to Europe because I can't make a liveable wage where I grew up.

It's easy to believe in a country when you don't have to sacrifice anything to be a part of it.

I look up at an enormous blue and gold flag of Kosovo spread across one of the municipal buildings ahead of the event. The borders of modern Kosovo spread across a blue field with six stars hovering above it. Each of the stars represents one of the cultures contained within the borders of Kosovo: not just Albanians, but Serbs, Turks, Roma, Gorani, and Bosniaks. Many stories, and not a single one of them simple. Maybe once you have a country, the only thing left to do is to try and tell a singular tale in spite of the past.

I spend the rest of the day snapping photos on the sidelines. The crowd gathers at a stage draped with Kosovar flags. The pop star Rita Ora comes on stage and plays while the crowd cheers for one of their own who has gone on to international fame. The stage lights cast across the crowd, a small part of a new nation has gathered to celebrate. In Northern Mitrovica, Gračanica, and all of the Serbian towns in Kosovo, it's just another night. When you make a nation everyone has to recognize it, even the citizens themselves.

Tomorrow, the stage will be taken down. Rita Ora will

jet off to perform somewhere else. The electrical plant will continue poisoning the air until it makes good business sense to forget the war. Trojan will keep waiting for half-time to come to an end. The standoff between Prince Lazar and Isa Boletini will continue until their statues crumble. The rest of the newest country in Europe will go back to navigating the uncertainties of the future on the island they fought for.

Tomorrow I will leave Kosovo to the Kosovars as I travel back in time to...

PART 3 TRANSNISTRIA

UKRAINE

MOLDOVA

RIBNITA

TIRASPOL

BENDER

SOVIET DREAMLAND

Transnistria goes by a lot of names. It's also known as Pridnestrovia and the Pridnestrovian Moldavian Republic. This is the least confusing part of a place that defies many modern conventions of statecraft. It gets the name Transnistria because it occupies a small strip of land near along the Dniester River. Basically, Trans (across) + Nistria (the Dneister River) = Transnistria.

Unlike Kosovo, Transnistria has been recognized by only three other nations, all of whom are unrecognized themselves. The Republics of Abkhazia, Artsakh, and South Ossetia are the only areas which see Transnistria as independent rather than being a part of Moldova. To make things more complicated, The Russian Federation protects Transnistria, hosts pirate elections within its borders, and yet, it does not see the little slip of land between Ukraine and Moldova as a country. Still, Russia counts Transnistrian votes as Russian votes, a political logic which can only make sense in a place where the USSR is frozen in time. But how did we get here?

For once, we're not going back to the fall of the Ottoman Empire, but don't worry they're still involved. This time we're going to the Russian Empire. In the 1700s Catherine the Great came to lead Russia and as her name indicates, she was pretty darn good. Namely, she was stellar at expanding the empire sphere based on Enlightenment values, large public works, and of course, warfare. It's worth mentioning that Catherine the Great was not Russian and her name was not Catherine, it was Sophie. She was born to German nobility and grew up in modern day Poland. It just goes to show that national identity is often defined by how we're seen rather than the hard facts of our birth.

Catherine the Great's reign was so successful that she inspired a mass migration to Russia which was gaining recognition as a leading European nation. Still, expansion required access to the water and taking land that was already spoken for. She saw the Black Sea as a critical choke point between Russian and Ottoman spheres, so she sent her general, Alexander Suvorov, south to do some conquesting.

And conquest he did.

The general pushed the Ottoman Empire back from the borders of Russia, taking a critical river which empties into the Black Sea. The Dneister River. But remember, taking land and holding it are two totally different things. Catherine the Great had to Russian-ize the area. Remember when Saddam Hussein Arabized Kirkuk? Same deal, but with Russians. Due to its cultural history of handicrafts and wine making, it became a hub for artisans and cognac vintners who either showed up on their own or were forced to migrate.

Developing an empire means exporting people who can build national identity in a place where it doesn't yet exist. The moment a person calling themselves a Russian moved to Transnistria the story became married to the land. When they worked the soil, raised their family and died, it became a fact as undeniable as the color of the sky — At least until another tale comes along at the end of a treaty or a gun.

And that's what happened. In 1917, the Bolshevik Revolution kicked the aristocracy to the curb and installed a supposedly working-class led government across the former Russian Empire. Once again history weds irony and tragedy. Catherine the Great was led by Enlightenment values which professed reason over religion and progress towards equality over ossified hierarchies. However, the same philosophical discourse which expanded the empire held the seeds of its undoing.

The Bolshevik Revolution, inspired by the writings of Karl Marx and Fredrich Engels, sought to create a multi-cultural workers paradise free of royal strongmen and spiritual zealotry. But when individuals have unchecked power over one another and the state becomes a religion, very few people end up in paradise. This is not only the case with Russia, all nations can fall victim to their own ideologies and die chasing what they thought they were after in the first place. For 70 years the USSR chased the dream of a stable communist nation.

The United Soviet Socialist Republics was a collection of 15 republics spread across the former Russian Empire and it was the largest country on earth by landmass. Soviet means *council*, a reference to a governmental system dependent upon elected legislative assemblies rather than all powerful strongmen. But, it didn't work that way. Sadly, installing an egalitarian governmental system required the work of some all powerful strongmen.

Vladimir Lenin was the first leader of the USSR. His goal was to take the reins of power only to return them to the people once resources were redistributed, workers were organized, and the bourgeoise dethroned. He also saw it as his duty to gather together Russian speaking people, their slavic cousins, their borderlands, and everyone in between under one red flag with a hammer and sickle on it. This included the area that we now know as Moldova.

Galvanizing a singular national identity out of hundreds of cultures, languages, histories, and desires doesn't happen by waving a magic wand or rifle. The Moldovans, Ukrainians, Romanians, and Turks living along the Dneister river left the Russian population nervous about separatist movements. What if the bureaucrats from Moscow were unable to convince the majority Moldovan and Ukrainian populations that they all shared a collective identity? What if mutual language, culture and history were more important to the people than the flag flying outside?

Moldova shares a similar language and culture with Romania. Ukrainians, though slavic, are not Russian and have more reasons to hate Russia than to love it. So, we have an isolated area of Russian Soviet culture hovering between two different ethnic and language groups, Moldovans and Ukrainians. The area that would become Transnistria began organizing its own governmental structures in the 1940s in case greater Romania had any funny ideas taking Moldova from the USSR. As Ertran from Kosovo reminds us, sometimes we define ourselves more by what we are *not* then what we *are*. Never was this more true than in the Cold War.

By the 1980s USSR entered into the Era of Stagnation which forced Mikhail Gorbachev to unveil a policy of openness and transparency followed by rapid restructuring. This meant that the central planning authorities of the USSR loosened restrictions on independent political parties, public discourse, and international cooperation. But by 1989 this policy failed to boost the economy of the United Soviet Socialist Republics and its satellite states. Pro-democracy revolutions tore through Eastern Europe in Bulgaria, Poland, and Hungary. The Berlin Wall toppled and the Iron Curtain dissolved like a meteor falling to earth. Meanwhile, in the USSR independence movements arose in Armenia, Estonia, Latvia, Lithuania, Azerbaijan, and of course, Moldova.

The USSR was shaking apart as republics tore themselves free from the failing empire. Eventually, the de facto Moldovan government declared Moldovan its official language. In response the Russian community of Transnistria established their own de facto government. Remember, if you want an insurgency or civil war, try and stop people from speaking their own language. With Moscow scrambling to keep the republics together, conflicts between Russian and Moldovan speaking populations ignited. No amount of astroturfed Soviet nationalism could turn a Moldovan into a Russian.

And then the illusion vanished. Like house lights coming up in a crowded theater the Soviet Union dissolved as constituent parts voted themselves independent. It was 1991 and 250 million people were left wondering, what am I now? I think this is an important moment. If your country disappears tomorrow, who are you? Where are you from? Are you your ethnicity, your language, or your history? Who are you?

More importantly, what are you willing to do to chisel these answers into stone?

A NEW SHERIFF IN TOWN

Transnistria was willing to fight. From 1990 to 1992 a civil war broke out across the Dneister River between the Russian speaking population of Transnistria and the soldiers of a new independent Moldova. It left 700 people dead but the fighting did not end with the drawing of a new border. Instead, it resulted in a protracted ceasefire and the creation of a demilitarized zone protected by Russian soldiers. The Transnistrian forces won which meant they could create a de facto independent country. But that didn't mean anyone had to recognize them.

Remember, at the most basic level there are two parts

to making a country: declaration and recognition. Transnistria declared, and declared, and declared again for good measure. They declared by writing a constitution, creating a national anthem, postal service, military, police, and even a currency of their own which features none other than Aleksander Suvorov, and Catherine the Great. Transnistria remained unrecognized but international agreements allowed companies to operate within the pseudo-state as long as they were registered with the Moldovan government.

This next part is a weird open secret in Transnistria. Let's do it as a kind of thought experiment: So, let's say, you were a former Soviet police force and suddenly you have control over your own unrecognized nation. You want to hang onto power and wealth but all the business in your new country has to go through the folks you just fought a war with. So, how do you ensure total domination over a population while looking like a legitimate business enterprise?

If you answered: start a grocery store brand, then you are correct. Sheriff is the grocery store brand that runs Transnistria. Its logo is the five pointed star of a wild west law man, because the grocery brand store is the *Sheriff* of this town. If that sounds funny and strange, that's because it is. But it's also brilliant. Grocery stores do a lot of things that governments do. They hold valuable central real estate, control supply lines, partner with hundreds of businesses, and a large population is dependent upon them. Political power comes in many forms, sometimes it's in the voting booth, sometimes it's in the frozen food aisle. But Sheriff didn't stop there, it's also a publishing company, a television network, a gas station chain, and even a football team.

Sheriff is a state of mind.

THESE BOOTS WERE MADE
FOR HIDING VALUABLES

I have a couple hundred dollars and my camera's memory card in my left boot. I stop flicking it back and forth with my toe when my bus stops in front of a Russian tank. The door flings open and a soldier wearing a kalashnikov boards the bus. The driver hands him a stack of passports and he flips through them. He stops at a blue American passport and I rise from my seat.

"Eric, Zooleger. Outside, now," he says. I follow the soldier into a frosty no man's land between Eastern Moldova and Western Ukraine. It's an unbroken horizon, gray brushland and bruised sky. Shocking that so many people have fought and died for this bit of land between nowhere and nowhere. I walk to the guard booth where I find two very different soldiers. A tall Russian soldier sporting a crisp, modern camouflage jacket and freshly shined boots next to his paunchy Transnistrian counterpart draped in ill-fitting Cold War olive drab. On his shoulder is the Transnistrian red and green, hammer and sickle flag of Transnistria.

"You are going?" asks the Transnistrian, flipping through my passport.

"Tiraspol, for a couple of weeks."

"Camara? You have?" he asks, eyeing my bag. I take out my Cannon and hand it over, giving the memory card a happy little jiggle in my boot.

"Who do you know here?" This is a bit of a problem because the only person I know is an American that goes by a fake name. Since you need to register an address and a contact to cross the border I just found the cheapest hostel.

"He calls himself Transnistria Terry?" The officials look at one another and smile.

"Welcome to Pridnestrovia," says the soldier.

I board the bus again, take the memory card from my boot and begin snapping pictures. The highway into Transnistria isn't really a journey back in time so much as a trip to a reality diagonal to our own. Onion-domed Russian Orthodox Churches stand across from an Ottoman fortress as we rumble over a rusty bridge spanning the Dneister River. The statue of a square-jawed worker with a bushel of hay eyes the landscape. The crumbling Soviet imagery is both inspiring and sad; it feels like trying to hold onto a flying dream in a waking life where gravity is all too real. When I get off of the bus, I expect to see a rogue's gallery of secret police and whirring security cameras. Instead, I find two old men sharing a cigarette on a park bench on a sun dappled winter afternoon with nothing much to do. Either this totalitarian microstate has such perfect control that it is invisible, or the news has sensationalized the story of a pseudo-state that likes Soviet artwork.

"You looking for Transnistria Terry."

I turn to find Terry, a bald middle-aged man wearing a beanie and glasses sipping a cup of tea. He looks like Stanley Tucci if Stanley Tucci was in the movie STALKER.

"That's me. Any problems at the border?" He gives me a firm handshake, turns on a heel and begins walking towards a waiting bus.

"No, super easy. I heard security was pretty tight." We hop on a city bus and edge our way to the back.

"Yeah, ever since the government changed, things have been a lot more open."

"That must be good for business."

"More tourists, less journalists but business is business. The last guy who was in power tried to lock everything down. Oligarch versus other oligarchs. Things got bad for a while. But this new guy decided to play ball with Sheriff, so it's a lot calmer." He says looking out the window of the bus.

"Do you have any problems living here?"

"I was thrown in KGB prison like three times, but that was about it."

"How was KGB jail?"

"Sucked. Oh, by the way, I'm going to put you in an apartment with my friend Dave for the night. He's American. It'll be just you guys cause I've got an Italian tour group coming through. No internet in there but you'll move to the hostel tomorrow." The bus stops in front of a Sheriff superstore which takes up a half city block. It looks like a Russian Walmart, but does not radiate the malevolent energy I expected from a store that runs a country.

"Come on, you'll see plenty of those around here. You should meet your new roommate," says Terry.

SEVEN FRIDAYS WITH
DAVE THE WHITE SUPREMACIST

I follow Transnistria Terry into one of the most perplexing restaurants I've ever encountered. Seven Fridays is an Asian fusion/Italian cocktail bar with a tropical flare. Russian pop music blasts through the cavernous restaurant which includes a full bar, children's area, and dance floor. Families enjoy plates of sushi and pizza next to old men chain smoking and knocking back vodka under paper cutouts of tropical birds. It's as if David Lynch designed a P.F. Chang's China Bistro. I follow Terry to a booth and sit down across from a skeletal, hollow eyed man with stringy hair parted down the middle. He types at a laptop and pays me a passing glance

"This is Eric, he's living in countries that don't exist for some reason. Dave is a programmer, he comes to hang out here every once in a while."

Dave glances up from his laptop and reaches a bony hand across to me.

"I've got to get out of here and meet these Italians, but Dave has the keys to the apartment. Welcome to Transnistria."

Terry leaves me sitting across from Dave. After a moment he looks up to me from his laptop and closes it.

"I haven't spoken to my father for a year since I attacked him. I threw him against a wall because he got brainwashed by the liberal media," says Dave with the blank enthusiasm of reciting a grocery list.

"What?"

"Yeah, I was just telling him how the world is and he got really close to me, and he growled. Seriously he growled at me. I shoved him against this wall and left. We haven't spoken since," says Dave as he picks up the laminated Seven Fridays menu and waves the waiter over. "Where else doesn't exist?"

"I was in Iraqi Kurdistan," I say, trying to get my brain to catch up to reality.

"Must have been crazy there with all the death cults," says Dave pointing to a picture of a beef teriyaki salad which the waiter writes down.

"Cults?" I ask.

"Yeah, Islam. It's a death cult."

He hands me the menu but I'm too stupefied to be hungry. I let him know that I was unaware that Islam was a death cult which invites Dave to begin a short diatribe about how the white European race is historically the *best stock.* He informs me of the shadowy cabal of minorities, bankers, homosexuals and homosexual bankers that are attempting to enslave the world with its communist agenda. He then asks if I am Jewish, because I certainly look like I am. At this point his teriyaki beef salad comes.

"You should try the food here, it's really good and it's really cheap," says Dave the White Supremacist.

"Can I get the key to the apartment? I just want to put my stuff down."

"Sure. But are you Jewish?"

"No," I say.

"Okay, cool. I hope I didn't offend you or anything, I say some pretty wild stuff sometimes."

I take the key, grab my bag, and walk out of Seven Fridays. I feel like I need a shower after being hosed down by Dave's ideas. I've registered the address with the authorities, made Terry my contact, and paid for a month of hostel life. It looks like I'm going to be stuck with Dave the White Supremacist and Transnistria Terry. I find myself grasping for something around my neck. I realize that I've left my camera on the bus.

Things are not going well.

THIS IS THE WORST, I HATE IT HERE

I mount crumbling concrete steps into the dark labyrinth of a block apartment building. There I find a metal door next to a shattered window that looks out over a rusted playground. The key squeals in the lock as the door shrieks open. The pitch-black apartment that I will be sharing with Dave for a night comes complete with a shuddering green light and two lawn chairs covered in filthy blankets.

I drop my bag and lay on my lounge. I want to text Savannah and tell her that I have made a series of poor choices which have landed me in a dungeon, but the dungeon does not have internet. I take deep breaths and remind myself that it is only one night.

The sun is not yet down, and it is a Saturday night in a new city. Normally, I would be surrounding myself in a kaleidoscope of novelty, meeting strangers and asking questions. But right now, I feel hollowed out, a victim of my own foolish choices that have led me to a lounge chair in a soviet crackhouse. I want so badly to go home, but I have no idea where that is. I decide to put my passport and remaining money in my boots, wrap my jacket around myself, and attempt to go to sleep. It is 7 p.m. I hope I wake up in a better reality than this.

"Why the fuck do you have your shoes on?" I wake up in the dark apartment with Dave the White Supremacist looming over me. I can see his sinewy outline clutching a two-liter bottle of beer. I don't want to tell him that I have money in my boots or that I have them on incase he returns home drunk and we have to engage in combat. Instead, I say:

"I just like wearing shoes when I sleep,"

"That's weird man."

Given our circumstances, I feel that neither one of us has a reliable barometer for *weird*. Dave mumbles to himself, puts the bottle of beer down, sits on his lounge chair, opens his laptop and begins typing. It is 3 in the morning. Instead of asking him to please put his laptop away and stop typing loudly I crawl into my soiled blankets, curl into the fetal position and hope that sleep will come.

Since I'm in the fetal position, cocooned in soiled blankets a foot away from a white supremacist, it might be a good time to tell you about the difference between traveling and vacationing. A vacation is a break from the thousand natural shocks of your day-to-day life. Travel exposes you to a million natural shocks an hour but with a purpose. You vacation to unwind and you travel to understand. In the end, you return to a day-to-day life full of gratitude for every bit that you walked away from.

To put it another way: travel sucks a lot sometimes. If you can survive there is understanding on the other side of all that suck. I hope.

ME, MYSELF, AND A TANK

I wake up and Dave is gone. I emerge from my cocoon and find my boots still full of valuables. I'm ready to move to the hostel which has internet, a kitchen, and presumably, no Dave. I throw on my backpack and I'm greeted with a frosty Tiraspol day. I see row after row of brick apartments overlooking rusty communal playgrounds and Russian cars from the 1970s chugging down the boulevard. Women in green vests sweep the street clean while employees in red and blue uniforms file in for their shift at Sheriff. I feel like I've been transported to an alternate reality where the Soviet Union won the Cold War. I head towards the center because I have no idea how to contact Terry or where the hostel is.

Aside from the sweepers I am one of the few people on the street. My footsteps feel slower, sounds are muted and colors less vibrant in spite of the glorious sunny day. Walking through Tirasapol Transnistria is like meandering through a strange dream inside a city made of Legos. Signs for the same restaurants *Dolce Vita*, *La Placinta*, and strangely *Andy's Pizza*, repeat over and over again as if on a constant loop. It feels as if I leaned too hard on a building, the whole city would come crashing down revealing itself to be an elaborate set.

At the center of town I find a statue of Vladimir Lenin in front of a stern municipal building. His coat sweeps triumphantly behind him as he looks down from a marble pedestal. Across from him are a series of military monuments. A tank from the civil war poses atop a stone incline so visitors can climb aboard and have their picture taken. At a loss for anything else to do I sit on the tank and dangle my legs. In the distance a novelty train chugs around the park, except there are no children inside. Just a grown man driving a tiny train in slow circles, otherwise, it's just me and a bunch of military monuments.

General Alexander Suvorov rears on a horse forever claiming the city of Tiraspol for the Russian Empire. A shiny MiG fighter jet zooms off into the sky protecting the people of the USSR. An eternal flame burns in front of an obsidian wall with all the names of Russian war dead from Transnistria reaching from World War II to the war in Afghanistan. Even though Transnistria is an unrecognized country, a stunning amount of people have died defending it. I hop off the tank and meander towards the downtown area while the toy train toots its horn in the distance.

SUSHI FOR OLIGARCHS

I come upon a block of kitschy restaurants. A sushi place, a Mafia-themed Italian restaurant and a shisha bar. I take a table at the sushi place and strangely, I'm handed a menu for the restaurants on either side. It seems that they're not actually separate, just one big restaurant with different decor. The whole city is window dressing.

Transnistria is an oligarchy which means that business, education, and government have been captured by a handful of wealthy elites. This is fairly common as totalitarian states shift from communal ownership to private enterprise. The few with money and power snap up real estate and begin both legitimate and illegitimate businesses. A communist era cafeteria becomes *Andy's Pizza*. A state-owned pub morphs into *7 Fridays*, and a soviet coffee shop is now *Dolce Vita*. This leaves the population wondering how a democracy driven by capitalism is actually better.

I order coffee from the Italian restaurant next to the sushi restaurant and find myself grateful for private industry and plentiful choice back in the United States. But maybe this is my deep American programming playing tricks on me. In fact, many of the choices we have in the US are as illusory as those in Transnistria. The trick is just harder to see because it's a larger nation.

Back in the U.S. I can purchase one of a thousand available melon ballers. I can read reviews on those melon ballers to see which one will best serve my melon balling needs. Once satisfied, I can have it delivered to my door in less than 24 hours. I will be doing all of this on Amazon. I can complete my order on a smartphone so long as it's Android or IOS. I can watch thousands of films, shows, sports, and news broadcasts if they come from one of the six media companies. I can purchase a locally made microbrew if it's distributed by the national conglomerate InBev. I can drink Coke or Pepsi. I can vote for a Democrat or Republican. Most of the political decisions we make aren't in votes we cast but in dollars we spend. Maybe the feeling of freedom is just not being able to see that the sushi restaurant, the shisha bar, and the Italian place are all the same restaurant.

I hear a knock at the window of the restaurant and see Transnistria Terry. I drop a couple of rubles on the table for whatever restaurant I am at and I head outside to meet him.

SLEEPING ROUGH

"Thought we'd lost you," says Terry.

He stands next to a young Transnistrian guy named Simeon, he helps Terry run the hostel which makes me feel more comfortable. I was starting to believe that Terry was running a safe house for rogue Americans running from the law.

"We're going to take you to the hostel now. Simeon is from here, you can ask him any questions that you might have about things."

I do have a lot of questions about things. I walk with Terry and Simeon past a Sheriff, we turn the corner and walk by another Sheriff, then we turn into a block apartment. I'm looking forward to diving into my bed for a quick nap before venturing out again. Maybe if I get some sleep the world will feel more real.

Simeon opens the door to the hostel. It is a single room with two sets of bunk beds covered in second hand clothes and couches with their innards puffing out. I smell burnt oil and cheap vodka wafting from the kitchenette. Somewhere in the distance I can hear the toy train blowing its whistle. This is a very strange place.

"Huh," I say.

"You can sleep there."

Simeon points to a bottom bunk with a ball of sheets on it. As I enter the room I realize that the bunks are not covered in second hand clothes. They are in fact, draped in sleeping Transnistrian teenagers. I sit on my new bunk.

"Need anything?" asks Terry.

"No," I say, even though I need so many things.

I lay down on my bottom bunk. I look at the bed next to me. There I find Dave the White Supremacist.

"Hey," he says.

I roll over to face the wall as the teenager above me begins muttering in his sleep. My phone lights up with a message from Savannah:

Savannah: What happened to you? How is Transnistria?

Eric: Weird Savannah. It's real weird.

ARE YOU FOLLOWING ME?

I decide to track down my camera since I don't want to spend any more time at the hostel. Also, it's the most valuable thing I own. A bus schedule informs me that the number 3 line took me from the station to my stop. I have to go to the station and wait for each of the number 3 buses to cycle through until I find the one with my camera. This will be hard because I don't know the Russian word for camera and internet has been spotty.

I board a bus to the central station and two other men in their mid-30s hop on behind me. After one stop I realize that I'm going the wrong direction so I get off and cross the street. The two men also get off the bus and cross the street. When I get on the bus going the right direction they do as well. Either we have the exact same plans for the day or I'm being followed. Since I am doing nothing wrong, I don't really care. This is a terrible way of conceptualizing the relationship between safety and freedom, but it's been a rough 24 hours and I just want my camera back.

I take a seat at the central station and wait for each of the number 3 buses to cycle through. One arrives the door opens. I make camera noises and gestures at the driver. He shrugs, shuts the door, and drives off. Another number 3 arrives. I do a camera dance. The driver shrugs and off goes the bus. This process repeats itself several times to no avail. Then I notice my new friends sitting on the bench behind me. One is clean shaven and stick thin with high cheekbones, the other has piercing blue eyes and a short goatee. They don't look like secret police, but then again, by definition, I would not know what secret police look like. My plan is getting me nowhere, so I try a direct approach:

"Hey, do you guys speak English?"

I reason that if they are secret police trying to figure out what I'm doing here then they probably understand English and maybe know where my camera is. They look around as if I might be asking someone behind them.

"Yes, I do. A little." says the guy with the goatee.

"That's great," I say, walking over to their bench and sitting down. "I left my camera on a bus on the number three line and I'm trying to find out if any of the drivers have it."

The two men look at one another. They exchange some words in Russian and the guy with the goatee turns to me.

"Yes, you know, maybe, I have heard about this camera. It was on VK," he says, pulling up the Russian Facebook clone and showing me a picture of my camera sitting on the dashboard of a minibus.

"That's it," I say.

"I am sorry, but that driver is no longer driving today. His name is Nikolai Shevchenko, and maybe you can meet him tomorrow."

What a strange coincidence that these two strangers who happened to be following me for the last two hours would know where my camera is, the name of the driver that has it, and even his work schedule. Very. Strange.

"Thank you guys," I say, relieved and somewhat creeped out.

"It's nothing. So, where will you go now?" says the guy with the goatee. If they are secret police then they're pretty blatant about it.

"I don't have any plans until I get in contact with the bus driver. What are you guys up
to?"

POSSIBLE POLICE, VLADIMIR AND VICTOR

"For me, she is perfect. This is the perfect performance."

I'm back in Vladimir and Victor's apartment watching opera on YouTube. Victor is in the small kitchen preparing snacks while Vladimir mouths the words to Diana Damrau singing the Queen of the Night Aria from the Magic Flute.

"*Krasiva*, beautiful," says Victor, returning with thin pancakes, jam, and sour cream. He takes a seat across from Vladimir as we dig in.

"I was in Berlin for some time and I loved the Opera. I would go as much as I could. Diana Damrau sings arpeggios dressed as a ferocious otherworldly being.

"I thought that it was hard to travel outside of Transnistria."

"Of course it used to be. But now each person has maybe three or four passports, so they can travel if they want to. They just have to use another passport."

Vladimir and Victor both work for the government of Transnistria. I don't ask them if they have been following me and they don't volunteer that information. If they're interrogating me by serving me lunch and watching YouTube videos I'm more than happy to give up my information.

"I've got a Russian passport, Moldovan, and Transnistrian," says Vladimir before translating to Victor in Russian.

"Same," says Victor, putting some sour cream onto his pancake and explaining something in Russian to Vladimir.

"He says that he is very glad to have you and that he likes to cook for company." I smile at Victor and we all raise our glasses.

Nastravi

"This is kind of a weird question, but do you have a nationality that you *feel like?*" Vladimir refills our glasses.

"What do you mean?" he asks.

"You were born in the Soviet Union and that doesn't exist any more. You have three passports for different countries. So, what are you?" I ask.

Vladimir translates the question for Victor who replies: *Ruski.*

"I am the same. Yes, I was born in the Soviet Union. But I feel, inside, like I am Russian. I grew up speaking Russian, watching Russian television shows, so Tiraspol, for me, feels different from Russia, but Russian. Think, maybe if the United States was to go away tomorrow, would you still be American?"

The question gives me pause.

I had never really considered it. The USSR crumbled in a couple of years and then vanished in a matter of days. The stateside news keeps up a constant apocalyptic refrain about how the American Experiment is teetering on the brink of collapse. But, what if it did? Would I become a Californian? Maybe I would be an Angeleno?

"I think I would still consider myself an American if the United States didn't exist anymore."

"Because your memory is from there. It's your home maybe."

"It's weird, though, because I don't live there." Victor says something while spooning some jam onto his plate. "We don't live in Russia but here we are."

We eat pancakes as the Queen of the night finishes her aria in the background. When the video concludes some suggestions come up for a stop-motion animation cartoon.

"Have you ever seen *Cheburashka*," asks Vladimir.

"*Cheburashka!*" Victor choruses.

"What is that?"

"It is a Russian children's show that we grew up with," he says, reaching across the table and playing the video.

We zoom through a tiny claymation town to find a Crocodile playing the concertina. Vladimir and Vitor hum along while we watch the children's show from another dimension.

Growing up in the US, the Soviet Union is pitched to us as a sort of shadow realm diametrically opposed to everything we hold dear. It's a place where cruel politicians crushed the human spirit at the expense of the state. Its collapse is pitched as a confirmation of American exceptionalism.

But a country isn't just the darkest moments of its history or its greatest achievements. It's a home and an identity before anything else. It's a place where everyone watched the same cartoons as they grew up. Vladimir says something to Victor.

"He wants to know if you would like to learn how to cook Mamaliga?"

HOW TO MAKE MAMALIGA

To make mamaliga you must be among friends. It's a heavy communal dish and it would be weird and sad to eat on your own. Your friends might be secret police, but that doesn't matter. Now that you have some friends around you let's get to cooking. You will need:

A large pot…
Two skillets
A small bowl
Lard
500 grams of pork belly, the fattier the better
500 grams of cornmeal
A single head of garlic
Shredded white cheese
A medium sized red onion
4 eggs
Tomatoes
Sour cream
Ungodly amount of butter
A short wooden pole
Cognac

Fry your pork belly in a skillet that has been passed down since the time of Catherine the Great. The pork is the star of the show so we're going for crispiness. Keep it on a consistent heat and drain off additional fat into a container for later use. Let nothing go to waste. While the pork cooks, discuss the similarities between Russia and Transnistria. Is Transnistria a part of Russia? Is it a part of Moldova? The answer is: it depends on who you are asking. Open a bottle of the local delicacy, Kvint Cognac. Did you know that a bottle of Kvint went up into the International Space Station with Russian cosmonauts? It did. Drink more Kvint. Remember, if you're trying to figure out if a country exists or not it's best to be a little drunk.

Toss a knob of lard the size of a toddler's fist into a

frying pan. Add onion sliced lengthwise and cook until onions are caramelized, lower heat and add tomatoes. If you think there is too much lard, there isn't. Double it, triple it, live a little comrade. While the tomatoes are cooking, you should discover that the term *dick measuring contest* also exists in the Russian language. It can be used to describe the contentious relationship between the US and Russian Federation. Everyone agrees that it is dumb, dangerous, and unnecessary.

Raise a glass to this.

Add the cornmeal to boiling water slowly while stirring constantly. This is best done as a two-person job. Keep the cornmeal moving so that no clumps form. No one knows if this is a Transnistrian dish or a Moldovan dish. Frankly it doesn't matter because there is so much more that we all agree upon which has nothing to do with our passports. Remove the pork belly from heat and set aside when optimal crispiness has been achieved.

Remove the skin from an entire head of garlic, add the cloves to a small bowl with a generous helping of salt and a heavy pour of oil. Mash the hell out of this until it becomes a potent garlic paste and set it aside. Do not talk about the upcoming Russian elections because it is none of your business. Instead drink more cognac.

Introduce four eggs to the tomato and onion mixture. Stir constantly making sure to break up curds until you get a smooth texture. Finish your cognac, pour more, and begin talking about the upcoming elections in spite of your best judgment. Ask if Vladimir Putin will win and witness a chorus of eye rolls. Do not inquire about who the present company will be voting for because it's none of your business.

Ask anyway.

Remove cornmeal from the heat. It should have the

consistency of porridge with all the water absorbed. Take the ungodly amount of butter and throw it into the corn-meal. As it melts, take your small wooden pole and begin beating the cornmeal mixture like it owes you money. Continue abusing the cornmeal until smooth. Evade questions about politics in the US. Realize the same corruption, brutality, and ignorance you criticize in other countries exists in your own. Mention none of this. Focus on beating butter into cornmeal with a wooden pole.

Place tomato mixture, garlic sauce, sour cream, and crispy pork belly around a table. Upturn the pot of corn-meal. Hopefully it will fall out in one glorious loaf. Enjoy the cornmeal with all desired toppings. Admit that the further you have gone on this journey, the less you feel you know about the world. You know that people are generous, courageous, and wise. You know that nations can be selfish, petty, and dumb. You know that you have a long way to go and no idea where your destination is. You wrestle with that question privately as you thank your hosts for the best 24 hours in Transnistria so far.

That's how you make mamaliga.

FINDING NIKOLAI

I have a plan to get my camera back. Vladimir and Victor helped me set up a meeting with Nikolai, the bus driver with my camera. In the messages that the guys translated Nikolai said that he may or may not have my camera. I think this might be a ploy to get me to pay him. Normally, this would be something that I'd chalk up to *dummy tax* which is a certain amount of money I must pay every year for sheer incompetence. However, this year I have no additional money for *dummy tax*. Which is why I have a plan.

I approach the station and find Nikolai smoking a cigarette next to his bus. Mr. Shevchenko waves me over. He's an older man with a gray beard and thick fingers, he looks like a character from *Fiddler on the Roof*.

"*Foto-aparat?*" I ask, aping the word for camera that Vladimir taught me.

He shakes his head, puts his hand on my shoulder and tells me *nyet*. I expected that he might want to play hardball, so I've prepared a statement using my phone translator designed to tug on his heartstrings and make him give my camera if he has it. If he does not have it, my plan is a horrible mistake and I'm a jerk. I hand him my phone with the message:

Please, I need to get the camera, or just the memory card back because it contains pictures of my grandfather who recently died.

In reality my grandfather died 15 years prior, but I feel like he would be proud of my cunning in this situation. I put on my saddest face and look at the bus driver. He begins pummeling me with rapid fire Russian. When we both realize this isn't going to work he takes my phone and begins typing into the translator. Looks like Mr. Shevchenko wants to do some haggling. He returns the phone to me:

I'm sorry. I gave the camera to someone else who claimed to be you.

I put on my best brave and accepting face. He continues typing.

I am so very sorry. My grandfather just died too.

My brave accepting face turns to horror as Nikolai Shevchenko then pulls me into a bear hug and begins weeping on my shoulder. This was a huge miscalculation. As I embrace the crying bus driver, I realize that I have forgotten an undeniable rule on and off the road: take people at their best and never assume malice where ignorance is the likely culprit. I thought that he had ill intentions and my camera was more important than his feelings. I hold Nikolai while he sobs, crucified by guilt.

He takes a step back, wipes his face, pulls a cigarette from his pack and offers me one. We stand smoking next to his bus without much else to say. I curse myself for my stupid plan.

"Pridnestrovia, good?" he asks.

"*Krasiva,*" I say. Beautiful.

He nods and puts an arm around my shoulder. Then he puts me on the bus and we putter back to town. He doesn't charge me for the ride.

My camera is gone. That sucks. I'm a jerk. That's worse.

WE'RE THE ALIENS

I walk through town nursing self-recrimination when I hear someone call out to me. I turn to find Transnistria Terry sitting at a coffee shop.

"Hey man, sorry about your camera," he says as I take a seat.

"How does everyone know about my camera?"

"Small town, small country, eyes everywhere," he says in the same blank drawl. "I meant to tell you, we've got a couple of tours around the monastery or an old datcha. Not too expensive if you feel like doing that sometime."

"Can I ask you a question?"

"Shoot."

"Why are you here? How did you end up here?" I ask. As I do, I realize that I'm afraid whatever answer will too closely mirror my own itinerant existence.

"It's been a wild ride man," says Terry gazing out into the middle distance. "I'm originally from Nebraska, so that probably had something to do with it. Moved to Los Angeles to make it into the movies."

"How'd you like it?"

"Hated it. Full of energy vampires. Good in the beginning. I was even doing extra work and someone asks me: 'Hey can you ride a horse?' I grew up in the country, so I'm like 'Hell yeah I can ride a horse.' Turns out they wanted someone for this western. Next thing I know I'm dressed up like a cowboy on set with famous actors."

Terry pulls up a black and white photo of a much younger Terry wearing a sombrero straddling a brown colt.

"Wow."

"Yeah, but then I had a script stolen. It's better here where things are openly corrupt," he says sipping coffee and

"What did you write?"

"You know the movie *Deep Blue Sea*?"

"The shark movie with LL Cool J and Samuel L. Jackson?"

"Yeah, I wrote that, but I made the mistake of giving it to the wrong person, next thing you know, their name was on it and I was out. Energy vampires. Makes you wonder what's really going on. Who controls things? I run a couple of online groups that look into that kind of stuff."

"What kind of stuff?" I ask.

"Disclosure, UFOs, people with experiences." Terry leans in when he says *experiences*." Anyway, I kinda banged around Eastern Europe for a while and ended up here in Transnistria, doing the whole tour thing. I met Putin once."

"You met Vladimir Putin?" Terry nods and doesn't provide any additional information.

"What's a country, Terry?" I ask this point blank. He swirls his cup of coffee and gazes into it.

"Well, I'm sure they used to be something different. Now, they're basically businesses. They keep the global elite in power while making the rest of us a slave class locked into poverty and forever war. The two biggest arms dealers in the world are the US and Russia and they're always fighting proxy wars."

"Why do you think that is?" I ask.

"If you make doughnuts you have to sell doughnuts." Terry stands up and drops some rubles on the table. "With that being said, I've got some doughnuts to make. Showing a tour group an old bath house."

Terry leaves me at the cafe. Across the street there is a Sheriff department store with a constant stream of people going in and out. I march across the street and into the Sheriff supermarket. Automatic doors swing open and a breath of warm air conditioning welcomes me. People push shopping carts around well-organized aisles under fluorescent lights. Employees in red and blue uniforms mist vegetables with water. There is a surprisingly long alcohol aisle where a liter of vodka goes for around 50 cents.

I leave with a bag of pickles and very few answers. I sit and eat my pickles in a park facing the MiG fighter jet posed as if it's swooping off to battle. Is that all it is? Is a country just a big business hellbent on charging us for existence? Are taxes a subscription service that we opt into when we are born? Is the world just a series of department stores with different window dressing? What a depressing thought. Then it begins to snow.

BEARS

I feel like I'm stranded on an arctic substation. Snow falls in an endless sheet of white from morning to night. I haven't been able to contact anyone outside of the country for a week. It's like the whole world outside of Tiraspol Transnistria has been swallowed up. I'd love to spend my time relaxing in a clean hostel full of kind foreigners, the place I am staying is the exact opposite of all those things. So, I spend my days wandering through the snow like a lonely yeti.

I shuffle into a bar which occasionally has functional internet. The bar looks like Miami after Armageddon, but I'm not there for the nightlife. Russian pop music blasts across a sticky neon dance floor. Old men eating plates of fried pork sit in squeaking vinyl booths with cigarettes balanced on ashtrays. A single bedraggled waitress in heels limps drinks and food back and forth.

I get a vodka at the bar, find a cigarette-burned table in the quietest corner and set my drink down. The bass from the sound system vibrates the glass across the table. I am blessed with a half bar of internet and so my phone fills with messages. Savannah is supposed to join me in Transnistria for Easter but we haven't talked for a week aside from a random message or two from my bunk bed. I hope she hasn't changed her mind.

I call, jamming a finger into my ear and keeping my drink on the table with my elbow. The phone begins to ring with a hissing and popping sound in the background. This is the best connection I've heard in awhile. If the KGB is listening, I hope they can hear what's going on because I sure can't.

"Hello?" I hear Savannah's voice on the other end of the phone along with a crackle.

"Hey! It's me." I push the phone into the side of my head.

"Hello?" Savannah says again. Her voice fades

"Hold on, let me call you back," I say, yelling at the phone.

The line goes dead. The signal on my phone blinks out. I look out the window. Nothing but snow. I sip my vodka. I should have stayed in Bulgaria. A large Transnistrian man pushes through the door of the bar and shuts it against the frosty blast. Lost in thought, I don't realize that I am staring. He waves at me. I snap out of it and politely raise my glass then I go back to waving my phone in the air and trying to catch some internet.

My phone blinks to life, "Hey, are you there?"

"I can barely hear you." she says.

"Hold on," I say, moving to a booth at the other end of the bar, "Better?"

"Kind of," she says. Even beyond the static on the line I can hear that she's upset.

"Oh man, it's super weird here. My camera got stolen, well, given away. Also, I think I'm sharing a bunk bed with a white supremacist, and the dude who runs my hostel claims that he wrote the movie *Deep Blue Sea* with LL Cool J. How are you doing? How are classes?"

The line is dead. The waitress hobbles over to me and drops off another shot of vodka. I ordered no additional vodka. The waiter points to the large man who is now sitting in the booth next to me. He raises his cup of vodka to me, a broad smile across his face. I raise mine back.

Nastravi

We knock back our shots of vodka.

"Where. Are. You. From." The man grinds out each English word.

"I am from U.S.A.," I say.

"Welcome in Pridnestrovia," says my new friend.

"Thank you. It's very nice here."

I look out the window at the nuclear winter. I dive back into my phone and the Transnistrian man orders two more shots of vodka. My phone buzzes but before I can answer the Transnistrian has sat down across from me with the shots.

I pick up the phone.

"Hello?" says Savannah on the other line.

"Why do you hate me?" asks the man in front of me.

"What?" I say to both the man and Savannah at the same time.

"Eric, is that you?" Savannah is on the line, clear as day.

"Why do you hate me? He asks again, leaning across the table with genuine concern on his ruddy pockmarked face. He is in his fifties and has a face that looks like it was used to break down the Berlin wall. The lattice work of burst capillaries on his nose announce to me that he's no stranger to vodka.

I'm torn between trying to accept this stranger's kindness and talking with Savannah.

"I've got to call you back, there's a… guy here. Just give me like, five minutes."

"Okay." She says, followed by a cryptic silence.

"Five minutes."

"I don't hate you," I say to the man.

"Why are you afraid of me?" asks the man. "I am a Russian. I am not a bear. We are not bears."

"I know you're not a bear," I say, trying to find the right words and arriving at the dumbest. I glance down at my phone. I've got four minutes left.

"Why do our countries fight then? We are not bears," he says.

I don't feel prepared to unpack my feelings about US/Russian relations for this man. Both countries are regional superpowers that vie for global hegemony. Both project their power into proxy conflicts to protect business interests and militarized buffer zones. Both are proud nations with vastly different histories and shockingly similar goals. I can't dive into any of this so I go with the my standard answer:

"The news," I say, pointing to a television behind him. "It's bullshit. We have bullshit news."

The man laughs and slams his vodka into mine. There. We did it. We solved the Cold War.

Nastravi!

We drink. There are some universal truths from country to country. Everyone thinks that their government is full of corrupt jackasses. Everyone knows the media is lying to them. Everyone understands the word *bullshit* and sees drinking as a momentary antidote to bullshit. I recommend you test this hypothesis out for yourself.

My new friend Igor orders two more shots. I try to explain to him that I've got to call my girlfriend, that I have not talked to her in weeks and we live very far away. He makes his hands into claws, puts them up to the side of his face and growls at me. Like a bear. He cracks up. I have got to get out of here.

Nastravi!

We drink. I grab my phone off the table and excuse myself from Igor. I stand in the doorway of the bar shivering as I am blasted with snow. I call Savannah back. It rings. It rings. It rings. Voicemail.

I try again.

"Hello," she says.

"Hey, sorry, this Russian guy came over and I didn't want to be rude. I'm trying to get away, but this is the only place with internet." I hear a moment of silence on the other end of the line.

"It's fine," says Savannah in a tone which is the opposite of fine.

"Sorry."

I look back in the bar. Igor makes eye contact with me again. He puts his bear paws up to the side of his head and growls. Oh Igor.

"Look, if you want to just call me tomorrow, it's getting kind of late here. Keep hanging out with your Russian friend" says Savannah.

"No, I wanted to talk to you. I'm trying to get out of it. Just give me another five minutes and I'll leave."

"Okay," she says.

It is at this moment that I find myself wondering exactly how letting Igor throw free vodka down my throat is helping me. Is this trip worth losing my job, clothes, money, apartment, and possibly someone I love? I'm going to thank Igor for his hospitality and leave. It is in this second that I turn around and realize that Igor has been joined by a friend. They have ordered a plate of food, and a bottle of vodka.

"I get you mamaliga," says Igor, pointing to the dish in front of me. The new guy takes a seat next to me and clamps an arm around my shoulder.

"You know mamaliga?" asks the friend.

"Mamaliga good," says Igor.

"Mamaliga good," says the new guy.

"Mamaliga good." I pick up the fork and prepare to wolf down a brick of cornmeal and fried pork in less than five minutes.

"Igor, you eat too?" I ask hopefully.

"No. Just drink," says Igor, pouring a round of shots. This mamaliga is all for me.

Nastravi!

We drink. My new Russian friend's arm brings me in tighter. I slam down my shot of vodka and begin pummeling my way through bite after pork-filled bite of mamaliga.

"Mamaliga good!" says the new guy, hugging me close.

"I am not a bear." says Igor as he does his bear impression again.

I am cramming fistfuls of buttery corn meal into my mouth with spoons of sour cream and garlic oil. I can see my phone ringing. It's Savannah, but my hands are too covered in pork fat to answer. Besides I've got half a mound of mamaliga left and two more minutes to finish it.

Igor pours another round. I wash the vodka down with more pork. Soon, I am looking at an empty plate. I am drunk and full of cornmeal. The men look satisfied that they know, that I know… mamaliga is in fact… good. They rise from their seats.

"I am not a bear. I am good man." says Igor, shaking my pork greased hand.

"No. You are not a bear. You're a good man," I say. Then, as fast as they came they gone out into the blizzard. I look down at my phone. A text message reads:

Gone to bed. Talk tomorrow.

I stagger back through the snow to listen to Dave, the White Supremacist, snore.

VOTING DAY

"Don't speak English at the polling booths. Also, maybe don't go near them."

Simeon tells me this as we are hunkered under the overpass of a Sheriff department store. Driving snow blanketed the city overnight and it's showing no signs of stopping.

"Why not?"

"They will think that you're a foreign agent," he says, putting his hood up.

"Who are you voting for?" I ask.

Instead of answering he smiles and pushes his bike off through the snow. I tromp through the fresh powder towards the center of town. It's doomsday winter gray. At the center of town the statue of Vladimir Lenin stands with a coat flying behind him vibrant billboards that say *VOTE!* Next to a photo of Vladimir Putin. Two Vladimirs and two very different Russias.

Lenin's vision was to take power as the leader of the USSR so that resources could be redistributed and an egalitarian communist dream realized. Handing complete power over to a dictatorship and party loyalists was a necessary, painful step in the creation of a society without hierarchy. Maybe the people of the USSR believed in his message, maybe they were threatened into acting like they did. Regardless, he held the collective power of millions of people in his hands and promised them a future.

Vladimir Putin has served as either Prime Minister or President of the Russian Federation since 1999 and shows no signs of relinquishing control. Since then, the former KGB agent has worked to restore Russia as a globe leading nation which meant crushing internal dissent in Chechnya, pushing out the borders by annexing Crimea and portions of the Republic of Georgia and carving out zones of influence in Artsakh and Abkhazia. Maybe the people here in Transnistria see him running across Ukraine to gather Transnistria into the Russian Federation. Maybe voting is just window dressing like everything else. Regardless, he promises them the past.

All nations have a single best time held in their collective imaginations. Sometimes it is in the near future like Lenin's USSR. Sometimes it is in the past like when Moscow was a globe shifting power player. In the United States there is a belief that somewhere between the end of World War II and the 1980s, there was a shining moment of American exceptionalism. There is a belief that we will someday return to this moment if only we make the right choice once every four years.

I wonder if I would feel compelled to vote if the outcome was a foregone conclusion like in Transnistria. Is having only one choice that much better than two? How many choices do you need to feel free? I watch as Transnistrians line up outside of polling places to cast their votes knowing what the future will already be. As I stand watching the polling place a teenager passes by and hands me a flier for a punk rock concert.

Sounds like the perfect thing to do after watching the elections.

PUNKSNOTDEAD

I descend from the snowy streets of Tiraspol and I'm hit with a hot sweaty blast of noise. The stairs take me under the street into the violent pit of a punk rock concert. The DIY stage bows and squeaks at the center as a singer screams into a microphone with the nasal wretch of the Dead Kennedys. The crowd of teens and twenty somethings jump and thrash to the aggression pumping from the electric guitar. It's a shocking, angry counterpoint to the Vicodin delirium of Tiraspol streets.

As I step into the crowd, I'm pulled off my feet and into the mass of sweaty humanity bouncing up and down. I don't know the words but when the lead singer opens his mouth to scream the world screams with him. I take an errant elbow to the jaw and get rocked sideways in the pit. I move myself to the side of the stage and in between dancing bodies I catch glimpses of the crowd. A woman with body modifications and black contacts paints nightmarish images of Osama Bin Laden and George W. Bush.

A teenager in a torn t-shirt punches a wall in time with the music. A young man has opened a cut on his forehead and droplets of blood are trickling down his face while he smiles and claps. It's a strange roar under the streets

The punk band leaves the stage to the appreciative howls of the audience and rap duo takes their place. The speakers rumble the floor with a thick trap beat. The rappers spit machine gun lyrics in Russian while the audience responds to the call and response. I don't have any idea what they're saying, but it's an angry and violent rapture that sends kids colliding into one another and leaving with bloody noses. Once again, the crowd is whipped into a violent frenzy.

Until 9:00 sharp.

Then lights go on. The musicians thank everyone and begin packing their kit. Everyone abruptly starts moving towards the exit. It's a Saturday night, and it seems the party is over. I ask someone what is happening and they respond with the word *Police*. I follow everyone up the stairs and into the snowy streets of Tiraspol.

This is one of the strangest places I have ever been.

THE WINNER IS

I emerge from the bus in the Chisinau market and it feels like there is light and color in the world again. It is as if the last month was a strange dream brought on by taking too much Benadryl. Or maybe it is just the fact that I'm going to see Savannah.

Either way I feel alive.

I sit in a cafe across from the station awaiting Savannah's arrival. She's ping ponged on busses from Bulgaria to Romania for the last ten hours to meet me in Chisinau. In a year we left Los Angeles for Erbil and got banned from entering Turkey, now we're meeting in Moldova to spend Easter in Tiraspol. If we keep going like this we'll have to go to outer space sometime in the next year.

The waiter turns on the television and Vladimir Putin appears. He walks on stage in Red Square in front of thousands of screaming Russians. As it turns out, he won.

The stage is doused in blue, white, and red colors and if the sound was off and I didn't know who Vladimir Putin was it would be indistinguishable from U.S. election coverage.

Putin cracks a bashful smile while waving to the crowd. He won the election with over 70 percent of the vote. The crowd chants:

Russia!

Russia!

Russia!

Even though everyone is chanting the name of Russia it occurs to me that they might all be chanting for something different. Someone in Moscow has a completely different understanding of Russia than someone in Tiraspol. Just like people crying out for Masoud Barzani in Erbil, or protesting for breathable air in Kosovo. It's a collective prayer for a future that is better than this one.

A bus pulls up outside. I see Savannah's backpack first. I leave Vladimir Putin to accept his nomination.

EASTER IN TRANSNISTRIA

"She says that I'm very beautiful and that you look like Jesus."

Savannah speaks to an old woman wearing a headscarf on the bus. Her statement is accurate, Savannah is beautiful and my hair situation has become pretty Christ-like in the last six months. The old woman places a hand on Savannah's arm as if she was her long lost daughter. Old women tend to fall in love with Savannah, particularly when she speaks their language.

The bus lets us off at Chitcani Monastery, a glorious Russian Orthodox church in the middle of a crumbling village. As we approach, we hear the ringing of bells. A monk high in the bell tower plays the brass vespers sending music through the village.

"Is this making you feel spiritual?"

"I'm more impressed that the monk can keep playing those bells. He's really going to town on those things." I say this as the monk begins jangling smaller bells while continuing the rhythm of the first. He's like a medieval DJ.

"Power of God," she says.

"Clearly."

Savannah is a devout Christian and I'm a missing and presumed dead Catholic, so while we can't agree on the divinity of Christ we can certainly celebrate Easter by attending church. We pass through the gates and the church yard feels like an anchor of base reality locked inside of Transnistria. While the streets and buildings of Tiraspol seem like fiberboard opulence or crumbling communist reliquaries, none of it seems quite real. In Chitcani Monastery there is color and light in the world.

We go into the church and pay a couple of rubles for beeswax prayer candles. I light mine and pray as best as an agnostic can. At times I find myself wishing that I had the unwavering conviction that some celestial power is always in my corner illuminating a path forward. Religious people have a certainty about their place in the billion things of the world and while I think it's beautiful, it doesn't feel like rock bottom truth. To me, unwavering faith is a double-edged sword.

The woman who was left paralyzed by a Serbian bullet in Kosovo was certain that she survived because of Allah. But the soldier who fired that gun was on a crusade to reclaim the holy land of his people. When God is on everyone's side he's on no one's side. To me, sometimes God is place to direct gratitude, unanswerable questions, and hope for a brighter future. On other days he's little more than a goofy superstition, no more real than the monster in a closet. Belief is a thing molded by your surroundings and your history.

Since we're in a church, we light our candles.

I thank God for keeping me out of Turkish prison. I apologize for upsetting Nikolai Shevchenko and pray for his grandfather. I'm grateful that Savannah is here. I'm glad we could split the cost of an apartment so I don't have to hear Dave the White Supremacist snore. I ask for guidance in the middle of this long trip, forgiveness for any thing dumb that I've done along the way, and patience for the dumb things I will surely do in the near future.

I ask God what he thinks a country is. I'm answered by the ringing of bells and the smell of incense.

SONGS FOR THE BLIND

"An old lady with a beard told me we should go to where the monks live," Savannah whispers to me as I look at the glowing candle.

"What?" I say, and she points out an ancient woman who certainly does have a beard. She points us to the back of the church with a broad smile on her face.

"We better do what she says."

We walk through the back of the church and into the monk's quarters. That's when we hear their music. The singing feels like it vibrates through the floor. Savannah and I stand speechless on the other side peering through the window as 30 monks sing in a swirling bittersweet chorus. Legato progressions emanate from a small chapel like honey dissolved in warm water. It is the sound of time stopping. A nun sees us and exchanges a few words with Savannah. She nods, takes me by the hand and we're guided into a kitchen with a long table.

"What's happening?" I ask

"They want us to eat here, I think."

Savannah and I sit down across from one another at a long wooden table. Nuns give us bowls of beet soup and crusty brown bread. The singing of the monks continues echoing off the stone walls. Images of saints line the wall in this simple cafeteria. Down the table from us, two blind men eat their food, sightless eyes cast upward at the benefi-cent faces of the saints.

We have punctured through time into another dimen-sion. We look at one another in stark disbelief. We could be having Easter lunch in this monastery in Czarist Russia, the USSR, or a couple weeks after the reelection of Vladimir Putin and it would look exactly the same. I thank whichever god might be listening for this strange and beau-tiful moment.

LAST DANCE

"We have to go in here," says Savannah, pulling me down an alley and into a restaurant in Tiraspol. We enter an old soviet dining hall where we find a middle-aged man behind DJ decks pumping 1970s Russian pop music while a disco ball rotates overhead. The room is draped in gold curtains and a portrait of Joseph Stalin looks down on a room of elderly people dancing with great approval.

We order drinks and watch Transnistrians dance like

rusty marionettes. Savannah asks the waitress what the occasion is, and she points out a couple in their 70s sitting at the head of the table. It is their 50th wedding anniversary. They've been together through the collapse of a country and the creation of a new one. Wars have been fought, dictators overthrown, the moon walked on, and the internet invented in the time that these two people have been together. Now they sit like statues with tiny smiles on their faces while their friends dance.

"Come on, you can't sit," says Savannah, pulling me to my feet. We move to the center of the cluster of old people and dance to the funkiest music that the USSR had to offer.

BUS BACK IN TIME

One of the little old ladies that Savannah befriended mentioned that we should go to the town of Krasna Gora because it's a beautiful place, so we grab some water bottles, fill a bag with snacks and find the bus to Krasna Gora. Any indication of modernity ends on the outskirts of Tiraspol. The last working communal farms in Europe pass by as we putter through the countryside on a rusted bus.

These farms are attempting to achieve the Communist dream of communal ownership where everyone is both a laborer and a beneficiary. Land was confiscated by the authorities and redistributed under socialized ownership and workers collectives, but this meant that central planners were responsible for creating economic equilibria from the top down. This was all a better idea on paper because instead of everyone rising to the level of a wealthy landowner they fell to the basement of a poor serf. They were equal in poverty as bureaucrats siphoned off resources for themselves. When the USSR failed, it left people with little idea of who owned what. Now the communal farms are fossils of an animal that failed to evolve.

"I think we're here," says Savannah.

"Where is here?"

I look out the window at a dirt road next to a couple of concrete buildings. We get out of the bus and look around. Aside from a cow and two old men smoking pipes there is no one but us. We walk into the only store open in Krasna Gora. It is stuck in the 1960s with mostly empty shelves except for a couple loaves of bread and some vegetables. An old woman snoozes behind the counter. We excuse ourselves without buying anything. If you ever find yourself in Transnistria, I do not recommend going to Krasna Gora.

"Well, should we wait for the bus to come back?" I ask, convinced that we had seen the whole town.

"Let's go check out that river," says Savannah pointing towards the Dneister snaking its way into the distance.

With nothing to see in Krasna Gora it only makes sense to follow the river.

A CABBAGE PATCH IN THE MIDDLE OF NOWHERE ON A TUESDAY

"This is my last vacation before the end of the school year," says Savannah as we wander through an endless field of cabbages along the water. Green heads stretch out for as far as the eye can see. We are the only people on earth right now.

"It's all gone so fast," I say, thinking about the typhoon that has been the last year. Only a couple of months ago I was teaching English in Kurdistan, now I'm in a field of cabbages somewhere east of Moldova. I have no idea where my next move will be but I know that I'll end up in Somaliland somehow.

"Do you want to go home after this?" She asks me the question and I don't know what she means. The United States? Albania? Wherever she happens to be?

"I don't think I'll be ready to go back to the US."

"Me neither. I mean, look at all we would be missing out on."

She gestures to the panorama of cabbages. She's right. It's a Tuesday afternoon, we have a backpack full of snacks and nothing to do but find our way out of this cabbage patch and back towards the city. Life is very simple at the moment.

We make our way to the river. Across the way a farmer has set the chaff in his field on fire. Flames creep across the land. White puffs of smoke catch sun rays turning them into golden beams across the river. A moment of casual pyrotechnics for us, and a million cabbages. We make our way along the river until we pop up onto the highway. All streets go to Tiraspol. We put our thumbs in the air and wait for someone to come along.

JOYRIDE

The car that picks us up has been stolen. I'm no expert, but the steering column has been cracked in half and the driver uses a screwdriver as an ignition switch. Since he is kind enough to pick us up, we're smart enough to not ask questions. We leave Krasna Gora and the cabbages in the rearview mirror and speed back to Tiraspol.

The driver is on his way to Chisinau, so he deposits us in a smaller city outside of Tiraspol called Bendry. Bendry has all the charm of a Detroit car park but it has been a frontline of every armed conflict in Transnistrian history. As if driving the point home, it is currently home to a modern Transnistrian military base as well as an ancient Turkish Fortress.

We set off to find the fortress since we're in town anyway. Signs take us through mud caked backroads and past snapping dogs chained to fences. Old Soviet factories sit long abandoned with vines crawling along facades featuring square jawed workers. We're about to give up on finding the fortress when we pop into an area controlled by the Transnistrian military. Between us and the Ottoman fortress are three seemingly drunk Transnistrian soldiers playing on a tank.

Their uniforms are in tatters and caked with mud, but they have access to a tank so I'm guessing they're real soldiers. One gets into the hatch while the others hang off the side. The engine guns and the tank begins whipping circles and drifting across the muddy ground. We walk carefully by the tank as it pirouettes in the mud and the soldiers laugh.

"Dude, what is Transnistria?" Savannah asks.

"That's what I'm saying."

SERIOUSLY, ARE YOU FOLLOWING ME?

Savannah and I stand at the pickle counter in the Sheriff. As I wait for Savannah to finish up, I notice that the deli section Sheriff has filled up with people. This is weird because moments before the store was almost empty. It's as if an entire apartment building needed desperately to go to the pickle counter in Sheriff at the exact same time as us.

This is not the first time something like this has happened. Over the last couple of days we've been seeing the same faces popping up behind us in restaurants and coffee shops. This leaves us with three possible conclusions: we are being followed, I'm being paranoid, or it's a small city and you run into the same people a lot. I duck behind the cheese case and disappear into another part of the store. My suspicion is confirmed and it appears that the only section of the store that has any people in it is where we were buying pickles. I go back to find Savannah waiting for me.

"Where were you?" she asks, bag of pickles in hand.

"Investigating," I say and then tell Savannah what I noticed.

"Do you think we're being followed by these people?" She drops her voice to a whisper.

"I don't know, let's just go to a random section of the store and see if they come with us."

I take her hand and pull her into the sporting goods section. We hide behind shelves of paraphernalia supporting Transnistria's soccer team, FC Sheriff. I keep a lookout while Savannah pretends to look at an oversized foam sombrero with the Sheriff logo on it.

"No, they're not following us," she says

"Wait."

I peak over the shelves and sure enough people are beginning to meander over to the section that we're in. Within moments, we're surrounded once again by the same people from the pickle section. We look at one another

"Yeah, this is a little weird." she says.

ORANGES

At some point I start sleepwalking. Savannah and I notice that I have been sleepwalking because every morning there are peels on the sink. We stand in the kitchen looking at the ravaged citrus and memories of the night before returning. I remember waking up with a start, feeling like I need to go somewhere. Apparently, I then sneak out of the bedroom and eat the oranges in the kitchen until falling asleep on the couch.

"Is everything okay?" she asks, picking up one of the orange peels.

"I'm okay. I think I'm just sleepwalking and eating oranges. I'm fine."

I smile and know that I'm not telling her the whole truth. The water boils in the kettle and the latch clicks up and I jump a bit.

"Are you sure about that?" she says.

I tap instant coffee into two mugs and pour water in each and take a deep breath.

"Sleeping has just been hard. I keep having dreams that I'm late for class in Erbil. Or I'm going to miss a bus or a plane and I'll be left stranded somewhere. Then I wake up in the kitchen eating oranges"

Savannah pulls me into an embrace.

"You've got a lot on that brain," she says.

"Yeah."

She's concerned, and frankly I am too. I feel rootless and hollow. When I wake up most mornings, I don't know where I am. Kurdistan, Kosovo, Bulgaria? The unreality of Transnistria isn't helping. I worry all the time that I will end up like Dave or Terry. I wonder when I'll just become an expat ghost looking for adventure when I should be on the first flight home. I don't know how to tell Savannah that I'm halfway through this journey with no clue where the next step is.

"I think I need to get out of Transnistria," I say.

"Me too Eczu," she says.

I kiss her on the top of the head and go to take a shower. When I turn on the tap, the water runs orange. I stop the flow and touch the bottom of the bathtub. Sand. It's time to go somewhere else.

Things have gotten too strange.

THE SAND AND LIBERLAND

"It says that a rare desert cyclone in the Sahara has kicked a bunch of stuff into the air and so it's snowing and raining orange sand all over Eastern Europe."

Savannah reads on her computer while munching a handful of popcorn. We decided to not go outside into Tiraspol today. Instead, we're watching Netflix and eating popcorn.

"So, a storm in the Sahara is why our water is orange?"

"Yes."

"Small world. Really, really small world," I say. My phone buzzes. A message from an unknown number.

Dear Eric,

I'm writing on behalf of Liberland. If you would like to meet the cabinet of Liberland and get an idea of what we are doing, then I would recommend coming to our three year anniversary in Novi Sad, Serbia. If you are able to make it here in the next couple of days I can arrange some introductions.

I show Savannah the message.

"I guess we've got to go to Serbia," she says.

Without another word we both take out our laptops and begin crunching the numbers. This is essentially a travel word problem. We have three days to travel the 600 miles between Tiraspol and Novi Sad. We can take planes, trains, buses, and boats, but we're limited by our dwindling budget. There is a travel triad of fast, cheap, and comfortable. Given that we're both on a tight budget it will be cheap, slow and uncomfortable.

"We could take a plane from Moldova or Odessa, but there's a layover in Turkey," says Savannah. We look at each other and grimace.

"Maybe we could just buy a really cheap car from Transnistria and drive to Novi Sad, then sell it when we get there," I say.

"No. That's a terrible idea for a lot of reasons," she says.

"It sounded a lot better in my head," I say as I'm still looking at a Transnistrian used car website.

"Busses and trains I guess." We cobble together a simple plan: We get up before dawn to take the 6am minibus from Tiraspol to Chisinau. From there we hop on another bus to a town called Iashi in Eastern Romania. After Iashi it's a 19 hour train ride across Romania to Timisoara where we'll find another bus across the border to Novi Sad.

Only 29 hours of travel. Easy.

We pack our stuff, check our passports and get to bed early. I sleep the whole night and I leave the oranges alone.

29 HOURS TO NOVI SAD

5:45 a.m.

Dawn breaks over Tiraspol. We pat our pockets for our passports and throw our backpacks onto our shoulders. We slug down the last of the instant coffee and say goodbye to our little apartment in Tiraspol. This is the beginning of 29 hours of uninterrupted travel. Today will be a very long day.

We march through the boulevard towards the bus

station. I assume that I will return one day to everywhere I have been before. I can't imagine that Tiraspol will be high up on that list, but life is long and full of unexpected journeys.

We load our bags onto the Mashtruka and putter out of Transnistria, past the Russian tank, and back into a world where the Soviet Union doesn't exist any more.

12:05 p.m.

We stop at the international bus station for pickled cabbage and bowls of cold potato stew. We eat slowly with our bags next to us like patient friends. Old men sip coffee out of paper cups and play dominoes. Middle aged women with faces out of the tin type photos in history books corral toddlers into their father's arms where they receive loud smacking kisses on their cheeks. Touts sell bus tickets to Kiev, Moscow, and Bucharest. Everyone is only passing through this place for the moment.

Savannah and I sit waiting for our bus to Iashi. We share a bag of chips. We listen to a podcast with one earphone stuck into each of our ears. It is a glorious day to watch people come and go while we wait for our next bus. We have no money, we are far from home, tired, and sweaty. We are leaving one country which doesn't appear on any map to find another. Nothing about our life is certain except for the fact that we have two tickets to Iashi and we believe that our bus will come. At this moment, on this afternoon, in the international bus station in Chisinau Moldova, we own a little bit of the world.

5:20 p.m.

Savannah and I run through the streets of Iashi

Romania looking for any thing that looks like a grocery store. A delay at the border turned an hour-long layover into 30 minutes. But we've got a 19- hour train ride across Romania and we're starving. Savannah spots a super-market and we bolt across a busy intersection.

"No longer than ten minutes in here," Savannah says, grabbing a basket and juking right.

"You go produce, I'll get chips and stuff in jars," I say.

With military precision we fan out through the Billa supermarket. Savannah gets carrots, cucumbers, apples and a fennel bulb. I get some sausage, pretzels, olives, and pickles. We run with our hands full of groceries to the train.

"We've got 5 minutes to get back to the train." I am huffing and puffing.

"I have to pee," she says.

"I do too."

"Did we get any water?" I ask.

"We can probably buy it on the train."

Savannah and I skid to a halt outside of our train plat-form. We high five and chest bump. We are expert travel-ers. We are all terrain human beings. We will end our long day of travel with a meal of cucumbers, carrots, olives and crackers. Then we will drift off to sleep in our overnight train from Iashi to Timisoara Romania.

6:10 p.m.

There is no bathroom. You cannot purchase water on board the train. Hell is the feeling of being thirsty and having to pee at the same time. I believe the fact that our bodies are capable of this sensation is an argument against intelligent design.

"This is pretty rough," says Savannah surveying our surroundings.

Humans are packed into every square centimeter of the brutal metal box. Teenagers play Eastern European trap music on their phones. Babies wail. Drunk old men seem to get drunker and older as the hissing clanking machine rumbles across the Romanian countryside. The smell of oil, diesel, sweat, smoke, and sausage whips into a funk so dense and impenetrable, it's almost visible.

I suck the moisture out of a cucumber and cross my legs hoping that the train will stop soon. It has been two hours. There are 17 hours left to go.

"You look terrible," she says, setting up a game of chess on the tiny table between the two of us.

"I feel terrible."

It has been a long day.

It has been a long life.

We are so far from everywhere.

8 p.m.

The train comes to a hissing grinding halt. Passengers file off to smoke so I know that I have at least the length of a cigarette to use the bathroom, buy water and return to my seat. Time slows as I hurl myself towards the station.

I get money out of an ATM because in Romania you have to pay to use the restroom. I feel that this is a human rights violation, but at this moment I will pay any price for relief. I slap some amount of Romanian money onto a counter in front of the restroom and I vault through the turnstile.

I finish and dash into a shop. The train is beginning to hiss and sputter. I will not be left in the middle of Romania with Savannah chugging away towards Novi Sad. I grab two liter bottles of water and leave the rest of my money on the counter.

I run back to the train and enter the second-class car holding the bottles aloft like the Olympic torch. I plop down in my seat across from Savannah. I feel like the richest man in the world because I was able to use the restroom and buy water.

2 a.m.

The fluorescent lights in the second-class train car do not go off. They buzz, nuclear white throughout the evening. I imagine us rolling along the dark Romanian hills like a bright beacon illuminating the countryside as we go.

Savannah and I tie the window curtains together in an attempt to create a makeshift dark tent where we can get some sleep. This does not work. We look across our tent at one another.

Only 7 more hours until Timisoara.

4 a.m.

An old drunk man is seemingly giving a lecture in Romanian to anyone who will listen. Given that it is 4 in the morning, he doesn't have much of an audience. This makes him speak louder and drink more. Savannah and I are crushed together on a small bench at the back of the car. I gather together all of my courage and go to confront the man.

"Shhh," I say, attempting to be firm yet magnanimous. The man then begins yelling at me. I slink back to the bench and huddle with Savannah for the rest of the journey.

. . .

9 a.m.

We are barely alive when we leave the train but we are here. This is a moment that you come to treasure as a traveler. You are bleary-eyed, bloodshot, and threadbare. You have everything on your back and nothing else. You have a place that you are going and a place that you have been but you own nothing else. You are right here.

However, for us, *right here* is sitting on hot plastic chairs in Timisoara, Romania. We've traveled for 600 miles across Romania only to get stuck an hour away from our destination. There are no buses which cross the border. Here is where we feel like our limbs can fall off and we can disintegrate into nothing. Here is where we know we have to move but can't think of the next step forward. Here is where the lady at the bus counter tells us that her cousin Cesar will drive us to Novi Sad for seventy-five dollars. Somehow, there is always a way from here to there. Somehow it appears. This time it is named Cesar.

The oppressive sun turns the rolling fields of yellow flowers to gold as we glide along in the backseat of Cesar's sedan. We're so thankful for our new friend and our good fortune that we buy cokes and share pretzels as we speed towards the Serbian border. Somewhere between our shared languages is enough to talk and laugh until a pleasant silence falls in the car. Savannah and I fall asleep with two earphones stretched between us. 30 hours later we roll into Novi Sad, Serbia.

We are right here.

THE FIRST MEETING

Our first morning in Novi Sad, I receive a cryptic message from the Liberland Instagram account.

. . .

Dear Eric,

 If you want to meet us you need to come to Apatin Harbor today. We are cleaning the boat for the festivities.

Who are we? What is the boat? What festivities? Most importantly, where is Apatin? A quick search reveals that I will have to travel by bus to the Northern Serbian town on the Danube River. I leave Savannah in Novi Sad, and head off to another bus station. I can tell that she is upset with me given the fact that I have just left her physically and metaphorically holding the bag in Serbia after 28 hours on the road.

While I'm at the bus station I realize that Savannah never signed up to run around Eastern Europe in search of libertarians. She never asked to be crammed into Romanian trains and left wandering through a Serbian city on her own. She agreed to be a Fulbright Scholar in a school in Bulgaria and on one of the last days of her vacation I'm leaving her to search for a boat full of internet strangers. Should I tell the Liberlanders that I'm going to spend the day sightseeing with my girlfriend instead? I probably should, but I've come this far.

My bus appears, and I get on board.

SMOKING CRACK LIKE A LIBERTARIAN

I arrive in the sleepy fishing village of Apatin Serbia on the banks of the Danube River. Since I'm looking for a boat, I head towards the marina. As I follow the sound of the water, I realize how little I know about Liberland.

The country is three years old and it was born from the same history that created Kosovo. After the fall of

Yugoslavia in 1997, the countries that made up Yugoslavia had to establish their own borders. The Danube River became the border between Serbia and Croatia. But on the river was a small island that no one wanted. Because neither country claimed the 7 square kilometer piece of land, it was declared no man's land.

As it turns out, if a parcel of land is declared no man's land by international treaty, it's basically up for grabs. So a libertarian politician named Vit Jedlicka decided to grab. He declared the island a country and is currently in the slow process of gaining recognition. Apparently, the Croatian authorities aren't keen on the creation of a new state in their backyard and they've kicked the citizens off of the land pending a legal battle. So Liberland now exists on a series of houseboats while the island remains empty.

Liberland also claims to be the world's first libertarian country. Its black and gold flag features a bird flying free over the island with the motto "To Live and Let Live," emblazoned across it. Previous to hearing about Liberland I considered libertarianism like flying a wingsuit through the alps. It sounds fun but should never be tried. Surely someone will get hurt.

A libertarian government is supposed to protect innate freedom and stand aside while market forces fulfill communal and personal needs. Essentially, a smaller, weaker government is meant to optimize for personal freedom. Want to drop acid and juggle chainsaws? Go for it. Feel like starting an artisanal cactus business. Well, if enough people want fancy cacti, the government isn't going to stop you. Feel like selling crack cocaine to school children? Now the government is going to put a stop to that. Smoke all the crack you want, but don't make it someone else's problem. That might be a good motto for Liberland.

I arrive in the marina and there I see a houseboat with a black and gold flag.

ALL ABOARD

A shirtless blonde man and a Serbian woman in a bikini top sun themselves on the top deck under the Liberland flag. Is the boat Liberland? Is that Vit Jedlicka? Should I have brought a swimsuit? I don't know what introduction I expected from the world's first libertarian state, but this is honestly pretty close.

"Is this Liberland?" I call out, startling the blond guy out of his lounge. He comes to the side of the boat and lifts his sunglasses.

"Yes! Are you a Liberlandian?" he asks with a slight Western European lilt. I don't know what to say or if I'm addressing a government official, or just a guy on a boat, or both.

"Not yet," I say.

"We'll have to change that! Come aboard."

And with that I arrive to...

PART 4 LIBERLAND

UNBANKING IN THE SUN

"I had my own country. It was part of Liberland. It was one square meter of Liberty Island and I called it *Wonderland*. I was living there for months, then they took me off to Croatian jail. I could have gotten out if I had paid the fine, but I don't have a bank account. I am unbanked."

Enter Yoshi, Liberlander, founder of Wonderland, and shirtless Dutch anarchist. For the record, he named himself Yoshi and his name has no relationship to the dinosaur that Super Mario rides. We're basking in the sun on lounge chairs with his Serbian girlfriend Ana. As it turns out Yoshi had no idea that I was coming, but I was welcome aboard.

"If you didn't tell me to come here, who did?" I ask.

"The government of Liberland is decentralized. It can be chaotic."

"Sounds like it. So, why did you become unbanked?"

"I realized the Euro is funded by death."

I can't tell if we're about to deep dive into conspiracy theories or if the European Union has a harsh fiscal policy that I am not aware of.

"How does that work?" I ask. Yoshi sighs and casts a look to his girlfriend.

"A single Euro is printed out of nowhere. It's backed by the military and a history of colonization. Death. We play this game where central banks issue currency to winners and debt to losers. Winners keep winning and losers get poorer."

"Who starts their own country, winners or losers?"

"People who start their own country refuse to play a crooked game. I used to work in finance. When I realized this, I had to change my life."

It's hard to imagine the shirtless anarchist working in finance.

"How do you support yourself if you don't use banks?"

"Bitcoin."

He says this as if that should answer all of my questions instead of generating more. I go to the file labeled Bitcoin somewhere in the back of my mind, open it, and a moth flutters out.

"To be honest, I have no idea what Bitcoin is."

"You don't know anything about Liberland then," Yoshi sits up on his lounge. This is clearly one of his favorite topics.

"It all began with Satoshi Nakamoto-" He launches into a brief history of Bitcoin.

Back in 2008 a mysterious cryptographer or group of cryptographers calling themselves Satoshi Nakamoto released a scientific paper about an anonymous peer-to-peer digital currency called Bitcoin. The first financial instrument detached from nation-states and banks. Nobody knows who Satoshi Nakamoto is, but Bitcoin became the de facto currency of the underground because it could be transferred across the world with no middle man watching over your shoulder. Want to buy guns and drugs anonymously? Great, get some Bitcoin, log onto the dark web, and wait for a discreet package in the mail.

"But it wasn't just about buying drugs. That was the beginning. With Bitcoin came the opportunity to remove yourself from the corrupt international banking system. As the price went up, our freedom went up," says Yoshi, gazing out at the water.

"Meaning that when Bitcoin became valuable enough, you could buy a boat, land, and even create a country?"

"Exactly."

Liberland was beginning to make sense. Black markets have a tendency to move towards legitimacy as they grow. NASCAR is a multi-billion-dollar business started when rum-running bootleggers realized they could make a buck by racing their souped up booze wagons. The black market alcohol business became a gray market gambling ring, and eventually a beloved family friendly motor sport. If you want to speed up that process, buy some land, make your own laws, and then you can determine what is legal.

"But you still have to trade Bitcoin for another currency. Doesn't that just put you back in the same system?" I ask.

"For now." Yoshi removes his sunglasses, and looks at me. "There are two ways to have a revolution. You can fight a war, or you can build a parallel system that works better."

"And that's what you're doing here?" I ask.

"Of course." Yoshi shrugs, lays back on his lounge and pops on his sunglasses.

I do feel strangely free. It is a Tuesday afternoon and I am sitting on a boat in a glittering harbor. Nations are shackled by their past but individuals can change their story. Pick a new name and move to Estonia. Meditate on a mountain in Nepal. Individually, we're free to dance between borders. If you get enough individuals together you can draw a new border. But, usually that involves a lot of bloodshed and less lounging on the deck of a houseboat.

"Hey I have a dumb question: where is Liberland? Is it the island? Is it the boat? Am I in Liberland right now?" I ask.

"Liberland is in your heart," says Yoshi.

"Oh," I say.

I CAN BE A LOT OF THINGS

Yoshi offers me a ride back to the bus station. As he gets his car Ana and I sit on a park bench overlooking the Danube. The day has cooled to a breezy twilight. River birds float by singing as the night approaches. Every once in awhile a fish takes a leap out of the water into the sky. Meanwhile the Danube rolls on.

I don't know what to say to Ana since most of the afternoon has been dominated by Yoshi talking about libertarian political theory. I compliment a pin on her bag. It's a blue lacquered face of a bodhisattva with a placid smile.

"Thank you," she says, removing her sunglasses as the sun tucks behind the trees. "Where has this journey taken you?"

She's in her twenties or early thirties which means she grew up in Serbia during the war. I'm hesitant to mention Kosovo. In this moment by the river I realize that the choice to rewrite your own story is not afforded to everyone. Maybe being born in a safe, wealthy nation, with a career in finance makes Yoshi's revolutionary lifestyle possible.

"Iraqi Kurdistan, Transnistria, Kosovo," I say.

"I'd like to go there sometime. To Kosovo. We don't have any problems with the Albanians. That's all politics," she says, watching a bird snag a fish out of the water.

"Yoshi seems to think that politics is the problem. Which is a pretty political statement."

"People aren't their governments. For instance, I don't mind the United States. Your nationalism I mean." She answers a question that I didn't ask.

"No?"

"Because the world knows who they're dealing with.

No reason to lie about it. If you want to put America first, put America first. You're not the only country in the world that thinks like this."

She says *you* meaning *the United States*. Still, I still feel like she is talking about me. I never landed on the moon or rolled a tank into Iraq, but somewhere my identity plugs into the larger story of the U.S. Regardless of how far I am from home, that will always be the case. The same is true for Ana and Serbia as well as Yoshi and the Netherlands. You can change your identity, but that doesn't mean the past is done with you. A car beeps behind me.

"Yoshi is here," I say standing up.

"For luck on the rest of your trip," she hands me the blue bodhisattva pin and gives me a hug. I leave Ana watching the flag of Liberland fly over the Danube.

BITCOIN RENTBOY

As it turns out, Yoshi is also a car. His sedan features an enormous decal cartoon of himself giving the thumbs up. It's painted with the Liberland flag and some kind of symbol which looks like two Fs with a double line through them.

"What is this mark?" I ask.

"That's the digital currency I created. It's resistant to 51 percent attacks and quantum computing exploits."

He says as I slide into the passenger seat. If you're keeping score at home Yoshi has created a country, a name, a religion, and now a currency. You have to hand it to him, he has a vision. We roll through the sleepy fishing village and onto a country road. The last bits of the sunset ignite the sky electric violet in the rear-view mirror.

"How did you get your Bitcoin?"

"I used to be a rentboy in the Netherlands," he says without taking his eyes off the road.

"What is a rentboy?"

"I sucked dick for Bitcoin. I used to charge one Bitcoin a blowjob." He says as we stop in front of the bus station. I don't know how long it takes to fellate a customer, but I would imagine you could knock out quite a few in a work day.

"Yoshi, you must have a lot of Bitcoin," I say.

"I do. And your bus is here," he says, smiling. We get out of the car and I thank him for an enlightening afternoon.

"You should come to the cryptocurrency conference this weekend. It will be your best opportunity to meet the president."

"I'll be there."

ALL ABOUT ME

"You just left me to move everything on my own," says Savannah standing in the kitchen of a new apartment in Novi Sad.

It's past one in the morning and there's a tired fury in her voice. The previous rental was booked, so while I was on the bus to Apatin, Savannah had to find us a new apartment and move our baggage.

"I'm sorry. I didn't know they were going to kick us out. I had to go to Apatin—" I say, sitting on the bed.

"These are my last couple of days of vacation and I spent it alone. I could have gone anywhere in the world but instead I came to get followed around Transnistria or on that stupid train across Romania."

"Which is why I didn't think you'd want to get on

another bus today. I couldn't tell them that I wasn't coming," I say rising.

"Why?"

This hits me square between the eyes. I've come such a long way that I couldn't imagine just giving up. But no one is asking me to be here and this stupid question is pointless to answer. It's my pointless question though.

"If I didn't get up there today, this whole trip would be for nothing," I spit back.

"This trip has been all about you."

The words land like an ice-cold anvil in the middle of the room. Savannah storms out onto the small balcony. I'm left with my pointless question to keep me company. She's right. While I was off lounging on the Danube she was moving our stuff and spending the day alone in a foreign city. I spend a few silent moments with her words echoing off the walls before joining her on the balcony.

The night is early spring warm. We stand on the small balcony looking at the air conditioning ducts of the adjoining apartments and a small square of sky. A silence buzzes between us as I stand next to her.

"I'm sorry. You're right," I say.

I was the one dragging us around the world. I got us banned from Turkey and wanted her to come to Transnistria. I'd be out on my own if it weren't for her place in Bulgaria. I was so busy with my own story that I forgot I'm an important part of someone else's. It was all about me.

We settle into an uneasy night of sleep. In the morning she tells me that she bought me some new shirts so I would look nice in case I met the President of Liberland. They fit perfectly. I give her the bodhisattva pin and she puts it on her bag. We decide to be regular people doing normal things in a country that totally exists. At least for a little while.

THE CHASE

We spend the days before the Liberland anniversary wandering through Novi Sad and knitting ourselves back together. We follow secluded alleys to eat ice cream in hidden palazzos. We explore fortresses and walk along the river ignited by spring flowers. We get drunk and play chess until the day has burned itself out and the night falls. It's like the city is telling us to shut up and enjoy being right here and right now.

After countless rakijas we find ourselves on a hunt for falafel. It is at this point that Savannah decides to run away. She launches into a dead sprint trailing laughter. I give chase without a clue of the game we're playing. Before I know it, she and I are in a city-wide game of drunk cat-and-mouse. I find her in parking lots, behind fountains, and hidden under picnic tables. Each time I find her she sprints off again.

We do this until we are breathless, sweating and shaking with absurd laughter. We embrace in the middle of a crowded avenue. We catch our breath and wonder why we did that weird thing just now. Savannah clicks herself under my arm and we continue our quest for falafel.

Savannah leaves on a bus back to Bulgaria the next day. I'll join her after I finish with Liberland. I see her off and walk back to our apartment. Somehow the place seems diminished. It's amazing how a person can change the way a city looks.

MAKING FRIENDS IN BARS

The Sheraton Hotel in Novi Sad is packed with crypto nerds. A black and yellow Liberland flag hangs behind the bar where the attendees clamor for a drink from overwrought waitresses. Everyone wears lanyards featuring various cryptocurrencies that sound like alien ice cream flavors like *Cardano* and *Ripple*. A new session begins, and the bar clears as the crypto nerds rush into the conference room.

When I find out the price to enter this conference is more digits than I have in my bank account, I try unsuccessfully to contact Yoshi. With nothing else to do, I'm stuck at the hotel bar wondering if anyone needs a rent-boy. I decide to do what brought me to Liberland in the first place: I make friends with strangers. I lie in wait listening to the mind-numbing hum of cryptocurrency chat.

An American voice booms through the murmur of the bar. People from the U.S. have many good qualities, but vocal modulation is not one of them. My countryman bellies up to the bar and orders a beer. He wears a Liberland lanyard and a shirt with the Bitcoin symbol on it. I scootch a couple stools down and ask him what beer he ordered.

"Some, Serbian thing? I don't know. It's beer."

I order one of the same.

"Put that on my tab," he says and introduces himself to me as Bitcoin Mike.

Mike is a head shorter than me and built like a keg. He has a powerful handshake and a remarkable ability to offend you, apologize, and crack another offensive joke at the same time. He is a Liberlander, purveyor of Bitcoin ATMs, owner of marijuana clubs, and elite world traveler. He rattles off his brief personal history like a diner waitress listing daily specials.

"You a Liberlander?" he asks, ordering a Jagermeister shot.

"Is it Liberlander or Liberlandian?" I ask.

"No fucking clue and I'm a diplomat for them. Call us whatever you want," he says.

I give Mike a rundown of my last year but he's become distracted by the waitresses. I clear my throat to try and get his attention.

"I'm trying to meet the President of Liberland," I say, snapping Mike out of his reverie

"Vit? Yeah, he's busy with the conference. I'm actually supposed to be speaking right now, but I think I'm going to stay here," he says as he begins scanning the bar, for the object of his attention.

"That guy is the Secretary of State if you want to talk to him." Bitcoin Mike points towards an elegantly dressed Pakistani man standing in the doorway of the bar.

"Thanks," I say, hopping off my stool. Mike claps me on the shoulder and says "Find me later, we'll drink more. You have weird stories."

High praise from Bitcoin Mike.

To my surprise the Secretary of State of Liberland approaches me.

"Excuse me, are you Eric?" He asks in a regal London accent.

"How did you know?" I shake his hand.

"You have been sending us quite a few messages. And it seems you've made it all the way to Serbia." He ushers me to a quiet table in the back of the bar.

"My name is Dr. Tariq, I am the Secretary of State of Liberland, the personal Lieutenant to the Queen of England, and otherwise, a businessman."

A characteristic of Liberlanders appears to be complicated and impressive resumes. Trying to assimilate all of this information at once feels like shoving a loaf of French bread in a single toaster slot.

"I have a lot of questions," I say, taking out my notebook.

"I imagined you might."

THROUGH THE WINDSHIELD

Tariq tells me about working with the Queen of England while he drinks his tea like he's painting a masterpiece. He calls Queen Elizabeth II *The Lady* in an accent worthy of preservation in the National Gallery. Here I was thinking that every Liberlander was a shirtless Dutch anarchist.

"Can you be a citizen of the UK and Liberland at the same time?"

"We all have different identities simultaneously don't we?"

He's correct. Technically, I am still employed as a third-grade teacher.

"I am here because it's exciting to build something from the ground up. This might be the future of statehood that we are creating on this island. As they say, there is a reason that your rear-view mirror is small and your windshield is big. You're not going backwards," he smiles.

"So, where are we going?"

"We're making a country."

Tariq smiles. Simple as that. I'm frustrated by this answer. Other countries have bloody revolutions and hard won political battles. Liberland has a cryptocurrency conference, t-shirts, and a houseboat.

"What does Croatia think about this?"

Tariq stirs his tea and taps his spoon on the edge of his cup.

"They believe that Liberland is an affront to their national security. The Serbs are far more supportive because we're bringing tourism and business to an area that would normally have none."

"How do you gain their recognition? March the Liberland Army into Croatia?" I say joking, but also not. Tariq laughs.

"No. The border dispute is ongoing. We were renting houses to Liberlanders who wanted to stay on the island, but Croatia decided to destroy the buildings, which, mind you, they have no claimed authority over."

"Do they take Liberland seriously?"

"They're beginning to and that works in our favor. They've arrested our president twice. Once for entering Croatia from the island."

"Why does that work in your favor?"

"Because by arresting him for illegal entry to Croatia it insinuates that there is a recognized border. You can't illegally enter a country from inside of that country can you? Either they have a claim on the island or they don't. An international treaty says they do not. Meanwhile, they are preventing people from entering Liberland and running patrol boats along the river." Tariq smiles like a trap snapping shut.

"So the more they try to stop Liberland, the more they recognize and even defend you?"

Tariq nods and sips his tea. Sometimes we define ourselves more by what we are not, and in doing so, the Croatian authorities have drawn a border. It's brilliant, like geopolitical Aikido.

"I assume that we will have our differences resolved in court soon."

Iraqi Kurdistan's referendum is snuffed out by military power. Kosovo gains independence after months of bombings. Russia keeps tanks at the borders of Transnistria after a civil war. Meanwhile, Liberland is taking Croatia to court and fooling them into recognition. There's no law that says a country has to be born of violence, but it's always worked that way. Maybe this is the future.

"Tariq, what makes a country? I mean, for you personally."

He takes a moment and tents his hands. He takes a deep breath.

"I'm sure there is an academic answer but I'm not certain that's what you're looking for." He considers a moment longer. "There is a feeling of home. We all understand this. It's something that we live for. It's also something that we are willing to fight for. It's a place that we miss when we are away from it. It's a part of you. I think that is what a country is to me."

"Is Liberland a home yet?"

"That depends on if the court decides in our favor. Until then we have to stay off of the island and deal with their patrols." He signals the waitress for the check.

"Will I see you on the boats?"

"What boats?"

"The boats to Liberty Island," he says.

AIN'T NO PARTY LIKE A LIBERTARIAN PARTY

"I was staying at the Four Seasons, in Hong Kong. Rented out the top floor. I'm with this programmer whizz kid—"

Bitcoin Mike is holding court while burning through a pack of Serbian Camels. Shots of Jagermeister arrive on a conveyor belt of waitresses clearing drinks. Sticky rings of liquor dot the table between empty bottles of beer and overflowing ashtrays. I sit in a circle of Liberlanders: Paul, a red-faced English journalist in his 50s,

Borna a Croatian talk show host and Elvie, a Scottish tech writer.

"Anyway, this kid is so smart and so rich he doesn't know what to do with himself. He's just knocking down bottles of Grey Goose in the penthouse. The staff calls me to see if I can stop him from rampaging through the hotel."

Across from me perched on a cushion looking out the window is Rose an elegant Swiss who works for Swarovski Crystal. She seems unamused by Mike's stories but unable to leave the smoking lounge. Next to me is Chris, a young Malaysian/Swedish filmmaker. I'm trying to figure out a single thing that bonds all these Liberlanders together aside from cryptocurrencies and a nicotine addiction.

"Excuse me." Mike corrals one of the waitresses with his hand on the small of her back. "Can we do another round? Who wants one? These are on me."

All hands go up. I suppose individuals can form a country without a common history, culture, or language. In fact, in modern statecraft, that is the rule and not the exception. The only country that demands heterogeneity of society is North Korea, but if you're choosing to live in a state rather than being born in one by chance, then some ideal must act as a bond.

"Anyway, I tell them that I'm renting a floor of their hotel, and the booze is included. If he wants to drink let him drink. So they kick us out. Also, it turns out that kid is wanted by the FBI, so any time I go back to the states they have agents waiting for me."

Everyone laughs and tired waitresses bring another tray of shots. We drink to Mike's tale of breaking all the rules. Then I realize what unites them all. They're rich. Maybe the spirit of Liberland is in the wallet and not the heart.

THE BALLAD OF BITCOIN MIKE

Young Michael was stuck in Spain. The serial entrepreneur had started a marijuana business in his native Colorado but decided to spend some time traveling in Europe. However, he'd overstayed his visa. That meant he couldn't leave because they might bar him from reentering the Eurozone. He couldn't stay because he had business back in the states. He was trapped between international laws and his own desires.

Pre-Bitcoin Mike decided to purchase a fake passport on the deep web. It cost a couple thousand dollars at the time, but buying anything illicit on the internet required a new invention called Bitcoin. Thinking nothing of it, Mike bought a couple thousand Bitcoin at the bargain basement price of a dollar a piece. But he never got his fake passport. Instead, he paid a fine to the Spanish government and returned home. Then, that couple thousand dollars in Bitcoin grew into a couple million. The price of the digital currency kept rising and before he knew it, Mike became Bitcoin Mike. He had reached the escape velocity of wealth where you go from being subject to the rules to making them yourself. If punishment for something is a fine and there is nothing you can't afford, then you are as free as you decide to be.

This story is common in the cryptocurrency world. When the price of Bitcoin leapt up it made a small group of early adopters very rich. Those people had shared values of limited government, free trade, and doing illegal stuff online. The internet dissolved historical borders like geography, ethnicity, and even language. This gave rise to affinity groups who had more in common with their online communities than their own countrymen. These digital pioneers dedicated themselves to a new political philos-

ERIC CZULEGER

ophy which rejects the state-based model of human organization as a fossil of the past.

CRYPTO-ANARCHY IN THE UK,
AND EVERYWHERE ELSE

Crypto-anarchy is like cyberpunk libertarianism. The
self-sovereign individual is the ultimate source of power
instead of banks, governments, and transnational institutions. It treats humans as essentially good moral actors who
will benefit their community if given the chance and
correct market incentives. Crypto-anarchists see peer-to-
peer networks, privacy, and decentralization as their
defense against the overwhelming power of technology to
manipulate individuals.

Social media Goliath's, search engine monopolies and
global telecom networks made a Faustian bargain with the
world: God-like access to data and communication in
exchange for your attention, data, and perception of free
will. Since we've all signed on the dotted line in some
respect, our data is used to make us look, click, buy, and
vote. Companies and governments work hand-in-glove to
manipulate us into compliance while creating value for a
small number of shareholders. To the crypto-anarchists, if
we are not emancipated from centralized systems we won't
be much different than a fleshy cog in a mindless machine
with little else than eyes to look, loins to desire, and a wallet
to buy.

The landscape of Iraqi Kurdistan is craggy mountains
punching up towards the sky and tumbling down into the
desert. Kosovo is a scatter of villages and brutalist cities
built on centuries of battlefields. Transnistria is a collection
of Soviet bloc Lego towns scattered among thick forests
and Communist datchas. The landscape of Liberland is a

glowing screen in the hand of an anarchist who knows how to use it exceedingly well.

Their idea is to stage a jailbreak from the cells we've built around ourselves. Encrypt your data and dance between international borders. Invent currencies, identities, and countries. Push the boundaries of governance, mathematics, and international law until nationality has about as much relevance as an astrological sign. Crypto-anarchy demands the individual be uncontrollable, beyond coercion and ultimately beholden to no state. However— and this is a big however— these crypto-anarchists are creating a nation in order to be free of statehood.

It's easy to be on board with this idea while I'm caught in a crypto fueled bacchanal. But it feels too utopian. I trust individuals far more than I trust organizations. You can reason with an individual soldier, but not an army. If left to our own devices without the guardrails of government to contain the negative externalities of human desires what would the world look like? Would it be a sublime vision of the fire dancers at Burning Man or A room of drunk people with different accents talking about how power corrupts while ordering another round of drinks from an underpaid waitress?

I don't know. I really just don't know.

THE MORNING AFTER THE ANARCHY

I arrive at the Novi Sad Sheraton bright and early in the morning and find Bitcoin Mike in an argument with the hotel staff and a beer in his hand. Elvie is chain smoking with bloodshot eyes and a hoarse voice from either crying or screaming or both. There is a single shoe left under the coffee table.

"What happened?" I ask Mike as I examine what

appears to be the aftermath of a small war. Before I can finish the sentence, Chris the filmmaker pulls me aside and tells me that I don't want to be a part of it. I agree and follow him outside to wait for transportation to Apatin.

Maybe man cannot govern himself.

Soon, a fleet of buses arrives to pick up 80 Liberlanders, blockchain entrepreneurs, crypto-anarchists, and me. From what I can tell, everyone is incredibly wealthy, very tech savvy, and a terrible dresser. One guy in particular sports a hand knit sweater with an Ethereum logo. For once, I am not self-conscious of being underdressed.

After a bus ride we are herded like cattle towards a waiting flotilla of boats. They range from the houseboat where I met Yoshi, to rubber dinghies and everything in between. I scan the crowd for the president and see him standing on the top deck of the Liberty and make a beeline towards the houseboat pushing past a crush of crypto nerds. To my surprise it is blocked by men with security t-shirts. I hold up Savannah's camera and say *press*. They stand aside and allow me aboard. You can be anything you want to be if you just lie. Remember that.

I enter the belly of the boat but I can't get through a clot of Liberlanders so I decide to find him later. It's a boat, he's not going anywhere. Instead, I get caught in a discussion of Ayn Rand between two millionaires. Eventually the security hands us all styrofoam boxes full of what are supposed to be sandwiches. It's just a box with some bread, a stray slice of cheese and a leaf of lettuce. If ever an anarchist made a sandwich, this was it.

The engines kick to life while I am assembling my DIY sandwich. I look out the window and it occurs to me that I have no idea how long our trip is or even where we are going. The guy with the Ethereum sweatshirt sits across from me checking his phone.

"How long is this trip?"

"Liberty Island is three hours away." He does not look up from his phone. "We're just going to look at it though. If we step on it then the Croatian police will arrest us."

"How will they know?"

"Those are their boats," says Ethereum guy as a Croatian patrol boat buzzes by the porthole.

THAT'S THE SOUND OF THE POLICE

I work my way to the top deck of the boat but Vit Jedlicka is nowhere in sight. I wonder how he could have gotten off the boat but there are more pressing concerns. Everyone watches the police boats encircle our flotilla of cryptoanarchy.

Someone cranks up the volume on a boombox. The officers pull in front of our lead boat which cues someone to break out a case of *Terra Nullus,* the official wine of Liberland. The police flash their lights, which only adds to the yacht party atmosphere. We all raise a red party cup of Liberland wine to the Croatian police, because it seems like we're having a way better day being anarchists than they are working for the man.

A cheer comes up from a boat behind us. Then another. I look over the railing into the water and Vit Jedlicka, president of Liberland tearing through the Danube on a jet ski. He wears a cream-colored suit jacket, a button-down shirt, jeans, and a blasé expression that I would associate with attempting to purchase the right detergent. On his aquatic steed he carves a perimeter between the police and the Liberland boats, drawing a line between us and them like a real leader. He doubles back and weaves through the speedboats, dinghies and yachts. He circles around the Liberty and

spins out a wave of water. I realize two things simultaneously:

1. I support Vit Jedlicka for President.
2. I have incredibly low criteria for a potential
   leader. Riding a jet ski is enough to get my vote.
   This is why America is a mess, people like me.

Still, I want to get on that jet ski.

MR. PRESIDENT

I watch the President rip between boats in our flotilla,
stopping only to give a short speech and speed off again. I
wait on the starboard side of the houseboat abandoning all
self-respect as I wave and beg for a ride.

"You trying to get on the jet ski?" asks an American
voice from behind me.

I turn around to find a middle-aged, bearded man
smiling with a cup of *Terra Nullus* in his hand. He looks like
the soccer dad that would bring good snacks rather than
basic orange slices.

"I am," I say.

"I'm Tom, the Foreign Secretary of Liberland." We
shake hands.

At this point a hobbit could introduce themselves to me
as the Prime Minister of Liberand and I wouldn't bat an
eye. Turns out Tom works for a travel website when he's
not busy starting a country. He lives in Florida and enjoys
being an amateur DJ. He seems to treat starting a country
less like a fight for independence and more like starting a
Rush cover band. It's fun. Vit comes whizzing by on the jet
ski and Tom can tell I am distracted. He puts down his
plastic cup of wine and walks towards the edge of the boat.

"Hey Vit!"

The President of Liberland whips around to see his Foreign Secretary yelling at him. He slows down and pulls alongside the boat.

"Got someone who wants a ride."

He turns and winks at me. Vit slows his engine by the side of the Liberty and Tom helps me step down off of the boat. I plop down onto the seat behind Vit. Given that there are no handles, I am forced to bear hug the President around his waist. As I hold onto Vit Jedlicka with my cheek pressed to the back of his jacket, I realize this is how I meet my first head of state. Clutching them like a spider monkey. Between the roar of the yacht, the gurgle-clack of the jet ski and the Lady Gaga tunes blasting from the top deck I can barely hear it when Vit speaks.

"Hold tight," he says with a Czech accent.

He guns the engine, the jet ski rears like a stallion, before blasting off into the Danube. We carve by the Croatian police threading through the fleet of party boats filled with crypto currency junkies and blockchain millionaires. We pull up to the very front of the pack facing down the biggest patrol boat. The jet ski speeds along with the shores of Serbia on one side and Croatia on the other. Blue and red police lights shimmer across the water while the Liberlandians roar with delight in back of us.

I have become so entranced by the jet ski ride that I am missing out on my precious opportunity to ask the President a question. I had so many but they're back on the boat with my wallet, keys, and Tom. I choke up on the President and try to get closer to his ear so I can yell my question above the roar of the engine.

"My name is Eric and…"

"I know who you are. Email guy," he says.

We yell back and forth between the jet ski's regular beat

on the water. I don't know if I will see (or embrace) the President of Liberland again so I decide to scream my one question in his ear:

"I've been living in stateless countries for almost a year now. They have to fight so hard and sometimes die in order to draw a line on a map! You're the only person that I've ever met who has started a country. I just have one question! Is it worth it?"

Vit chokes the engine between the Liberty and the Croatian police boat. He turns to me as best he can while wrapped in my arms. He answers in the only way that the president of a crypto-anarchist micronation could:

"Everyone should start their own country."

He punctuates this by burning out a u-turn and sending up a wall of water between the Liberty and the Croatian police. We bound at full speed towards the oncoming boats and whip around once more until we're chugging next to the houseboat. The foreign secretary pulls me back aboard and I watch as the president speeds off again to do more presidential stuff.

Am I a crypto-anarchist now? No. I'm not wealthy. The rules still apply to me.

THE WORLD ACCORDING TO CRYPTO

There are a lot of terms in the crypto world. Here are some that I have learned:

Decentralization: Removing third parties like governments, corporations, and banks to make a better global economic system. Maybe.

Blockchain: A way of storing and transferring information and wealth without a central server. All data is maintained on an unchangeable and public ledger.

Hodl: A misspelling of *hold* made by someone on an

early crypto message board. It means, just hold on to your Bitcoin until it's worth millions.

Moon: Short for *moonshot*. A time in which a cryptocurrency increases in value several hundred percent.

Lambo: A Lamborghini.

Early Adopter: The rarified ranks of individuals that purchased Bitcoin early. It originally sold for around a dollar and spiked to $15,000 by 2017.

To use these all in a sentence, one could say:

I'm no early adopter, but I knew the blockchain revolution was going to lead to massive decentralization, so I bought big. Now, I'm hodling waiting for it to moon so I can get my Lambo.

One could say all of this. It would make one absolutely insufferable. I spend the rest of the journey to Liberty Island interviewing the new natives of Liberland.

EVIE THE ARMS MERCHANT

"I used to work for an arms manufacturer in Glasgow," she says with a thick Scottish accent. "But you know I was sick of working on things that just exist to kill people."

Evie hangs over the prow of the boat with the wind in her face.

"I started getting into the whole crypto thing because it seems like a way out of the same cycle of war all the time. I attended one conference and then just started traveling around the world to the others. Are you going to the one in Acapulco?"

"No, I didn't know there was one there."

"It's called Anarcho-pulco. It's a lot of fun," she says before leaving me to top off her wine.

It seems like all of the Liberlanders don't trust governments, like parties, and somehow took a skydive out of society with cryptocurrencies as their parachute.

Freedom is the ability to choose.

WELDON THE DRUG DEALER

"I was the leading importer of MDMA in the late 90s and early 2000s. If you popped a pill of ecstasy in Southern California during that time period, you probably took one of my pills. Great shit, I stand by it to this day."

Weldon is a tall, heavyset guy from Southern California. He has the goofy giggle and childlike curiosity of someone who has been to a decent amount of raves.

Weldon would have continued his life of crime until his headquarters in San Diego were raided. He was on vacation in Mexico and all of his friends and collaborators were busted. His girlfriend at the time called him and told him not to come back for fear he would be busted.

"It was a lot of ecstasy. I would have spent decades in jail. So, I decided to leave and never come back. I ended up kicking around Thailand for a couple of years."

"Do you speak Thai?" I ask. Weldon answers with a small monologue of what I assume is quite proficient Thai.

"Anyway, I was living out of the country, pretty much just living off of Bitcoin. Then the price, like, explodes. Suddenly, I can hire a good lawyer to look at my case. It's been long enough that they can't prosecute me anymore, so I come back to the states. Crazy."

Freedom is a high-priced lawyer

DOUG WHO ALMOST DIED

Doug and I stand on the prow of the boat looking at the horizon between the police boats. He asks me if I have any Bitcoin. I tell him that I do not. He takes my phone, downloads a digital wallet and transfers me $5 worth of Bitcoin.

"Now you're part of the club," he says.

Doug was dying of cancer eight months before standing on this boat. He shows me a picture of himself from what he thought would be his deathbed. He was an anarchist originally from Orange County California. Though he's middle aged with a shock of white hair, he sports a goatee that looks like it was born out of a counter cultural movement.

After a stint in the military, he got involved with the anarchist movement. Everything from hidden technologies and underground parties to working to educate prisoners and writing for the local alt-weekly. Cryptocurrencies were a natural fit for him because he, like so many other people on this boat, was curious, smart, and more than a little angry about how power tended to stay at the top. Then he ran face first into the hard wall of cancer.

"I was just laying there. You know, dying. I thought to myself, I gotta do something. I can't just lay here and die. So I call up a couple of my friends. I've got some ideas for crypto businesses and I start two businesses from my deathbed."

"Was that hard?" I ask.

"Probably not as hard a dying," he says.

Now Doug runs a blockchain-based private airline service and a crypto ATM company. Eight months ago he was dying, and now he's on this boat on the Danube.

Freedom is surviving.

IMAGINING FREEDOM ISLAND

In the distance we see a puff of green trees and a slip of sandy beach. When Freedom Island appears on the horizon everyone stands at the prow of their vessels. All of the boats, including the police, cut their engines outside the tip of the island. Someone kills the music and all we can hear is the sound of water lapping the sides of our boats and the sandy shore.

Vit makes a speech and awards *the first order of Liberland* medals to some of the Liberlanders. Cheers fly up from all the boats. We raise a cup to the first order of Liberland, to the police, and then to the island. Freedom Island is a tree-filled sandbar under a cobalt sky. The wild shore disappears over the horizon with Serbia on one side, Croatia on the other, and opportunity on its virgin soil. I hear the Liberlanders whisper to one another imagining what the island will one day look like

That's where the waterfront will go.

Light rail will connect us to the mainland

I could see like a sort of Sydney concert hall thing, right there at the tip.

80 people on a handful of boats fill the empty island with daydreams of a truly free country. They erect dreamy apartment buildings and promenades. They can see cranes fitting solar panels onto schools and grocery stores. They live and let live.

Liberland is an anomaly in the world of statecraft. Nations are fought for with blood and treasure. They're protected with standing armies and an origin myth more bulletproof than the nation itself. They are usually taken from others by a group that has enough weapons and money to eclipse the story that was already installed on that land.

But Liberland is different. No one wanted this island. It is no man's land. So that means that whoever can take it can make it their home. It is equal parts inspiring as it is sobering. I've been taken with the jet skis and the bitcoin millionaires and the crypto-anarchists this entire time, but this is just one story of how a country gets to be born. Most aren't so lucky. Will the countries of the future be fought for in court rather than on battlefields. I don't know. But I doubt it. After all, we are looking at an empty island.

After the ceremony Foreign Secretary Tom comes up to me.

"Where's the next stop on your trip?"

"Somaliland," I say, and then clarify. "In Northern Somalia."

"Yeah, I've been there!"

"Why?"

"We have an embassy in Somaliland. Do you want to stay at it?"

Just when I think I'm done being surprised, I find out that Liberland has embassies all over the world.

"Yes. I do want to stay at your embassy."

ONE LAST STOP

Back in Bulgaria Savannah looks over my shoulder as I book my ticket to Hargeisa Somaliland. When I complete the purchase, she tackles me across the couch.

"That's your last stop. Ramadan in Somaliland and then you're done," she says.

"I guess so," I say.

"So, what happens next?" she asks.

I don't know what will happen next. I hadn't thought that far ahead.

AN OFFER I CAN'T REFUSE

I am sweating. I am pacing. I am sending polite, but firm, but desperate emails to my editor and to the President of Liberland. My bank account is dwindling in the low triple digits. While I have been freelancing articles payments are painfully slow. On top of that, I have not heard from Liberland since their offer to couch surf at their embassy. I leave for Somaliland in three days and I am running the very real risk of being homeless and penniless in Somaliland.

My emails contain phrases like:

I just wanted to drop you a line to confirm...

I'll be arriving in Hargeisa in three days, so I'm curious if there are any further instructions.

I have not been paid.

The problem with traveling to Somaliland on a budget is not that it is an expensive place to stay, but that it is an expensive place to stay safely and within the law. Foreigners are not allowed out of their lodging downtown after nightfall. Furthermore, there are only a few fortified hotels in the area. The safest of these goes for $150 a night.

I wonder what $5 worth of bitcoin will get me in Somaliland. My email pings. The President of Liberland has gotten back to me before my editor. He asks me for my phone number which I find somewhat odd, but when the President of Liberland calls you must pick up. My phone rings a second later.

"Hey Mr. President," I say, pacing Savannah's bedroom.

"Hi Eric, Tom told me that we had offered to house you at the embassy in Hargeisa."

And you're still going to right?

"He did say that."

"So there is a small problem."

If I can't stay I'm going to be wandering the streets of Hargeisa and I literally have no backup plan because I am not a smart person.

"What's that?"

Please let me stay over at the embassy.

"Yeah so we lost our Ambassador to Somaliland."

No ambassador means no embassy. No embassy means I have nowhere to stay. I'm screwed.

"Oh, dang."

I'm screwed. I'm screwed. I'm screwed. Maybe I can stay at an NGO. Maybe I can find a family to host me. Maybe I can offer to mop floors for the Ambassador Hotel in exchange for housing.

"Look, I don't have much time to talk, but is that something that you would want to do?"

I'm going to be ransomed. That's probably an overblown stereotype. But I'm totally going to get kidnapped and ransomed.

"Do what?" I ask.

"Be the ambassador."

Wait what?

"Like the ambassador to Somaliland?" I say.

"Yes," Vit says.

"On behalf of Liberland?" I say.

"Yes," Vit says.

A long moment passes in which I feel like the host of a strange hidden camera show will pop out and let me know that this is all an incredibly elaborate prank.

"Can I stay at the embassy?"

"Yes. But it is empty. I will try to get someone to put a bed inside for you."

"Like, what do I have to do?" I ask.

"You have to establish diplomatic relations with the government of Somaliland."

Totally, I do that all the time.

"Okay."

"You also have to buy furniture for the embassy. As I mentioned. It is empty."

I don't know how to do that.

"I can do that," I say.

"Great, I'm glad this worked out."

Vit hangs up. I think I just became an ambassador from one stateless nation to another.

"Hey Savannah!" I yell to the next room.

"Yeah?"

"I just got a call from the President of Liberland."

"Great! What did he say?"

PART 5 SOMALILAND

I AM NOT QUALIFIED TO DO THIS

I'm thrown sideways as my airplane banks, waking me from a drooly slumber. I try to figure out where I am and what I'm doing. I look around the small airplane and find that it is full of Somalis. Right. I'm doing the ambassador thing.

I wipe the sleep from my eyes and go over the notes that President Jedlicka sent me. Once I land in Hargeisa Somaliland I will be met by a Syrian expat named Wassim who serves as the Liberland attache to the UAE, whatever any of that means. Wassim runs a construction business in the area. He will connect me to the political infrastructure of Somaliland, and let me use his office for the next six weeks while I'm serving as ambassador.

I have never done anything that qualifies me for this other than being on the right jet ski at the right time. I have been a third-grade teacher, a journalist, a summer camp director. I have telemarketed theater tickets, served coffee, and for a brief period of time, taught acro-yoga. Like most things in life, I said yes because I couldn't afford to say no. Like most things in life, I intend to make it up as I go along.

The tiny aircraft rattles as it takes another steep turn. I open the window shade and a fire hose of sunlight blasts me in the face. My eyes adjust to the orange light reflecting off the desert and I see the insinuation of organized human society creeping across the arid plain.

"Hargeisa?" I ask of the man next to me. He gives me a thumbs up and a broad smile.

Two mountains define the horizon watching over a small East African city. I see orange sand dotted by craggy boulders and stippled with green bushes. Shepards

245

maneuver gangs of goats and tan SUVs crawl down the road. The plane whips into a final descent and digs into the sandy tarmac for a screeching halt. Everyone claps and begins filing off in a chaotic rush.

I step off the plane and I'm hit with a gritty blast of desert wind while I make my way towards the small terminal building. Upon telling friends and family that I was going to an unrecognized nation in Northern Somalia I heard a consistent refrain about Somali pirates, Islamic extremism and the *failed states*.

Sliding glass doors creak open and I hop in line to get my passport stamped.

The term *failed state* is as ambiguous and absurd as a *stateless nation*, or even *the third world*. These are concepts used by global powers and transnational bodies to define regions against standards which they themselves are setting. *Failed state* conjures the image of a rubble filled wasteland in Mad Max devoid of human life. While there are rubble filled wastelands in Somalia, they also exist in California, and pretty much anywhere else there is rubble.

The most charitable reading of the term refers to a place where central governance is too weak to deliver services to citizens and too chaotic to engage in international relationships. Lack of foreign investment and the inability to stimulate growth of private industry means a plummeting national currency, weakened central government, the rise of informal economies, and the constant threat of violence. This becomes a death spiral for a country as it moves closer to being referred to as *a failed state*. But of course, the Horn of Africa was not always like this.

A woman wearing a full abaya stamps my passport. When I go to collect my bag, I find that instead of a luggage carousel they have a crew of young men dressed in white button down shirts hurling bags into the center of an empty room. While I wait for my bag to be hurled it might be a good time to talk about the history of Somalia and Somaliland.

The Horn of Africa has been inhabited since the Paleolithic era. While nation states didn't exist back then, human beings tend to self-organize based on the demands of the land they inhabit. Somalia is a dagger of desert that juts into the Red Sea which gave rise to a clan-based nomadic culture that thrived off trade with neighbors. Since geography is destiny, the landscape of Somalia has been both a blessing and a curse.

The Horn of Africa is packed with natural resources and positioned for international trade. This means that its history is largely defined by larger powers fighting for regional influence while native populations attempt to self-determine. While The Horn of Africa was subsumed by our old friends the Ottoman Empire, the origins of Somalia and Somaliland began in the 1800s with the European *Scramble for Africa*. During this period from 1833 and 1914 European colonization in the African continent rose from 10 percent to an eye-watering 90 percent.

Italy had its eye on East Africa and began snapping up territory in modern day Eritrea and Somalia. Meanwhile, the British wanted to protect their trade routes through the Red Sea, setting up shop in the northern portion of Somalia which would eventually become Somaliland. However, the Somali-led Dervish movement attempted to unite the clans against foreign invaders. Remember, no one likes to be colonized and a common enemy is a great way to get people to work together. The guerilla fighters were eventually crushed by colonizers, the movement acted as an intertribal galvanizing force and built the foundations of the modern multi-tribal Somali state. It showed that regardless of clan affiliation, the Horn of Africa could act unilaterally in its own interest.

In the 1960s the Italians and British decided to hand control over the region back to Somali leadership. The British-held Somaliland became an independent state for five whole days before joining with the rest of the Horn of Africa and forming the modern borders of Somalia. Decades later, Somaliland would try to regain its independence with a bloody civil war.

After Somalia gained its independence from European powers in the 1960s General Mohamed Siad Barre seized power and installed a system of government of his own invention which he termed *scientific socialism*. This system was neither scientific, nor Socialist. It mashed together the worst ideas of Marxism, tribal oligarchy and Islamic law into a brutal dictatorship. He built his center of power in the current capital of Federal Somalia, Mogadishu. Barre's government enjoyed a close relationship with the Soviet Union which was trying to spread the good word of Communism throughout East Africa.

However, during the Cold War, Barre broke ties with the USSR and formed an alliance with the United States which paid his regime handsomely for establishing a base of operations on the Red Sea. The U.S. was more than happy to overlook the fact that Barre was a genocidal dictator in exchange for access to the Horn of Africa. Global powers prefer predictability over justice, so hopping into bed with a dictator like Barre is often the rule rather than the exception. Throughout his reign Barre carried out imprisonment, torture, and starvation campaigns against the Isaaq tribe, dominant in Northern Somalia. Once again, attempting to eliminate a culture from existence led to catastrophe.

In 1988, Somaliland declared its independence with

Hargeisa as its capital. This metastasized into The Somali Civil War in 1992. Barre's military sought to end what he termed *The Isaaq Problem* by killing hundreds of thousands and leveling over 90 percent of Hargeisa with aerial bombardment. As fighting spun out of control Barre's regime was ousted from power, leaving him to escape over the border to Kenya. The power vacuum left by Barre led to infighting between tribes, the growth of Islamic extremist groups, and the collapse of institutions. The Somali Civil War is currently a frozen conflict between de facto states, each claiming their own independence.

Puntland occupies the tip of the Horn of Africa straddling the Indian Ocean and the Red Sea. Federal Somalia sits to the South with the capital city of Mogadishu on the Indian Ocean. Somaliland, where I am currently in the airport waiting for my luggage to be hurled, occupies the top half of the Horn of Africa along the Red Sea.

My bag plops down in front of me. It's time to go do ambassador stuff.

DOWN THE AIRPORT ROAD

I emerge from the airport into the smoldering sunlight. As my eyes adjust I see Wassim. He looks like a mix between Jim Belushi and Ray Romano. He stands out in Somaliland. Wassim leans on a dust caked 4x4 with a massive exterior exhaust. He playfully raises his eyebrows behind sunglasses and waves me over with a bottle of water.

"Wassim?"

"Mr. Ambassador?"

"That's me," I say, accepting the bottle of water.

"You're a CIA agent," he says, his smile falling dead on

his face. I choke on the water as I try to put my first impression in reverse.

"No, just happened to be in Liberland at the right time."

"You're right. You don't sound like a spy at all!"

I can't tell if he's joking or not. He pops the passenger side door for me and gestures for the driver to grab my bag.

"Come on, let's get coffee. I'll interrogate you and then we'll get you to the embassy. Hop in."

I climb into the SUV with Wassim and his driver. The engine guns and we shoot out of the airport parking lot. Our car immediately takes a huge pothole, sending my head into the roof.

"Best to hold on tight. Hargeisa is pretty safe, but the roads will kill you," says Wassim as the Somali driver pilots our 4x4 onto an asphalt road cratered with suspension-crushing potholes.

Airport Road is the main artery of Hargeisa and leads into the heart of downtown. Driving into the city feels like witnessing the lifecycle of a country. It's a mixture of construction, destruction, improvisation, and reimagination. Fancy hotels hugged by scaffolding sit next to tin shacks and crumbling restaurants from a time gone by. Old men leaning on canes in traditional dress stare as our driver whips around a bus packed with school children. It's hard to imagine that just a couple decades prior Hargeisa was known as the *Dresden of Africa*.

"Since the English occupied Somaliland all of the cars have their steering wheel on the English side, but we drive on the European or American side. It's a mess. You'd think they would have changed that after the city was leveled," says Wassim.

I roll down the window as we come to a knot of traffic.

Cooking oil, gasoline, incense and goat fill the air. I can taste the dry chalky dust on my tongue and my mouth starts watering when I see a woman cooking samosas in a vat of oil on the street.

"I go to her a couple times a week. Probably should do that less," Wassim pats his stomach.

His phone rings and he chats in Arabic as we pull onto a residential side street. It's a neighborhood of small fortresses. Squat stone buildings are boxed in by high walls with broken glass bottles jutting out of the top as makeshift barbed wire. Heavy metal gates are manned by guards in stone booths.

Lining the dirt road are a series of small shacks with corrugated tin roofs. Each shack is painted with a cartoonish bushel of green leaves with brown stalks like something the Jolly Green Giant would pitch in the frozen food aisle. Each shack has a three-digit number and one of two words:

GAFANE 346 or WHITE HORSE 482

Inside, I can see men lazily chewing at branches full of the green leaves. They lay, catatonic on rattan mats next to plastic tea jugs. I meet their glassy eyes. Lights are on, but no one is home.

"What is going on in there?" I ask Wassim as he hangs up his phone.

'Khat. Local narcotic,' he says peeking out over his shades.

"Legal?"

"The Koran didn't say anything about khat, just booze. By the way, I've got some bottles of black market vodka in the office if you're interested. Hargeisa gets pretty dull during Ramadan."

"Have you tried it? Khat?"

"Yeah, in Yemen. Gives you a good buzz, but you can get addicted. Causes problems around here. The men spend all their money on it. Also, the goats get stoned and stand in the middle of the road." The truck pulls up to a compound with barbed wire lacing the top of its walls.

"We're here."

The driver honks his horn and a steel door rolls open revealing a small villa. I hop out of the SUV into the garden courtyard. My new office for the next couple of months.

THE POLITICS OF DIRT

Wassim opens the office door greeting his staff in a mixture of Arabic, English, and Somali.

"Come on, in, you should get to know everybody. Sorry to leave you but Hargeisa is too quiet for me during Ramadan."

The office is a small house converted into a construction company with chunky wooden desks surrounded by blueprints and charts. I'm introduced to Khader, a soft-spoken Somali project manager in his mid 20s who looks about as confused to see me as I am to be here. Yahia is a Syrian from Idlib who moved his family to Africa during the Syrian Civil War. He's lanky, with deep set eyes framed by dark circles. He wears a jumpsuit and looks like a cast member of the Sopranos if they hadn't slept in a couple of days. He gives me a tour of the office. The walls are lined with construction plans that are as unintelligible to me as Arabic.

"Wassim, what is it that you do, exactly?"

"I build. I'm a builder. The schematic that you're

looking at is a dam. But right now we're working on the road from Berbera Port."

I'm surprised to hear about Berbera Port. I studied it as an analyst, and it's an important geopolitical point in East Africa.

"Can't show you those blueprints though," Wassim says. "Politics of dirt."

"What's that?" I ask as he steers me back to the patio. We sit and he replaces his sunglasses with spectacles. He looks and talks like a professor that always has full classes wheeling easily between topics, languages, and people.

"Politics of dirt. Any time you put something in the ground, there are politics. I tell you where that road goes, suddenly you buy a plot of land on either side. Or maybe a government official bribes me to make sure that the very important road goes by his very empty hotel in the middle of the desert. Politics of dirt. Everything is political. Even dirt."

A housekeeper brings us coffee and a plate of fruit.

"I'd imagine there is a lot of politics around Berbera," I say.

"Which is why I don't keep those blueprints out for everyone to see." He dumps a small mountain of sugar into his coffee.

Berbera was originally built as a Russian naval base in collaboration with the Somali government. It was eventually turned over to the United States when the Soviet Union shrunk into the Russian Federation. The U.S. then expanded the port to service ships going through the Red Sea. But the civil war came and everyone pulled out and an upstart nation calling itself Somaliland took hold of the territory. Berbera Port was open for business and investors came running.

The UAE jumped on Berbera with the goal of turning

it into a shipping port that could service Kenya and Ethiopia. However, having a port full of goods is one thing, if you want to move, and sell those goods, you need a road. Enter Wassim. His phone rings and he clicks from New York intellectual English into Arabic. He puts the phone down with a *Yalla bye.*

"Your bedroom has been furnished Mr. Ambassador. I'll have my secretary take you up to the embassy."

THE LIBERLAND EMBASSY
TO SOMALILAND

Wassim's secretary steps out of her SUV talking on a cellphone with a *Hello Kitty* cover, wearing a long black abaya with neon green tennis shoes. She finishes her conversation, drops her phone into her purse, and opens a brilliant toothy smile at Wassim and me.

"This is Fathia, she'll take care of anything you need while I'm gone."

I place a hand over my heart in greeting and she extends hers covered with the cloth of her abaya. Somaliland is run both legally and socially under Islamic law. Women wearing full length abayas are generally only touched by their families or their husbands. While some devout Muslims don't shake hands, others will drape the cloth of their abaya like Fathia. I take her hand.

"I'm going to finish up some work here, why don't you two head up to the embassy? Come back tomorrow and I'll make introductions."

Wassim and I say our goodbyes and I climb into Fathia's SUV, it seems that if you want to drive in Somaliland you need 4-wheel-drive. She puts on some bug-eyed sunglasses and steps on the accelerator. We spray dirt as she pulls off of the side street and whips us back onto the Airport Road.

"So, you are the ambassador of Liberland?"

I feel like she's asking if I am an astronaut because I watched *2001 A Space Odyssey*. I give her the short version of how I ended up in Somaliland.

"I am confused," she says.

"Me too," I admit.

"What happened to the original ambassador?" I think about this for a long moment. It never occurred to me to ask.

"I have no idea," I say.

"It sounds like you are the real ambassador then."

I will have to practice saying it in the bathroom mirror before I get used to saying it.

We turn onto the dirt path running past an opulent white hotel fittingly called *The Ambassador*. She brings the car to a stop in front of a makeshift checkpoint. Four middle aged men with AK47s and tattered green clothes guard a heavy metal gate crossing the road. Compared to the car bomb checkpoints in Iraq this one looks prehistoric. The men with guns surround the car and give me a slack-faced stare. Fathia rolls down the window chats with the men. They accept whatever Fathia said because one of the guards unties the twine holding the metal gate closed and pushes it open.

"This is a very safe area of Hargeisa, it is called Masala. There is a hospital, the Ambassador Hotel, and many other embassies. You will be very comfortable here," she says.

"Looks safe," I say, watching the men tie the gate together.

Fathia's SUV rumbles between fortified compounds wrapped in barbed wire, entombed in concrete bearing the logos of organizations like the United Nations, Doctors Without Borders, and The Norwegian Refugee Council. We roll to a stop outside of a boxy mansion behind high walls with a thick metal gate.

"You are home," she says, beaming a bright toothy grin. She honks the horn. "Your guard will open the gate."

My guard? I had no idea that I would be protected. The gate pulls aside with a screech. I imagine a Somali Rambo, ready to snap necks for Liberland. I wonder if I can have my guard hold people over my balcony by their ankles if they disrespect me. I am already drunk with power. This is the beginning of corruption. The metal gate rolls back revealing a concave middle-aged man with an ancient machine gun. He smiles and waves.

"He is called Eid. He will make sure you are safe," says Fathia. It doesn't look like Eid could protect me from a light breeze but I do feel safer.

"How do I say hello, how are you in Somali?"

"*Eska waran*," she says as I get out of the car. "I will leave now. See you tomorrow."

Faithia whips the car around and peels out of the driveway.

"*Eska waran*," I say to Eid.

"Ahhhh, *nabad geleeoo*," says Eid.

I laugh and nod. Eid laughs and nods. We shake hands, both of us laughing and nodding. A long moment passes and we have gone as far as our shared language can take us. Eid shoulders his rifle and takes me by the forearm for a tour.

He shows me to a detached marble banquet hall complete with chandelier. We walk through a small papaya grove and pass by the maid's quarters. Eid takes me to his guard house where he has a bed, stove, and prayer rug. We enter the mansion under a soaring portico to find a dining room which is empty except for 12 metal chairs. Our footsteps echo along the stone walls as we explore each of the nine rooms, empty except for a bare lightbulb. I assume that my official quarters will be the only room with a bed and dresser.

Eid takes me to the roof. There is a warm breeze pulling up off of the hills below. I can see the whole of Hargeisa. There are clusters of nomadic homes along the hillsides and the electric lights of downtown are beginning to blink on. Eid points at the mountains in the distance. The sky is a shout of rose quartz. We watch in silence as the sun begins its slow descent.

The call to prayer rings out from the valley below. Eid pats me on the back and leaves me with the last of the sun, and the eternal mountains. I am so full of gratitude for Eid, Faithia and Wassim. I am saturated with it. I am thankful for Vit, Bitcoin Mike, Vladimir, Terry, Astefano, Claire, and Savannah. My body barely contains me. I realize that this is my last home before the end of my journey.

I am so grateful for the world

FOOD, WATER, AND PARANOIA

I turn on the tap in my bathroom and a dark rusty dribble turns into a bright yellow spray. I turn off the tap. I will need to procure both food and water if I want to maintain the lifestyle and hygiene befitting someone of my position. It's time to venture out for supplies. I find Eid boiling tea in his guard house and listening to the radio. I pantomime drinking water and eating food followed by an exaggerated sad shrug.

He opens the metal gate and points down a stony path. I thank him and begin my quest. The ground is crowded with bushes covered in gnarly thorns which bite right through the sole of my hiking boots. A group of men pass by me effortlessly navigating the rocks in sandals heading towards a mosque in the distance. Down the road, I find a checkpoint where guards sit drinking tea. They look up as they hear me approach.

Eska waran?" I say, which is far less impressive to them than I was hoping.

I pantomime drinking water. I shrug my shoulders and look like a sad clown. The guards point to a metal shed with an electric light buzzing inside. They return to their khat as I continue past the checkpoint.

The shed contains powdered milk, tang, bags of rice and cans of tuna from Saudi Arabia. They also have Pringles. This is not strange. Pringles are everywhere. I was once camping with Berbers in the Northern Sahara. The last shop we hit before the endless desert had seven flavors of Pringles. At this point, it would be stranger if this small metal shack in Somaliland wasn't selling Pringles. What I'm saying here is; good job Pringles corporation. I literally have no idea how you do it.

I buy six liters of water, soap, a tin of tuna and tubes of Pringles. The man behind the counter holds up five fingers and I give him five American dollars. He returns my change in a small stack of Somali shillings. I thank the man and shuffle away loaded with supplies. The U.S. dollar is one currency used in Somaliland. After the war, the Somali Shilling became so depreciated that it was all but worthless paper. In order to pay for anything more expensive than a cup of tea you have to use a small brick of Somali Shillings or a couple U.S. dollars. Even though Somaliland can politically detach from Federal Somalia it can't separate itself from the global financial system.

It is a dark moonless night, and I begin my walk back

to the embassy weighed down with Pringles, tuna and water. My first night in Erbil was a spiced symphony of noise and disorder. Tonight is an ominous silent glare. Feral animals dart between shadows into the spiny bushes. I pass by high-walled compounds guarded by men with guns in pools of flickering light. An unknown animal wails in the distance prompting me to leap in the air. I come down hard on my toes and a searing pain shoots through my ankle.

I freeze. My eyes go large. My heart slams in my chest. I have dropped my Pringles. I level the light from my cell phone at my foot hoping that I don't find a scorpion clinging to my boot. There, next to a fallen can of tuna is a goat's horn. I stepped on it in such a way that it catapulted into the flesh above my boot. I gather my things and pocket the goat horn.

Maybe I need a reminder that fear is mostly in your mind. Maybe I think it will be a neat souvenir. I'm not certain why I keep it, but I vow that the goat's horn will never leave my side while I am in Somaliland.

SHOWERING OUT OF BOTTLES
AND YOU CAN TOO

Eid opens the gate for me. Once again, he takes me by the forearm and walks me through every room of the house, to show me that there are no terrorists waiting to kidnap me. There is no way for me to express how glad I am that he does this. I give him a tube of Pringles.

I go up to my new bathroom and with the liter bottles of water for a bucket bath. Given my time in the Peace Corps I know that it takes me exactly 1.5 liters of water to get passably clean. If you've never showered out of a liter bottle, below is a step by step process:

Step 1: Pour the first bottle of water over your head. It doesn't matter if it's cold, you have no one to blame but yourself.

Step 2: Use your hair like a water sponge. That will help you get the rest of your body wet. Make sure to work your hair-water into all of your dry parts.

Step 3: Stand there, naked and cold wondering why you are showering out of a plastic bottle. Consider all of the lives that you could have led besides this one. Remember, everything passes. Everything changes. Find some way to capture this moment. Look for the moments of joy and humor in the discomfort and anxiety.

Step 4: Get soapy! Don't be shy, it's been a long day.

Step 5: Use the rest of the water in your bottle to rinse off.

After finishing with my five-step process I realize that I have no towel. Naked and dripping, I penguin-walk on the slippery marble floors to my bag. I find a shirt that I hate and decide that it will be the Official Liberland Shirt Towel. Still damp and dripping (due to my impressive hair sponge) I eat tuna out of the can using Pringles as makeshift spoons. Once I have finished dinner I dive into bed. This is the life of a diplomat that I was meant to live. This is my absolute peak.

I am home.

EVERYONE IS COMING FOR ME AND I'M GOING TO DIE

I lay awake in bed listening to an air force of mosquitoes hover around my room. I was told by some people that I should be on anti-malaria drugs. I was told by others that I didn't need them. I listened to the others because:

a. I didn't know where to get these drugs.

b. I couldn't afford them.

The mosquitos above me seem to generate a small breeze given how large and plentiful they are. I regret rolling the dice on the Malaria drugs so I try to cocoon myself under the blanket. Problem solved. I quickly realize that my cocoon is as hot as a pizza oven at high noon in the middle of Burning Man.

SLAM!

I hear a door bang shut in the hallway. All of my senses go red alert.

Did someone just come in the front door? Could it have been Eid? No. I don't think he can close a door that hard.

I leap out of bed and press myself against the wall. I try to be more quiet than I have ever been in my life. I can hear my heart through my chest.

SLAM! Another door.

Are people looking for me? How did they get past the gate?

I open the door a crack and peer into the darkened hallway with the goat horn clutched in my fist. I am in my underwear and boots. If someone is trying to kidnap me it's going to be very weird for everyone. I push through the door to patrol. This is my embassy. This is an act of war against Liberland. A pleasant breeze blows through the house.

SLAM.

The breeze blows a door shut. As it turns out the hallways get windy causing the doors to open and slam shut at random intervals. Satisfied, I back up towards my room lowering the goat horn. I shove the damp Liberland Official Shirt Towel under the door and place my backpack in front of it. If and when someone comes for me. I will hear them coming. I will be ready, with my goat horn.

Only one month left.

DAY ONE DIPLOMAT

When I wake up I've been riddled with mosquito bites. I get dressed and go to my balcony hoping I don't have malaria. Outside a gang of camels meander across the sandy scrubland framed by the mountain range. I feel like I'm in *Jurassic Park*. I head out towards Wassim's office and introduce myself to the guards at the checkpoints along the way. I try out my new Somali phrases, I learn names, I shake hands, I diplomat like I've never diplomated before.

As I come onto the Airport Road, I notice a crowd of people gathered around an overturned truck. The front end is smashed to a metal pulp. The driver sits unharmed next to the wreckage washing his face with a bottle of water. I pass by the scene walking far off on the shoulder. Gangs of goats go by. Men sip tea in plastic chairs. Women manage children picking through market stalls. I get a couple of passing glances, but aside from the accident it seems like a normal day in Hargeisa.

Wassim's driver opens the gate to his office and offers me a big hug for some reason. I hug the man. I never turn down a hug and neither should you.

"Ah, the ambassador is here. Great. I've got someone for you to meet," says Wassim sitting with a cup of coffee on the porch. He says something to the housekeeper in Arabic and another cup of coffee and fruit appear.

"How was last night? Did the bed work out?"

"Totally random question—" Wassim's eyebrows go up as he lights a cigarette. "Do you take anti-malaria medication?"

"Mosquitos get you?' He laughs and taps his ash into a tray.

"Most of me, yes."

"No, you're fine in Hargeisa, there might be malaria in

other places, but not here." A wave of relief passes over me. I won't die but I'll be itchy for a month.

"I saw camels this morning," I say this as if I'd seen a leprechaun.

"You didn't touch them did you?" asks Wassim

"No."

"Good. People keep their money in their animals out here. The last thing you need is an angry shepherd claiming that you hurt his camel and demanding money."

I give it some thought. He's right. That is the last thing I need. There's a knock at the door of the compound. The driver opens the gate for a small middle-aged Somali man wearing a white dishdasha and neatly tied turban. He has round, golden rimmed glasses and a neatly trimmed mustache. The man greets Wassim with an embrace. I stand to introduce myself. He extends his hand with another over his heart.

"Hello!"

"*Eska waran!*" I say.

"Oh, you speak Somali already. Very good," he says, dusting off a chair and taking a seat with a deep sigh. He looks at us and then grins. He seems like a man who has never been in a hurry in his life.

"This is Abdulrahman. He is a man who can make anything happen." Says Wassim with a hand on Abdulrahman's shoulder.

"Who are you?" says Abdulrahman. Wassim grins and returns to smoking.

"I am the Ambassador from Liberland to Somaliland." It feels like I am claiming to be a wizard.

"Oh, okay, very good. I work with the government of Somaliland. What is it that I can do for you?" I let Abdulrahman know about my two-point mission for my time in Somaliland.

"While I am here opening our embassy. Liberland would like to establish a strong relationship with Somaliland. So I am hoping that I can meet with someone in the President's office." *This sounds right. This sounds like something an ambassador would say.* Abdulrahman nods, holding a steaming cup of coffee under his nose. A smile breaks across his face.

"Okay," he says.

"Also, I am trying to buy furniture for the embassy," I say followed by a decisive sip of coffee. Abdulrahman and Wassim say something to one another in Arabic. I scratch my mosquito bites.

"Everything is okay. No problem, no problem," says Abdulrahman. He gestures for my cell phone. He plugs his number into it and calls himself. "Now, we are in contact. I will call you."

Abdulrahman says goodbye and heads towards the front gate.

"Do you have any money?" Abdulrahman asks. I do not know if he means me or if he means the Embassy of Liberland. The answer is no either way.

"Not yet," I say.

"Ah, okay. Consult your president and we will talk. You have my number." Abdulrahman, the man who can get things done, shuts the gate behind him.

My president? Is Vit Jedlicka my president?

LIBERLAND CALLING

I buy a portable wireless router from a telecom store. The tiny black box slides open and connects my phone to the internet. African wireless companies have been leap-frogging legacy systems for a decade because it's easier to set up an antenna than to string a continent full of land-lines. Sadly, it's not so simple to rebuild critical infrastructure or create a growing economy in an unrecognized nation. Somalilanders often own a couple of cell-phones while living in nomadic homes.

I call my parents and Savannah to let them know I am alive, and then I dial Tariq. The phone rings as I watch a herd of goats followed by a shepherd urging them forward with a lazy rap of his stick. Each goat has a phone number spray painted across its back. This lets someone buy a goat or return one if it's lost since livestock is a critical pillar of the economy. With some spray paint, a flesh and blood animal can be turned into a tradable asset.

"Eric, Hello," says Tariq in his BBC English accent.

"Hey Tariq. I've met with Wassim and I have one contact in the government."

"Have you figured out how to buy furniture?" he asks.

"I am working on that. How do I get money into the country?"

"Oh." Tariq considers this, and then says, "I suppose you'll have to open a bank account."

"Got it."

I click my wireless router closed and watch the goats ramble off into the distance. I wonder what the U.S. government will think about my bank account in Somaliland. I wonder if I should invest in goats instead of Bitcoin.

DOWNTOWN HARGEISA

"Let's go downtown. I'll show you the ropes."

Wassim catches me by the arm as I return to his office later that day. We hop in his 4x4 and crawl through the potholes of the Airport Road towards the heart of

Hargeisa. The sun is starting a slow descent toasting each of the streets a dusty orange. We're swallowed up by a cacophony of activity. Men spark welding torches outside of mechanic shops. Women butcher thick slabs of ruby red meat while girls hem brilliant hijabs with pedal-powered Singer sewing machines. Shopkeepers shout at our passing car, holding their wares aloft.

"I'm going to point out the banks that might believe your story enough to open an account. Then we'll head over to the nicest coffee shop in Hargeisa."

"Sounds fancy."

"Hargeisa doesn't have a ton to offer in terms of modern conveniences, or nightlife for that matter. Good music, but you probably won't hear any of it during Ramadan."

We cross a bridge into the city center.

I poke my head out the window and look back at the bridge. A trickle of muddy water flows between the craggy rocks and piles of garbage. Teenagers play in the lengthening shadow of the bridge. Heavy with groceries, women pick their way down the side of the embankment.

"Don't come down here after dark unless you're with someone by the way. Technically, foreigners like yourself are not allowed down here without armed protection, but I guess you'll have to settle for me."

"They have international banks here?" I ask.

"Sure, there's a lot of money in Somaliland. Diaspora is coming back. That's the way it usually goes. Wait for a conflict to cool down, come in, and develop while the prices are low. I know guys who have made millions out of Somaliland."

Wassim drums on the steering wheel as we cut through a knot of traffic and park in a sandy lot. A young boy comes up to the window, Wassim hands him some money to watch the SUV as we step into the dusty nest of streets. The sun cuts rose colored prisms in the air as it ducks between the tallest buildings in Hargeisa. Trucks and buses chug by packed with people. We turn onto a wide boulevard and an impromptu market seems to spring from nowhere. Young men carrying tarpaulins heavy with goods drop their loads and open them as we pass. When an ancient army vehicle rolls down the street the hawkers wrap up their bags and disappear as quickly as they arrived.

"What are they doing?" I ask Wassim.

"Informal market. They're not allowed to sell clothes, so when the police come by they have to move it along,' He peeks over his sunglasses at the stacks of jeans.

"Everyone is a business person. Somalis are good at it. They've got it in their blood. They're nomads and traders. Drop them anywhere in the world and they'll find a way to survive and to make a buck while they do it," says Wassim.

We come upon a ramshackle warren of wooden market stalls selling everything from fresh fruit to cell phones. A young boy stands next to a speaker thumping out static beats while a Khat stand is mobbed by men buying small bushels. These are the last days of routine life in Hargeisa until Ramadan rings in a month of quiet and contemplation.

"Okay, so there are two banks here, but I'm going to send you to Dabshi, because it's where I go." Wassim, points out a shining modern building dropped in the middle of a crumbling block. "Can you tell who the billionaires in Hargeisa are?"

"Banks," I say.

"You just need to bring your passport. They're going to give you a hard time. So you just need to tell them who you are and they'll set you up." *All I need to do is tell them who I am.*

"And I'll be able to get shillings?"

"I wouldn't recommend that. They have a different system here." Says Wassim as we walk through the central square. He points out some old men sitting in front of metal cases filled with bricks of Somali shillings.

"You're going to get a Dabshi account on your phone and you'll be able to text one of these money changers to pay your bill in shillings. It's like digital money, but it's not, because it's real. A real guy brings real money to a real place, but people just use phones to make the guy move,' he says.

Technically this system is not that different from how banking actually works. Swiping your card doesn't send money from the card to anyone else. It sends a signal for your bank to get in touch with another bank and exchange some ones and zeroes. Here in Somaliland it's a guy on a motorbike with a stack of tattered Somali shillings rather than a piece of code terminating one of millions of trans-actions a second. I am fixated on the brick of Somali shillings locked in a box next to the man with the motor-bike. Is this all money really is?

"Coffee?"asks Wassim, jarring me back to reality.

Yes, I do need some coffee.

DAMN GOOD COFFEE YOU HAVE HERE IN HARGEISA

Deero Mall is a turquoise cube. The inside of the cube looks like the set of a zombie movie. The mall is empty except for a clothing shop with a couple haunting mannequins. Fluorescent lights buzz too brightly before flickering on and off in an irregular interval. A small sign by a defunct elevator reads *Berbera Coffee*.

"This is the best coffee shop in town. Owned by some wealthy people."

Wealthy people. The term takes on a grim connotation.

As we cross through a hallway spotted by pools of standing water, my expectations for the best coffee in Hargeisa lower. Wassim opens a glass door for me and the smell of woodsy, floral coffee perfumes the air. The shop features luxurious red upholstery, marble flooring, and flat screen televisions play BBC Africa. Families and a smattering of internationals enjoy delicate cups of coffee served by waiters dressed in black aprons. Berbera Coffee could give any hipster cafe in California a run for its beans.

"See? There's plenty of wealth here. It just doesn't make its way to everyone," says Wassim as we take a seat and order espresso from a young man in a chef's hat.

"So where's the government in all of this?" I ask. Wassim glances through pictures of ice cream on the laminated menu.

"Limping along. The only place they really have control is in Hargeisa and maybe some of the bigger cities."

I consider the libertarian ethos of Liberland. Does limiting government and relying on an unregulated free market lead to everyone acting in the best interests of their fellow man? Or does it just lead to brilliant coffee shops in the middle of post-apocalyptic shopping malls? Our espresso arrives.

Wassim smiles at his cup and looks up at me for confirmation that this is indeed a remarkable coffee shop. In the glass demitasse I see a thick layer of amber crema frosting over the ink black brew. It smells like a sunrise over fields of cocoa. I want to preserve this cup of espresso in a museum. Wassim and I take our first sips like a sacrament. Whoever owns Berbera Coffee makes a fine espresso for the people that can afford it.

"What are politicians supposed to do?" I ask.

"I think you're asking the wrong guy about what politicians should do. I'm a builder. Ask me about dams or how to run a business. I might have something to say about that."

"Well, as my fellow Liberlander, what do you think they should do?" Wassim considers for a moment over his cup of coffee.

"I think that the day every politician pops a cyanide pill, the world will start to get a lot better."

"What about the government of Liberland?"

"Liberland is an un-state-state. It's a place to have a mailbox in Europe. If you want to do business then fine, the world can sort itself out. Governments line their pockets and don't deliver. This is coming from a guy who has lived in Syria, the United States, Dubai, Germany, and Somaliland." Wassim perks his eyebrows.

"What do you think a country is?" I ask.

"You should be an expert by now, shouldn't you?"

I put my cup back on the table. I have never had the question turned on me. I take a long moment looking at the Somali waiter in a French chef's hat making Italian espresso from Ethiopian beans. My mind is blank.

"I don't know. I used to think that a country was a landmass connected with a similar culture, language and shared pool of wealth, but that's not really true anymore. Money doesn't care about borders and immigration to another country doesn't change your identity." I give my coffee a stir and watch a small whirlpool appear.

"Millions of people live in diaspora communities that have never stepped foot back in their homeland, but it is still their country. I think the closest I can get is this: A country is a shared memory. Memories give us an identity, they change over time, and they don't exist without recognition. They have to be shared to keep them alive. We do that with flags, songs and ideology."

Wassim lights a cigarette and leans back in his chair. I keep talking.

"By teaching new people about this shared memory, we make this illusion that becomes our identity. When something happens to our country, it happens to us. So we'll die and sometimes kill for this thing that doesn't really exist." I take a sip of my coffee.

"Hmm," says Wassim.

"It's not geopolitical, but that's the best I have right now.""

"Maybe you'll find some inspiration over Ramadan."

Wassim and I leave the last beautiful dregs of our espresso sitting on the table at Berbera Coffee. We emerge into the flickering hallway full of puddles and walk back to the car.

Wassim pays the boy watching the car another couple of shillings. As he starts the engine, there is a knock at his widow. He rolls it down to see a young woman begging. She has the gummy green mash of khat between her teeth and in the corners of her mouth, Wassim hands over some money.

Night has fallen, but the rodeo of cars and buses kicks up impenetrable dust into the headlights.

We inch back to the office through a tangle of cars. Goats with phone numbers written on them wander through traffic. Men stoned off of khat stagger wild eyed down the sidewalk.

At some point, we will make it back to our guarded compounds and high walled mansions. For now, we're at the mercy of the street, even though we're clearly the wealthy people.

Maybe Somaliland is a libertarian paradise.

ALONE IN AN EMPTY EMBASSY

Eid greets me at the front gate of the embassy. Once again, he takes me through every room in the house to show me that I am safe. I crack open a fresh liter of water and use it to shower. I sit on my balcony watching the sparkling city below while I eat tuna and Pringles. Tomorrow, Ramadan begins and so will my fast. I upturn my can of Pringles to leave no crumb behind.

I dive into bed with my goat's horn for protection and listen to the mosquitos buzz overhead. I think of my mission here in Somaliland. I stay awake that night wondering if I am working for a convenient mailbox for wealthy people to do international business. I'm answered by the sound of the wind blowing through an empty mansion.

THE FIRST DAY OF RAMADAN

I finish my last tube of Pringles at four o' clock in the morning. I chug a liter bottle of water and listen to the morning call to prayer echoing throughout Hargeisa from my balcony. Below, I can see men making their way through the crescent moonlight to their local mosques. The Holy Month of Ramadan has begun in Somaliland.

During this month Sunnis rise before dawn to eat an early meal called *Suhoor* because they will be fasting until sunset. The Holy Month of Ramadan remembers the 30 days (or so) that the Quaran was imparted to the Prophet Mohammed. Practicing Muslims abstain from food or drink, pray five times a day, and give to the less fortunate. They do this to honor the prophet while experiencing the pain of hunger and the gratitude that comes from breaking their fast with family and friends in a meal called *iftar*.

Fasting begins on the first crescent moon in the lunar calendar and it ends one month later. Some exceptions for fasting during Ramadan include: illness, traveling, and pregnancy. I've lived in Muslim countries for many years, but this will be my first time fasting. It's possible that I will get ill or travel during the next month, but I don't think I'll get pregnant. In the interest of full disclosure for safety sake I will be drinking water in private on particularly hot days. Also, if I am offered food or drink by a Somali I will take it. There's no reason to out-fast a practicing Muslim.

The final call to prayer rings out and I bow my head to pray in the way only a heavily lapsed Catholic can. God to me is not a consciousness that I can petition. He is a silent friend to thank for star-filled nights and a stoic listener when I feel life has become irreconcilably bent. If you put a gun to my head and asked me I would tell you there was a God. If you demanded that I tell you what he thinks about human life, you'd have to pull the trigger.

I bow my head and send my silent thanks to whoever hears these things. I am grateful for Eid, for my bed, for cans of cheddar Pringles and clean water. I am grateful for Savannah and my family and friends. I am grateful to be on this balcony before sunrise celebrating Ramadan as best an agnostic can.

With my first prayers of the day done, I shower out of a bottle of water.

MYSTERY ROAD FRIENDS

I say goodbye to Eid and pass through checkpoints

towards the main road. Other than opening a bank account I have nothing to do, so I decide to explore downtown. I'm lost in thought as I make my way down Airport Road when I realize that a middle-aged man has begun walking beside me. I don't know how long he has been there, but I look over and smile.

"*Ramadan Kareem*," I say. Happy Ramadan.

"*Ramadan Mubarak*," he returns. Blessed Ramadan.

We go on in silence for another couple of moments and then he asks me where I am from. I tell him that I am from the United States. He tells me that Somaliland is a peaceful place and that I should tell people back home. I assure him that I will. My new friend then disappears into a nearby market.

Less than a minute later a new man is walking next to me. We wish each other a happy Ramadan. He then holds me by the wrist and we walk together chatting. After a few minutes, he tells me to let the world know that Somaliland is peaceful. Then he disappears. This happens no less than three times on my walk downtown.

Every time I find myself walking alone a new Somali friend arrives and then disappears as quickly as they came. I'm used to locals approaching me to find out what I am up to, but this is the first time it feels like a formalized process complete with a message to report back to my people. There are some experiences that you will have when you travel that you won't ever get additional clarity on. Why a new Somali man would always show up while I was walking anywhere in Hargeisa is still a mystery to me.

BECOMING MARBLE

There is a Russian MiG in Hargeisa's Independence Square. This fighter was shot down during the civil war and it's kept suspended over a mural as a memorial to the war dead. This monument is different from other monuments that I've seen.

In Europe and the United States conflicts turn into marble once they've passed from memory into legend. Statues of men on horses with square chins gaze out over a spent battlefield. Wreaths and flags indicate that what we've always been fighting for is a mutual peace. Lengthy inscriptions give a poetic summary of a war that was fought with courage, honor, and dignity.

This mural in Hargeisa's Independence Square depicts a nightmarish landscape of war and atrocity. Cartoonish images of men carrying AK47s parade over bodies in the street. Hands are chopped off of figures leaking cherry colored blood. The ever present fighter jets fly overhead spraying death at the ground like an uncaring god. The eyes of the human forms are all wild with fear, or bloodlust, or the heartbreak of industrial death.

I think back to the MiG jet in the square in Transnistria. It was silver and polished to a gleam, set in such a way that it looked like it was zooming off into the sky to protect Soviet values. It tells a story about a country where ingenuity and technical prowess keeps everyone safe under the watchful eye of a military powerhouse. It says: *we're safe because of this.*

In Hargeisa, the MiG flies parallel with the earth, battle scarred and looking for targets. Below, humanity tears itself to shreds in the last moments before they are snuffed out by falling bombs. It says: *we survived this.* The same jet, thousands of miles away tells a different story. A symbol is just what you fill it with. A statue, a person, a flag, or even a border. Placeholders for the stories we tell ourselves. A freedom fighter can be a terrorist. A dictator can be a great leader. It all depends on which side of the

275

story you are on. I wonder how long it will take for this monument to turn into marble.

BANKING THE UNBANKED

Every culture has their own way of standing in line. The English are the undisputed champions of standing in line. They are polite, efficient, quiet, and evenly spaced. Albanians cut in front of anyone who is not actively defending their position in line. Americans stand in a scatter plot while speaking loudly about personal matters or playing on their cellphones. This gives rise to the common American colloquialisms: *Are you in line?* Or *Is this the line?*

There is no line in the Dabshi Bank. A mass of humanity spills from the lobby out into the street. As I approach the mass I am enveloped into an amoeba of men in button down shirts and women in abayas. At random intervals, a person is taken from the mass to a desk by another person who might be an employee. I stand and sweat, waiting until I am deemed worthy of being taken to a desk. I could really use one of my mystery friends to appear and explain.

Eventually a man with a lanyard enters the mass and pulls me out. I have been chosen. While at the desk I explain that I would like to open a bank account and hand him my passport. He eyes me and then my passport.

"You can open an account which will hold $500," says the desk man.

"I will need to get an account with a higher limit," I say.

"Why?" I take a deep breath and prepare for my first official act as ambassador:

"Because I am the Liberland Ambassador, and I would

like to use Dabshi bank to hold our official account as I set up the Embassy in Hargeisa."

The man at the desk looks around as if he is on a hidden camera prank show. He picks up the phone on his desk while keeping his eyes on me and says something in Somali.

"Come with me," says the desk man, grabbing my wrist and pulling me through the mass. He takes me to another building, points to the door and says:

"Go to the man with the biggest desk in there. Tell him what you told me."

I thank the man. He laughs and claps me on the shoulder. At this point, I don't believe myself when I say that I am an ambassador. The question is: do they? As I continue my quest, I wonder if it's a crime to impersonate an ambassador. Since I'm already doing it I suppose I'll just keep going.

I find the man with the biggest desk in a nicely appointed office filled with half cubicles. He seems to be waiting for me with a grin hidden behind his hand.

"Hello. I am the Ambassador from Liberland to Somaliland. I would like to use your bank as the official treasury of our embassy, so I will need a higher deposit limit," I say, using my most diplomatic tone.

The man calls the rest of the office to his desk. I am asked to repeat myself. Eventually I am giving a short lecture about Liberland to a group of Somali bank employees while illustrating my main points with photos and videos from my phone. I include the bit about the jet ski. I leave out the job description of a rent boy.

A piece of paper is stamped, copied and stamped again. My passport is photocopied and handed back. I shake the hand of every man in the office and I walk out of Dabshi Bank. The Liberland Embassy officially has a treasury. Much like the Liberland Embassy and Island of Liberland, it's empty but it exists.

NAUGHTY BOYS

I snap pictures as I head out of downtown. It is early but dark clouds are gathering on the horizon. As I approach the bridge, I notice that the trickle of water has changed into a small stream. A group of teens are diving off the rocks into the water and I think that might be a good shot.

I climb down the rocky embankment. I hold up my camera and give a questioning shrug to see if they'll let me take a quick photo. One of the teens gives me a thumbs up and leaps into the water. I thank them and then turn to go back up the embankment when I am blocked by two older boys. It's still daytime but the bridge casts a dark shadow over me and the growing group of teenagers. I hear a chorus of voices saying *dollar.* It becomes clear that they are not asking.

My hands go to my pockets and I let out a nervous laugh. The largest teenager lunges towards me, twisting my collar into his fist. Adrenaline jolts me. Coming down here was a mistake. I wheel back, breaking his grip and push through the group to escape up the embankment. The gang of teens close in grabbing my clothes, shoving me forward to the largest boy. He pulls me face to face with him and rubs his fingers together.

"Okay, okay," I say, reaching deep into my pocket for dollars that aren't there.

I pull out a wad of Somali shillings and shove them into his hand. The circle around me opens up as they count the money. I make a break for it, vaulting over spiny bushes and scrambling on hands and knees up the sandy hill. In seconds the teenagers realize they haven't gotten much and start chasing me.

I pull myself over the ridge and notice a woman sitting in a plastic chair frying samosas in a huge pot of cooking oil. I run towards her waving my arms with the gang of teenagers snapping at my heels. She stands up from her vat of oil and narrows her eyes. She then regards the boys chasing me. She flicks the oil off her slotted spoon into the sand and unleashes a fusillade of Somali verbiage at the boys. I don't know what she said, but they're stunned. She spits out a couple more phrases and the boys melts back towards the bridge. Their shoulders slump as they recede, they mutter what I can only assume are apologies.

The woman sits back in her chair and begins tending to her samosas again. I thank her as best I can. She gives me a barely perceptible nod and returns to the pot. She points to the space under the bridge and wags her finger at me. She points decisively at the top of the bridge and waves me on. I walk quickly over the bridge on adrenaline pumped legs. I almost jump out of my skin when I notice that a new walking friend has appeared beside me.

"Don't go under that bridge," he says to me. "There are naughty boys under there," he says. Then he tells me to let everyone know that Somaliland is a peaceful place.

The world is full of naughty boys.

THE COMING STORM

As I walk back to my place I see a thunderhead rising in the distance above the Airport Road. Black clouds swallow up what is left of the sun's dying light.

I smell wet stone and sand before hearing the patter of a downpour. The storm overtakes the land with such ferocity that I don't have time to find cover.

I make a mad dash to Wassim's office. Rain turns the dust in the street to sucking mud. I slog between bits of cover as men and women watch me sliding in the muck of the road from their store fronts. I huff through the rain until I see Airport Road in the distance. I hope someone is home.

I knock on the metal door. The driver opens it up and chuckles at my condition. He pulls me into a big hug and gives me a couple wet back slaps and hands me a towel. I am soaked and starving. I squish through the office in drenched shoes.

Yahia prays in the corner of the conference room. Over the white noise of the rain, I can hear the Maghreb call to prayer. The first day of Ramadan has gone by. I shut my eyes and bow my head as the call to prayer concludes. I'm thankful for this towel, for being warm, for the woman with the samosas. Thanks God, or Allah, or whoever is steering this boat.

"You eat? Iftar? Yes?" says Yahia with a prayer rug under his arm.

He gestures to his mouth. I realize that I must be interrupting his dinner plans. I am tempted to make an excuse and go home, but I am stuck.

"Okay," I say.

He gives me a thumbs up and a smile. Americans tend to be independent to a fault. This makes accepting the kindness of others excruciating because we think of ourselves as an inconvenience. I am not exempt from this, but accepting the charity of others with grace is a kindness itself. Besides eating something other than Pringles, tuna, and water sounds good.

Yahia opens the door to the kitchen and the smell of fried chicken, curried rice, and sumac billows out. I am famished. I grab some silverware and set the plastic table on the covered patio. Yahia brings out two non-alcoholic beers. Then he presents a plate of the most beautiful fried chicken I have ever seen. It's followed by a bed of yellow rice with roasted vegetables and a cucumber salad with sumac and lime juice. Seeing the table full of food after a chaotic day I'm surprised that the clouds do not part and pour white light on this plastic table.

Yahia brings a plate with two gooey Mahjool dates and sits down across from me. Per tradition we break our fast for the day by saying *bismillah* and eating a single date. As my teeth separate the pit from the flesh of the fruit I feel that I have never truly experienced a date until this moment. The sweet syrupy fruit tumbles down my throat, my face flushes and my pulse quickens. Life blossoms in me. It tastes like the physical realization of a prayer. I feel like I am high off of a date.

The meal passes in a blur of fried chicken, rice, and salad. The crackling unctuous skin of the chicken dances with the acid and salt from the salad. Spiced rice perfumes the air with cardamom, cumin, and curry. The non-alcoholic beer quenches, crisp, refreshing and sweet. While tearing through iftar, I found myself almost chuckling with joy.

Yahia and I exchange a few words while demolishing the meal. I try to remember the Arabic words for *very good* and succeed in telling him that *he is very big*. I just say thank you again and again until all of the chicken is gone and I am on my second non-alcoholic beer.

Yahia and I finish our meal, laying back in our chairs like we've been shot with tranquilizer darts. We nod at one another. *Allahu akbar*, I say. God is great. We finish the meal by watching the rain come down and smoking shisha.

God is great.

AND THEN THERE WAS A CYCLONE

I wake up to a brilliant orange sunrise over the mountains in the distance. A pack of camels tromp across the craggy horizon. The call to prayer sings in the distance and the familiar sounds of morning swirl up from the valley. Goats muttering, workshops tinkering, trucks chugging down the Airport Road. Everything is the mix of familiar and foreign that lets me know that I am settling into a temporary home.

I open my little wireless hub ready to report my successful mission to the bank. My phone struggles to connect for a moment. The internet service bars disappear. I check my messages and realize that I've been offline for a whole day. With no connection to the rest of the world I feel an intoxicating mix of dread and freedom. Anything could happen at any moment and I would remain oblivious. For all I know Cleveland disappeared into a nuclear fireball, North Korea reunified with the South, and the United Nations has come clean about aliens. This must be what it was like to live in the 90s.

Fortunately, the Ambassador Hotel has a working internet connection. At this point I care less about sharing the good news with Liberland and more about making sure that my family doesn't declare me missing in Somaliland. I swing out of the Embassy and through the checkpoints to the Ambassador Hotel. At the entrance two guards frisk me for weapons, give my bag a once over, and let me pass.

The Ambassador Hotel is a collection of villas all painted dazzling white. Given its security and proximity to the airport it is the only game in town to host foreign dignitaries, airline pilots, and the occasional mercenary or crypto diplomat. Much like the bar in Erbil, the hostel in Transnistria, or the houseboat in Liberland, this is a place where strange people doing strange things make awkward small talk while wondering what everyone else is doing in a place like this.

The smell of fresh bleach and lingering cigarette smoke greets me as I enter a lobby stuck in the 1970s. It's all lacquered hardwood and mirrors, decorated with dusty paintings of vast plains and roaring lions. Next to a lion painting I see a sign announcing that armed guards can be rented for excursions outside of the city. That's right, for $200 you can hire humvees full of dudes with guns the same way you can get a snorkeling excursion in Cancun.

I go up to one of the sharply appointed bellhops and inquire about their internet.

"No internet anywhere, because of the storm," he says.

"Is there any way that I can call out of the country?" I ask.

He says something in Somali to another bellhop who rummages behind the front desk until he produces an enormous brick of a phone with a satellite antenna poking off of it. I reach for the brick but he does not hand it over.

"It is very expensive to call out of the country on this," he says, indicating that some money would help him part with the phone. I hand him a couple of dollars and receive five minutes with the brick.

I punch in Savannah's Bulgarian number. She picks up on the third ring. The line is fuzzy but I can hear her.

"Oh my god. Hello," she says through the static.

"Hey Savannah, I'm fine, everything is fine. I don't have long to talk though."

The two Somali bellhops begin to look impatient even though I just began talking.

"Okay, wow, I had a dream about you last night and I hadn't heard from you for a couple of days-"

"No, I'm good. Hey I need you to-" The line fuzzes in and out.

"And I was getting worried, like, oh man, did Eric die and he was visiting me in my dream?"

"No, I didn't die. But can you call my parents and let them know—" More static.

"And I saw all of this stuff on the news about the cyclone in Somalia."

"Wait, what cyclone?" I ask.

"So you're not in the cyclone?" Savannah asks.

I look at the sunny day outside and then to the bellhop approaching me with his hand outstretched.

"I gotta go. Don't worry about me, everything is going fine!" I say into the phone. "I love—"

The line goes dead. I hand the brick back to the bellhop.

Is everything fine?

What's this about the cyclone?

NAKED MEDITATION

I spend the next internet free days asking if anyone has heard news about the cyclone. This doesn't go well since I know five phrases in Somali and none of them involve cyclones.

I swing by the office to say hello to Kahder, and Fathia. Both of them sit at their desks awaiting the return of email. It's amazing how little we can do without being connected to one another. It's amazing how we can't understand each other with more communication than ever. It's all just amazing. I realize that I am pacing around the office because I am full of nervous energy which would normally be disposed of by scrolling the internet. I decide to stop bothering everyone and go buy a jump rope.

I find the fluorescent green thing in a small bazaar across from the office and walk back to the embassy. I will spend my long Ramadan days learning to jump rope. I will jump rope so much that I will emerge from Hargeisa with visible abs, astounding agility, and a slew of other life problems solved. I will look back at this day as the beginning of my life changing jump rope journey. I will write a book called *Jumping Rope for Diplomats*. It will be a staggering success.

I choose one of my nine empty bedrooms to be the new Liberland Gym. I begin jumping rope. I am not good at it. I jump two or three times until it catches my shoe or whips my ankle. I try again and fail. The sun glares angrily at me through the window. I am doused in sweat. I keep jumping. With each *whap* of the rope I consider my situation:

WHAP! WHAP! WHAP!

I need to get in touch with the government of Hargeisa. I need to find a furniture store. How much furniture should I buy for a mansion? How do I introduce myself to a president?

It snags my shoe. I take a deep breath and start again. I see Eid watching me in the front yard. I wave. He waves. Another man joins him in the yard.

WHAP! WHAP! WHAP!

I need to call Tariq. I need to call my family. I need to get out of Somaliland.

WHAP! WHAP! WHAP!

I need to find out about the cyclone. Did anyone die? Am I safe here? It doesn't look like a cyclone is coming, but then again, what does it look like before a cyclone? I need to stop getting lost in foreign countries and do something with my life.

WHAP! WH-

I stop, huffing and puffing. A small audience of men has gathered in the front yard to watch me jump rope. This was enough for a first workout. I hear the midday call to prayer. Eid and his friends lay out prayer mats and pass around a bucket of water to wash. I rattle off a quick prayer too.

I am grateful for probably a lot of things I can't think of right now. I am very confused, disoriented, and bad at jumping rope. Please help me make contact with the government of Somaliland. Please help me find furniture. Please, just help. Thanks Allah.

I shower out of a bottle. The Liberland Official Shirt Towel is still wet from being left out in the rain. It's hot enough to air dry. I wander around my bedroom, naked, wet, and anxious. Between the cyclone, the attempted mugging, and the fear of being found out to be a fraudulent ambassador, a panicky crisis rises inside of me. After nearly a decade of living abroad, this isn't my first international anxiety rodeo. I inhale deep measured breaths while listening to my heart beat out a rapid SOS.

My pulse speeds, my palms sweat. The walls of the room hug inward on me. Too hot, too close, too much of everything. Traveling can be equal parts revelatory and disruptive. When you recontextualize yourself you risk losing a tenuous grip on the things that make you, you. There are cases of a phenomenon called *India Syndrome*, a condition in which a tourist to India experiences a profound, almost spiritual psychological breakdown. This leads casual tourists to join monastic orders or turns exchange students into babbling maniacs. It's common enough that embassies in New Delhi have protocols put in place to deal with backpackers who have lost their minds.

I stand wet and naked in my room in Hargeisa Somalia sucking at the hot air and trying to keep everything together. It feels like my skeleton wants to jump out of my skin and run for the horizon. Instead, I decide to meditate. At this moment it seems like the only choice to keep myself sane. If you find naked meditation to be an odd choice of activity, you clearly have never tried it. I encourage you to do so. However, I also encourage you to never admit as much in the written word as I have done here.

I put down a new dry shirt on the bed, sit down cross legged and close my eyes. I breathe in and out slowly through my nose. I try to let the million sensations of the world pass through me without sparking my increasingly rapid internal monologue.

I hear creaks in the house. That's not a big deal, it's a creaky house.

I focus on my breath and only my breath.

I'm going to stop thinking now. This is my last thought. This one right here.

I'm safe. I'm in Somaliland, and I'm safe. I'm also present, at this moment. I'm done thinking. I'm just breathing. Breathing and thinking about how much furniture costs. What do I need? Like a couple of couches. Why am I here? This was a stupid and dangerous idea. There are nine rooms. Are they all going to be bedrooms? What goes in a bedroom? I've got to get out of this country. Is it a country? Beds go in bedrooms. But also, dressers. I should get dressed. I'm still wet though. This is stupid. This is all so stupid. I'm so stupid. But I'm breathing and my pulse feels like it will break me in half. I'm not thinking about that. In fact I'm not thinking about anything.

What is that creak?

It's just a creak, keep breathing.

Do you remember that Super Nintendo game Smash TV? Stop! Inhale. Do you want to check the door, I think that's where the creak came from. Exhale. Just look at the door, you're not going to achieve enlightenment by meditating naked on a bed in Hargeisa. You're never going to be anything, you're going to die friendless and alone.

INHALE.

Would you look at the door? Someone is there and they are going to kill you.

Shut up!

I open my eyes. Standing in the doorway is a woman in a purple abaya. I am sitting there wet and naked. Monumental embarrassment turns time into taffy. In slow motion I leap up to close the door while yelling all of the words that I know in Somali. I plant a foot on the handle of my new jump rope and fall to the marble floor with a wet naked slap. The housekeeper tries to close the door but my wet naked body is blocking it. Instead she disappears down the hallway. I hear the front door open and slam shut. I lie on the cool dusty tile assessing my situation from her perspective:

She walked in on a hairy, wet, naked, American meditating on his bed. He then leapt up and yelled:

"HOW ARE YOU? THANK YOU! YES! NO! BATHROOM!"

He then fell onto the floor where he currently is. He wishes he could go back in time and throw his younger self down a well so that this would never have happened. He is ready to get off of the ride. Today was not the best day.

That night the internet clicks back on. I tell Savannah everything.

She laughs.

She laughs a lot.

HUMANITARIAN AID

"So you are currently safe?" asks Tariq.

"Yes."

I am sitting in the Ambassador Hotel nursing a lump on the back of my head from where I fell. I'm also totally cheating Ramadan by having coffee because I had to buy something to use the internet.

"That's great to hear. When the Internet went down, we thought that maybe we'd lost you."

I imagine Vit Jedlicka ordering Liberland special forces to extract me from rising flood waters.

"Nope. All good here," I say, hoping that Tariq doesn't somehow know about the naked meditating.

"Cyclone Sagar, as it has come to be known, wreaked havoc on the nomadic communities towards the coast," says Tariq in an accent that should read every audiobook.

I look up maps of the affected area. A red circle radiates along a path from Berbera port. While we got a touch of the rain, Sagar punished the desert population. Countries with underdeveloped infrastructure don't have the capacity to deal with natural disasters. The initial loss of life and destruction is usually just the beginning. Problems cascade down to the most vulnerable communities like a cruel joke.

For the nomads, livestock and people are killed during the event. This means that their finances and important community members are wiped out. On top of that water pumps and homes are torn from the desert. Now, people have to band together and find water from pools in the desert. This leads to an outbreak of cholera. With crippled finances, paying for transportation, medical care, and subsistence supplies become impossible.

"We see this as an opportunity to build relations between Liberland and Somaliland We're going to make a donation of international aid to the affected area. In fact, we're one of the only countries with a team already in Somaliland," he says.

"That's great." Who is the team?

"You."

"Oh."

Deliver international aid. No problem.

"Great, we will see about getting you a budget. Transferring money to your bank account will take too long, so we're devising another plan.

I go over my missions:

1. Establish diplomatic relations between the nations of Liberland and Somaliland.

2. Coordinate a delivery of international aid to the affected area of Cyclone Sagar.

3. Buy furniture.

The call to prayer sounds. I push away my coffee. I bow my head.

I pray. I pray. I pray.

DOING DIPLOMAT STUFF

Wassim laughs at me on the other end of the phone.

"Well, at least you didn't get blown away in the cyclone," he says between chuckles.

"Yup," I say standing outside of his office.

"Look, just call Abdulrahman. He'll get everything taken care of. That's what he does. You'll see."

"But I need to get Liberland to transfer money to Somaliland somehow and they can't work with Dabshi," I say, venting more of my problems than I should.

"Taken care of. They're going to send me Bitcoin, I'm going to give you the money from my safe. Easy."

This is the first real world transaction of Bitcoin I have ever heard about.

"Do you know how much they're sending?"

"I think fifteen," he says.

"Hundred?" I say, nervous to carry around that kind of cash in Hargeisa.

"Thousand. Fifteen thousand. Anyway, enjoy the rest

of Ramadan. I'll text you when the money is ready."
Wassim hangs up.

Fifteen thousand dollars. So I can spend $5,000 on aid, $5,000
on furniture, and $5,000 to keep the embassy running. That makes
sense.

I call Abdulrahman. He picks up on the first ring.

"Hello. Where are you?" he asks.

"I'm outside of Wassim's office."

"That's fine. Wait there and I will come to you." I do
what I'm told.

I kick a rock down the dusty alleyway. A couple of
goats wander by with numbers spray painted on them.
School children bumble down the street after one another.
Birds croak in the trees.

It's just a normal day. It's hard to remember that every
day is a normal day for most of the world. People wake up
and drink coffee. They see friends and laugh at inside jokes
that are no longer funny. They wonder about the future.
There will never be a headline about there being a totally
normal day somewhere in the world.

I am grateful for today.

A large black Cadillac comes chugging down the alleyway.
Behind the steering wheel I can see a white turban and gold
rimmed glasses. Abdulrahman reaches up for the steering
wheel like a child that needs a booster seat. The car rolls to a
stop in front of me and the passenger door pops open. I get in,
Abdulrahman kills the engine and shakes my hand.

"So I opened a bank account, but they can't transfer
money to it in time. That's okay because Wassim is getting
Bitcoin and giving me $15,000. But now I need to figure
out a way to give aid to the people affected by Cyclone
Sagar. But I want to coordinate it with you and the government so that it goes to the right area."

Abdulrahman nods, placid as a Swiss lake at dawn.

"I will make a meeting with the Vice President. Then I will call you." He says.

"That's great."

I'm dumbstruck. Abdulrahman makes things happen. He and I sit looking at one another in the car for a moment.

"Okay. Goodbye." He smiles. We shake hands, because clearly this is my cue to leave. I get out of the car. I feel like I just did a diplomatic drug deal.

A BIG STACK OF CASH

I walk back into the office and sit down at an empty desk. As I'm staring into the distance thinking about furniture and cyclones when I notice that Fathia is hovering over me with an envelope in her hands.

"I think this is for you."

She hands it to me. I whip it open and dump out the contents. A small stack of crisp hundred dollar bills falls onto the table.

Faithia and I look at one another, it is obvious that this is the most money either one of us has seen in real life.

"I think that this is for the embassy," I say, gathering the bills back together and squaring them on the desk in front of me.

As I flip through the 150 bills, I am a bit disappointed that it did not come in a metal briefcase. Maybe they didn't have one in the office. I have Fathia count the money with me three times and then place it in the office safe. It's real. I have $15,000 for humanitarian aid and furniture.

CAMEL BURGERS AND DOOM

"I'll have the camel burger please."

I say this to the young Somali waiter in the white button-down shirt. Yahia has been out in the field building a road so I haven't seen him for iftar. After a week of eating Pringles and tuna on my balcony I decided to take myself to dinner at the Ambassador Hotel.

The restaurant at the Ambassador Hotel looks like a yard sale under Christmas tree lights. Plastic furniture is scattered across a terraced field made of gravel. This means that when you sit, the chair sinks about six inches into the ground. At this moment, there are about ten people eating at the restaurant and maybe 15 waiters. I have concerns about the design, layout and staffing of the Ambassador Hotel. I'm starving for questionable meats in my diagonal chair so I will leave them unanswered.

I gaze off into the distance as the $15,000 haunts me. Buying furniture used to be the biggest concern I had. Now, I have to turn money into food and logistics. I feel like I am moments away from being discovered as what I am. A fraud. I've been an intelligence analyst by name only. I've been a third-grade teacher masquerading as a travel writer. Months prior I literally pretended to be a journalist next to real journalists. For a moment I consider confessing to Abdulrahman, Liberland and the government of Somaliland. This was all a jet-ski related mistake. I am incapable of helping them.

"I noticed you are both alone and looking at us," says a voice in a German accent which reminds me of Werner Herzog.

I realize that I have been staring at one table for a long time and they have sent an emissary to find out why. This is how I meet Hans, who, as it turns out, lives across the road from the embassy. His formerly blonde hair is settling into a silvery gray but his bright eyes and tan skin tell me that a life outside has kept him younger than his years.

"Would you like to join us for dinner?" I stand up from my sunken chair and join their table.

I am grateful not to be alone with my own thoughts.

THE BUSINESS OF SAVING

"The problem," says Saida, tearing open the flesh of an orange. "Is that we are not, in any way, prepared for climate change. That means pastoralists and nomadic communities will suffer. They know that a drought will occur every five or ten years. But now we have a drought every three years. And, of course, events like this cyclone." Saida's prognosis is followed by a round of solemn agreement from the rest of the table.

Saida, Amsale, and Jonathan are saving nomads, or at least trying in spite of the odds stacked against them. The group of NGO workers breaking their fast across from me are ensuring pastoralists can continue practicing their ancestral culture as the world spins forward, trading bits of data instead of heads of goats.

Saida is the regional head of PENHA (the Pastoral and Environmental Network on the Horn of Africa). She wears a floral abaya and a wary expression as I explain why I am in Hargeisa. Across from her are Amsale, a middle-aged Eritrean woman with a vibrant yellow headscarf which matches her jubilant personality and Johnathan, a British-raised Ugandan with a wit as dry as a bone.

Amsale chimes in.

"We help with replenishing livestock, or building new water pumps. We fund our work through handicrafts or our salt harvesting farm on the Red Sea," She opens her phone and shows me brown paper bags of sea salt. Tiny sacks tied with twine that wouldn't be out of place in a Beverly Hills boutique.

"But most of it comes from donations and partnering with other organizations. It's hard to compete. Since we're small it's a difficult sell." Jonathan adds this between sips of his non-alcoholic beer. The word *sell* hangs in the air.

While the life of an aid worker might seem eternally fulfilling due to its high moral aims, often it becomes a difficult business with uncertain returns. Poverty, disease, hunger, and climate change are global issues but solving, or even alleviating, some of the suffering caused by them doesn't equate to soaring profits. This means that NGOs have to compete for a limited pool of donations which is filled by a mixture of good intentions, guilt, and tax write offs.

"So, Mr. Ambassador," says Saida, dripping with skepticism. "Have you delivered aid before?" She tears a piece of bread and chews it slowly in my general direction. I am embarrassed to talk about my adventures in Somaliland with real humanitarians, but I'm also aware that their expertise could help me with my new found mission.

"I was a Peace Corps Volunteer," I say.

"What is that?" asks Amsale.

"It's like the opposite of the American Army. Volunteer teachers, that kind of thing," I say.

Saida is unimpressed with my joke or my pedigree. She puts the bread down on the table and dusts the crumbs off her hands with two quick swipes and folds them in front of her on the table.

"Where is this money coming from?" she asks. I put my burger down and take a deep breath.

"Bitcoin," I say. Everyone exchanges a glance.

"So, what is your plan to deliver this aid?" says Hans as

if he were throwing me a life preserver. It turns out to be an anchor, but I grab it anyway.

"I have a contact named Abdulrahman who is going to introduce me to government officials." I'm drowning.

"Abdulrahman who?" says Saida.

"I don't know his last name," I say.

A long silence that falls across the table. I can feel my chair sinking a couple more centimeters into the gravel. I only have wrong answers. After a few moments Saida exhales audibly and signals for the waiter to bring the check.

"I would also make sure that you know where the money is coming from and going to. You might be laundering money for someone."

"That's a good idea," I say, sipping my water bottle.

There isn't any water in it. I just want to do something with my hands because I feel like I am rightfully being interrogated. I realize how little I know about Vit, Wassim, and literally everyone I met on that Bitcoin party boat.

Hans pays for the meal and Saida, in spite of her frosty treatment, invites me to Eid dinner at the end of Ramadan. I accept. I thank everyone and let them know I am heading back to the embassy, with plenty to think about.

"I will walk with you," says Hans, "After all, we are neighbors."

He shoulders his backpack. We click the lights on our phones and cross through the checkpoints on the way back home.

HANS VERSUS THE MESQUITE BUSH

"This is the *prosopis*," says Hans, raising the thorny vine for me to examine.

"What is the *prosopis*?"

Hans and I are crouched in the darkened road between our two houses. The lights on our phones, trained on the tendril of the thorny plant that crowd every available piece of real estate in Hargeisa. Apparently, it is known as *prosopis*.

"I think that you would call it the Mesquite bush. He turns over a waxy leaf and reveals the gnarly thorns. My only experience with mesquite is BBQ sauce related so I'm having a hard time understanding why this bush matters to Somaliland, let alone this german man.

"Goats learn to eat the bush when it first starts growing. That's when they can pass the seeds. But later on it develops thorns and kills the goats. This is a huge drain on the economy," says Hans, his voice low in the hushed evening.

"How long have you been working on this Hans?"

He lets the vine fall back to the earth and stands dusting his pants off. He puts his hands on his hips and does some mental math for a moment.

"For the better part of five years."

We click our lights off and we're dipped into violet darkness. Our gaze travels to the dome of the sky above our heads. I feel very tiny at this moment, and I assume that Hans does as well.

"Any luck fighting *prosopis*?"

"No, it's everywhere," Hans laughs. "But we're not just getting rid of it. We're teaching people how to turn it into something they can sell. Helping them trim the bushes until they develop into trees with shade and hardwood."

A trickle of moonlight across the mountains is all that separates dark sky from land.

"It's a small thing, but it's important. Not everything is a big world saving gesture, it doesn't need to be."

We take a couple more moments quietly watching the night between our two houses. Hans seems fulfilled doing battle with the mesquite bush.

"I'm going to go to bed. Please come by for tea soon." He shakes my hand and clicks on his phone light to pick his way back home.

"I will. Thanks, Hans."

I stand looking down at the prosopis on the ground. I poke it with my boot. The Mesquite bush in Somalia is a master class in unintended consequences. In the 1970s the desert was expanding. It killed pastoral animals and encroached on the cities sending Siad Barre to the international community for a solution.

Advisors recommended planting mesquite. The nitrogen fixing plant would keep the critical element in the soil while sinking deep roots that would help in case of flood or cyclone. But the plant spread like green wild-fire across the landscape. While the plan helped slow desertification it killed livestock. Another domino in an endless chain of good and bad. Sometimes atrocities breed peace makers, sometimes nitrogen fixing plants kill goats. It's all just impossible to know what little thing will matter most.

The moon rises over the mountains. Soon it will be full, Ramadan will be over, and I will leave Somaliland. I'm not an aid worker, a journalist, a teacher, or a travel writer. I'm not an ambassador. I'm also not a fraud. I'm here. I'm going try to help, whatever that may mean.

MY NICEST SHIRT

"Where are you?"

It's Abdulrahman. I am face down on my bed riddled with new mosquito bites and clutching my goat horn. I'm so dehydrated that I feel hungover even though I've been drinking non-alcoholic beer for two weeks.

"Just doing some work." I lie, searching for a fresh bottle of water.

"Meet me in front of the Ambassador Hotel in a half hour," he says.

"Okay. Why?" I've got a half liter left. I whip off the cap and cradle the phone in my shoulder.

"We are meeting with the Vice President of Somaliland," he says.

"Today?" I ask, looking at the bottle in my hand and realizing that I have to make a choice between drinking it or showering with it.

"Yes."

He hangs up. I take a sip of the water, run to the bathroom, dump the rest on my head and save a couple drops for my toothbrush. I find my least wrinkled button up shirt whip it in the air to iron it through sheer inertia. It does not work but flailing around my room helps me air dry. I hop into my only pants and knock my boots together off of my balcony to dislodge some mud and goat droppings from the tread.

When I am fully dressed, I look like someone who has survived a nuclear apocalypse on their way to Sunday school. This is not how I would have liked to meet the Vice President but it's the best I can do. Eid waves as I rush past him through the gate. I pick my way down the rocky path towards the hotel while trying not to sweat.

BOOTS ON THE GROUND

Abdulrahman wears a dark blue, two piece suit. It is pressed to perfection. A national pin shines on his lapel next to a brilliant red tie, and a blinding white shirt. When

I sit in the car, he looks me up and down and I am very aware that I look like I was just saved from a desert island.

"You look great!" I say to Abdulrahman.

"Thank you," he says, not returning the compliment.

It's good to know that he is not a liar. He kicks the engine on and we putter down the road into the heart of Hargeisa. He begins briefing me while I try to pick some stray pebbles out of my boots.

"So, you will tell the Vice President, who you are. You will also tell him what you would like to do."

Great. I'll tell him who I am and what I'm doing here. No problem. I'm the Ambassador of Liberland and I'm here to help the nomads affected by Cyclone Sagar. Also, if he could hook me up with a decent furniture place that would be great.

We stop at a checkpoint manned by uniformed Somaliland soldiers. Both guards seem to know Abdulrahman, so they lean into the window and chat before lifting the gate and waving us through. I take deep breaths attempting to muster the unearned confidence of a real politician.

We step out of the car. Abdulrahman brushes his suit jacket clean. I give my shirt a couple of tugs to see if the wrinkles will come out. They don't. We stop outside of an ornate banquet hall. It is upholstered with a couch that wraps around the entire room and thick pile rugs with intricate designs. Inside, the Vice President sits in the corner with two other government-y looking folks.

"You are ready?" says Abdulrahman.

"Yes." I lie and put on my best diplomat face.

WHY ARE YOU LISTENING TO ME?

"I'm here on behalf of the people of Liberland to build diplomatic relations between our two nations."

I am listening to myself say these things. To me, these things sound like things a government official would say. The Vice President appears to be listening. The other two people I found out are the Vice President's Secretary and the Canadian Diplomat to Somaliland. No one has interrupted me so I keep talking:

"We believe that between our two nations there is a bond through our goal of gaining international recognition." I do my best presidential half-frown and solemn nod with a small fist pump in their general direction.

"So, in an act of solidarity with the people of Somaliland, we would like to deploy an aid delivery of food to the affected area of Cyclone Sagar."

Deploy. Yup that sounds like what a diplomat would say.

"I will be working closely with Abdulrahman to dispense a donation of $5,000 to get the necessary supplies. All we ask of your office is help coordinating delivery and locating an area of most need. Otherwise, we hope this will be the beginning of a strong relationship between Somaliland and Liberland." Half-frown. Concern-eyes. Fist pump.

The Vice President and Abdulrahman exchange words in Somali. They nod. I nod.

The Vice President speaks:

"We are happy to meet you and for your assistance with Cyclone Sagar. My secretary will be made available to you as your translator. Also, my personal security detachment will accompany you into the desert where you will meet with the nomads."

We all stand up from the couch. We all shake hands. There is a round of thank yous and slight bows. I have become a politician. I think I am full of shit.

But also, maybe I'm not.

I AM YOUR FATHER

Abdulrahman and I sit in his car outside of the Ambassador Hotel. I have thanked him 40 times in the ten minute ride from the Vice President's compound.

I don't know if I am laundering money, embroiled in an international bitcoin gang, or actually delivering aid, but I met the Vice President of Somaliland so that seems like a win.

"We will buy supplies together. You will bring the money and we will load up the trucks."

"Okay, sounds good." I think of the 15 grand just sitting in the back of a safe at Wassims.

"And then after that, we will go for furniture," I remind him.

"Yes. Thank you." Abdulrahman nods. He takes a moment and it looks like he is trying to piece together the perfect words in English. He pats my knee.

"While you are here. I am your Somali daddy," he says. It's a weird turn of phrase but I'm touched by it.

"You are Abdulrahman." I shake his hand and step out of the Cadillac.

DITCH WEED

There are new cars in the dirt alleyway outside of Wassim's office. Small neighborhoods in countries like Somaliland have a certain unchanging routine. Goats pass by in the morning. A white truck leaves in the early afternoon, it comes back after the call to prayer. The same men gather at the same plastic table for the same cups of tea. I've even fallen into the same rhythm of the street as I bounce between Wassim's office, the embassy and the

Ambassador Hotel. Somehow, the very strange becomes very normal.

I knock on the metal gate and receive my hug from the driver. Fathia opens the safe and hands me $5,000 while she mentions that her sister is visiting and waiting in the car outside. I tuck the money into my notebook and zip up my backpack. I am suddenly aware that my backpack contains far more than my bank account.

I thank Fathia and tell her to have a good time with her sister and walk into the courtyard of the office. The sun is shining and a breeze rustles through the prosopis bushes. I can smell cooking in the distance as someone prepares for iftar. I have just been promised a security detachment to escort me into the desert where I can deliver aid to nomads. Everything feels like it is falling into place.

The guard closes the gate behind me as I walk down the alley. When I turn towards the Airport Road, three men pull up in a truck and wave me to me. I wave back. Given the fact that I make a new walking friend every day, it's entirely possible that I have met one of these men before.

"Hello," says one of the men getting out of the truck and putting his arm around my shoulder. I'm trying to place where I have seen any of them before, but nothing is clicking into place. The rest of the men emerge from the vehicle and leave it running for some reason.

"We're going to smoke some hashish, you want to come?"

I find this strange given the fact that it is the late-afternoon during Ramadan. They shouldn't be smoking anything. I certainly don't want to go with them.

"No thanks guys."

I edge back out of the circle and cut towards the

airport road. The alley is empty except for a couple cars and an old man staring dreamily out of a khat shop.

"We'll go quick. No problem."

Their hands are on me again and they're starting to turn from back pats to fingers gripping onto my shirt. I can feel them gently urging me toward the truck at the end of the alley. Something snags in my stomach, and the moment has pivoted from probably harmless to very bad. I need to get away from these men.

"We go now."

Their faces are smiling, but they pull a bit harder. I am about to break and run when my cell phone rings. It gives me the opportunity to disengage and get their hands off of me for a moment.

"Okay, yeah we will go." I try to keep my voice light. I pick up the phone.

"Who are you talking to?" asks Fathia on the other end of the phone. I look back towards the men, they are edging back towards the vehicle.

"I don't know, some guys in the alley," I say.

"My sister is in the car facing you right now."

I look at an SUV parked in the alley. A woman who looks vaguely like Fathia sits in the driver's seat, her eyes wide with concern. She shakes her head slowly as Faithia's voice crackles on the other end of the phone.

"She says that she heard those boys talking in Somali about how they are going to take you."

A bucket of ice water spills down my back. I bolt back to the metal door outside Wassims. Before I can knock, the driver flings the gate open and slams it behind me. I take a couple of deep breaths in the courtyard and the driver pats my back. Once I compose myself, I walk into the office.

"Fathia, thank you."

"Maybe, you should have someone drive you today," she says.

"I think so."

I sit at the plastic furniture outside of Wassim's office. The housekeeper brings me a cup of coffee, but I don't touch it. I should have been changing my route home more. Bad things can happen anywhere. Sometimes the best protection you can have is a community. Fortunately I will never know what they wanted because of Fathia's sister.

I am grateful to be here.

NOWHERE HOME

That night I lay in bed with my goat's horn in my hand and the buzzing mosquitoes flying circles above me. My cellphone is laid on the side of my face. Savannah is on the other end.

"I'm going to be done with Fulbright a couple weeks after you get back."

"I know."

The two weeks left in Somaliland feels like years to me right now. There's a long pause on the other end of the line.

"Do you want to go back to the states?" she asks.

I sit up, scratch my mosquito bites and walk toward the balcony. The moon is filling up, a dish of warm milk. It was just a sliver when I got here, but that seems like an impossible memory to me now.

Time moves in dribbles and waves when you're traveling. The only real thing is where you are at any given moment. Somehow it's easy to think that it will never end. Somehow it always does.

The moon will be full soon, Ramadan will end, I will

leave Somaliland and somehow become normal again. The whiplash of going from Somaliland back to the United States feels like it could break my mind.

"No, I think I want to chill out somewhere else for a while." I think about the map, and the globe and the solar system, and the galaxy and the infinite universe. I will go anywhere in the universe. I just can't go home yet.

"I had an idea," she says.

I picture Savannah laid out on her bed in Bulgaria. The sheets are covered with shotgun blasts of little projects that she tinkers with. A bit of writing here. A couple of photos there. A book on Russian grammar. One cup of tea, and a long cold one from the night before. I don't care where she says she wants to go. I will say yes. She is the home I want to return to.

"How about France?" she says.

"Eww!" I say reflexively.

"Marseille. You hate Paris," she says.

"It's not that I hate it. I just don't ever want to go there again."

"I found a cheap sublet there." If she wanted to go to the bottom of the ocean I would say yes.

"Okay. Sounds good. I'm ready to come home,"

"Yeah. Quit messing around. You need to get over here," she says.

"I'm on my way," I say.

SEVEN TONS OF AID

It's raining and I have $8000 in my backpack. I decided to add an extra $3000 to the aid budget because I'm the Ambassador and Liberland doesn't need another couple of sofas as bad as nomads need food. Abdulrahman and I whip through the center of Hargeisa in the pouring rain. The Cadillac swerves to a halt outside of an industrial warehouse.

I get out of the car holding my bag and thousands of dollars over my head to shield myself from the rain. Every sound in the city pings my fraying nerves. I notice every backfiring car and loud conversation as if they are threats leveled directly at me. Carrying around a backpack with eight grand stuffed inside makes me feel very kidnappable.

I want to buy the food, get it out to the nomads and spend a summer watching the sun creep across the wall in a French cafe. I jolt when a man takes my arm. He says something to me in Somali and points to Abdulrahman. I signal to him that I don't understand what he's saying and he switches to English.

"He is a very good man," he says before going to greet Abdulrahman who gives him a couple of shillings to watch the car.

"You are okay?" Abdularahman asks, putting a hand on my shoulder.

I assure him that I am and I follow him into the warehouse. My senses are on high alert all the time, but Abdulrahman's endless calm is infectious. The smell of damp concrete and sweat mixes with olive oil and sweat as my eyes adjust to the inside of the building. Stacks of rice, flour, beans and lentils the size of houses. Men in jumpsuits scramble over the piles of bags easily hoisting 50-pound sacks of cornmeal over their heads. Tall glimmering cans of oil stand next to pallets of water and tins of fish. The workers slow to a crawl as they notice Abdulrahman and me enter.

A foreman comes over to Abdulrahman and greets him like an old friend and confidant. I watch as they dance through exchanging pleasantries bowing their heads to one another. Abdulrahman gives this foreman the same deference that he gives to me or to the Vice President of Somaliland. He is someone who I wish every politician would be. He shows up on time, he gets things done, he respects everyone, and he listens. I feel very lucky to be in his presence. He brings the foreman over to me and introduces us. The only thing I can make out is 'Liberland.'

The foreman shakes my hand and gives me an invoice. Numbers accompanied by words written in Somali. I look at it closely and pretend to know what I am seeing while I gesture to Abdulrahman.

"We can afford 7 tons of food. It will be brought to the desert and we will give it to the nomads."

"This is a good price?' I ask, opening my backpack and taking out a small stack of hundred dollar bills.

"It is the only price," he says with a smile.

I hand him the bills. He gives me the receipt. He takes $8,000 to the foreman who counts the bills and nods in my direction.

Computing power from anonymous people all over the world turned into Bitcoin stored by an unrecognized nation state in the Balkans.

Bitcoin was traded into dollars by Wassim in Somaliland. Dollars morph into 7 tons of food. 7 tons of food turns into political power. Everything is an investment.

Everything is a Ponzi scheme.

ADVENTURES IN INFRASTRUCTURE

Abdulrahman and I get back to his car to find it unattended by the guy he paid to watch it. He mutters under his breath and begins checking the tires. There is no real parking enforcement in Hargeisa. You pay a guy to watch your car while it is parked, if the police see that it is unattended they let the air out of your tires. In the same way that a ticket is essentially an institutionalized bribe to enforce good civic behavior, this system operates by making your life a lot harder if you don't have a guy to watch your car. We stand in the rain looking at the flattening tire.

Abdulrahman shrugs and we get into the car. He whips the car into the street and we bump along the road rolling on the partially inflated tire.

'This is Somaliland," he says and presses on the accelerator.

We dip into the Airport Road and the tire blows out sending us into a lazy 180 in the mud-covered streets. When we come to a stop Abdulrahman puts a hand to my chest presumably to see if I am still intact. I am.

"We are in luck," he says, pointing out the window.

Across the street is a tire shop. Employees in grease-stained overalls are already running out to provide us with their services. I'm amazed at our luck but not totally surprised given the amount of blown tires and disabled vehicles I've seen littering Airport Road.

If there were a strong central government in Hargeisa the police would watch parked cars and accept fines. Paved roads would mean less popped tires and fewer tire stores. It's not great, but it does function. I watch as Abdulrahman's big black Cadillac is jacked up by a team of automotive professionals in the pouring rain.

I am grateful for infrastructure

JUST A LITTLE BIT HIGH

The next day Abdulrahman and I are in a dusty warehouse on the outskirts of Hargeisa picking up the seven tons of food we purchased. A team of workmen clamber up a mountain of dry goods stored in the warehouse, whip them on their heads and toss them into the flatbed of the biggest truck I've ever seen. The rail thin Somali men have superhuman strength and speed, especially this far into Ramadan in the searing heat.

"They're working so fast," I say. Abdulrahman's lips tighten into a half frown.

"Khat. They are chewing." He points out some of the men stripping vibrant green leaves off of a branch behind the jugs of oil. They stuff the leaves into their cheeks and speed off back to the pile of food.

"Do you take khat Abdulrahman?" I ask. He shakes his head.

"No, never. I also don't let my son to take it. It's a drug."

I nod my head sober and pious as the Quaker Oats man.

"Have you tried it?" he asks.

"No, but I'm not against it," I say.

Abdulrahman calls a workman holding a small bushel of Khat and asks him for a branch. The workman has a plug of the vibrant green mash in his teeth. He seems to be on the verge of a constant giggle, glowing from the effects of the plant. He hands me some khat.

I look at Abdulrahman to see if he disapproves. He seems to think it's funny. I take a bite out of the plant, stem and all. The workman cracks up and takes the branch from me. He rips several leaves off and hands them to me and pantomimes jamming them into my cheek. I do as I am told and begin chewing the fibrous mash. Immediately all of the saliva leaves my mouth. I choke a bit as juice runs down my throat and cough into my hand. It is speckled with flecks of plant fiber and glow-in-the-dark green saliva.

The workman laughs at the foreigner's first khat experience and goes back to lugging bags of sugar.

"You like it?" asks Abdulrahman.

"It's not good."

I don't know if it is impolite to spit, so I swallow the battered mash. We watch the men fill the truck with food and somewhere there is a familiar tickle in my brain that announces a drug has entered my system. I can start to feel a kind of warm energy radiating inside of me. Like noticing the sun ready to burst through gray clouds after a storm passes. I stifle a small chuckle, I can't tell if it's just the placebo effect or if I am, in fact, a little high. Either way, I decide that when I am done with my ambassadorial duties I am going to buy an enormous amount of khat, take it back to the embassy and stuff myself so full of leaves that they're coming out of my ears.

For science.

TILTING AT MESQUITE BUSHES

I lay in bed staring up at the ceiling. After the stress of meeting elected officials, transporting thousands of dollars in Bitcoin, and attempted kidnappings I feel broken in half. I want a normal day in a quiet, anonymous city. I want to browse in a book store and buy something that I won't read. I want to stop looking over my shoulder every ten seconds worrying if I've wasted the last year in pursuit of little more than a decent bar story. I want to stop. I am catatonic in my bed.

I stare at the ceiling and I watch the sun creep across the sky. The mosquitoes wake up and go about their business. I can't be bothered to do much but swish them away when they want a snack. Though I am basically a deflated tire, inside of me I am trying to crowbar my lifeless form out of my bed and into some kind of action.

Just one thing. Do just one thing today. Go to the Ambassador Hotel or go for a walk. Just put your damn boots on and don't let a whole day of your precious life go by. Don't just lay here letting the mosquitos eat at you until something happens. Move.

I push myself up into a seated position and put on my boots one at a time. I look out the window. It is already late afternoon and my big accomplishment is sitting up and putting on my boots. My phone buzzes.

It's Hans.

Hans: Hello neighbor! I saw you return yesterday and I wanted to invite you to my house for tea.

Eric: Hey neighbor. That sounds great. I'll be over in a minute.

I don't know quite how it happens but sometimes if you give yourself the slightest push the rest of the world helps get you moving again. I wash up and look at myself in the mirror to see if it appears that I've been lying motionless in bed all day. It does.I don't think Hans will notice. I wave goodbye to Eid and walk out the front gate into the road. Hans stands in the middle of the road. The small German man opens his arms wide for a hug. I embrace my new friend and follow him into the front gate of his compound.

"I've been meaning to have you over for some time now, but it always seems that you're quite busy." He says stepping out of his shoes and into his modest home across from the Liberland Embassy.

"Yeah, we're doing an aid delivery to some nomads I think," I say.

"Fascinating, how are you determining the area of most need?" he asks, turning on his electric kettle. I know that this is something that I should have an answer for but I don't. I shrug.

"There's a guy named Abdulrahman. He takes me around and tells me what I'm supposed to do. Otherwise I just listen to what the government of Liberland or Somaliland tells me to do." Han's face falls and I can tell he is trying to find the most delicate way to tell me that I'm unprepared to do something like this. I answer him before he speaks:

"I'll be honest, Hans, I don't really know what I'm doing here or even if this is the right thing to do. I'm just kind of a dog chasing cars at the moment." Hans pours two steaming mugs of tea.

"Well, ya, aren't we all?" He claps me on the shoulder and we go to his modest sitting room and perch cross legged on cushions surrounding the room.

"I've been here for five years attempting to stop the prosopis bush, and I could be here for a lifetime more. What matters is trying. Besides, you're working with the government and you can't do anything they don't want you to do," he says in that matter-of-fact German way.

I sip my tea and nod, glad for Hans' company and advice. Throughout all of the years that I've spent abroad I've worried about being Don Quixote alone trying to answer a question that no one asked.

But then there is Hans, sipping his tea and battling his mesquite bush. Action mixed with belief gives things meaning. Time lets you know if those things were important.

There is a knock at the door. Hans jumps up.

"I forgot to tell you, I invited some friends over. I think that you will like them."

HANS AND HIS QUESTIONABLE FRIENDS

Chaos smells like Ethiopian gin and Chinese cigarettes. I'll come to find this out over the next couple hours. Hans brings three men into the sitting room. A slight Canadian-born Somalilander named Hassan is followed by an enormous glacier of a Somali man named Abdul who speaks with a curious South London accent. They're followed by a middle-aged Chinese man named David. He has small round glasses and a constant hacking cough. He shakes my hand and introduces himself as the Chinese Ambassador to Somaliland.

We all exchange pleasantries until Hans offers us tea. David swipes the offer away like an offensive insect. He takes out a satchel and produces a bottle of Ethiopian gin and a carton of black Chinese cigarettes.

"Cups!" says David, slapping the cap off the bottle of gin.

I do a bit of situational awareness math to assess if drinking with this group of strange men is a good idea. I have an empty stomach and I haven't touched a drop of alcohol for the last three weeks. I don't know any of these guys except for Hans. It's illegal to drink in Somaliland, but we're in a private home and technically two ambassadors are present so maybe we'll get diplomatic immunity. I judge this situation to be 5/10 dangerous. I probably shouldn't, but I'm going to anyway.

Cups arrive. Gin is poured. Before I go any further in this chapter, I want you to know that I am about to make several mistakes that will result in a life threatening situation. For those of you playing at home let's see if you can spot the poor choices I'm about to make. Anyway, David sets up 4 glasses of pure gin and lights a cigarette. We clink the glasses together. If you guessed that getting drunk with these men is my first mistake, then you're right.

The burning Ethiopian booze welcomes warm electric oblivion to my brain stem. A day spent staring at my ceiling and pondering my stupid existence is long in the rearview mirror swallowed up by a gulp of liquor. Suddenly, me and these three men are all fast friends. I share my bizarre story of becoming an accidental diplomat which lands in three different ways. Hassan finds it funny. David immediately begins refilling my glass and talking about how China and Liberland should form a strategic alliance. Abdul looks at me icy and silent across the smoke-filled room.

Another round. Glasses down. Cheers to Somaliland, to Liberland, to China, cheers to the mesquite bush. David begins shouting about the greatness of China. He declares that he will one day make me the President of Liberland in spite of the fact he's just heard about the country. I laugh him off and try to engage Abdul who continues to stare daggers at me from across the room.

"You've got an English accent," I say.

"I do. Had a bunch of business in South London before I came back here. You said you lived in Albania?" he asks, thorns all over the question.

"Yeah."

The air which was previously full of drunken yelling about political nonsense and Chinese cigarette smoke settled into an unsettling quiet.

"Ça bon?" he asks.

Northern Albanian slang to say *What's up?* My jaw drops. A Somalilander with an English accent saying hello in the Northern Albanian dialect while sitting in a German house next to a Chinese guy named David, is weird to say the least. It is concerning because Northern Albania has

315

connections to organized crime networks operating in South London.

"I've been to Albania. Used to move a lot of cocaine through London with the Albos," says the enormous man sitting across from me. Bingo.

"So why are you here?" he asks, but it is more a threat than a question.

From his perspective, I am an American with a dubious travel history and a connection to Northern Albania. It wouldn't be hard for him to believe that I was involved in organized crime myself. Or perhaps he thinks that I'm a spy like everyone else seems to. What is clear is that Abdul does not like or trust me. Unfortunately, the truth is the least believable story.

"Like, I said, I was a teacher in Iraqi Kurdistan-"

"Yeah, I know we've heard all of that. But, why are you here? Right now, in this room?"

"I invited him." Hans pipes up and sets his tea down in front of him. "He is working on making an aid donation to some of the pastoralists in the desert. He is working on aid like me."

I hear David's lighter snap to life. He begins muttering to himself, clearly annoyed that the good vibes have left the room.

"You've been here for how many years? Five years and still there is mesquite bush everywhere," says David. International shots fired. The evening is taking a sharp left turn and smashing the accelerator towards a cliff.

"Progress is slow, but we are trying," says Hans.

"China comes and gives whatever they need. They want roads? We build roads. They want a port? We build port-'

"China's trying to fuck us without a condom! How many Somalis do you employ? Who owns what you build,

China or Somaliland?" Abdul is unmoving cold rage behind the cigarette.

"It's for Somaliland," says David, suddenly defensive. Hassan shifts uncomfortably next to me waving his hands back and forth and trying to calm the situation without saying a word.

"Who owns you, David? Do you work with Xi Jin Ping or for him?' says Abdul and the question lands like a burning cinder block. I think we all want to know the answer. A silent smoky room.

"I don't understand the question."

"You understand the question. You all do. You come here trying to do your little things to help Somaliland, but really all you do is take a little bit every fucking time you do. And that's why I want to know why the fuck this guy is here."

"I'm a fake ambassador," I say, trying to bring down the temperature of the room. "Liberland is a fake country. I met the President on the back of a jet ski in Serbia. I'm just here to buy furniture for a fake embassy which is right across the street. You can see it if you want." I look at Hans who has begun quietly collecting cups in a bid to get us out of the sitting room. David upends the bottle of gin into his glass and then knocks the dregs back into his mouth.

"No more gin." he says.

"The ambassador invited us over. You got anything to drink there?" Abdul asks under a good-natured chuckle. I look over to Hans, it appears he wants me to do anything to get these people out of his house.

"Yeah. Come on over," I say.

We all get up.

If you're keeping track at home, this is my second enormous mistake. Inviting three strange drunk men into your home after a geopolitical screaming match is rarely a recipe for a great evening. Please take notice of how each mistake compounds in order to create a dangerous situation in the near future.

I drunkenly lead a parade of gin-soaked internationals from Hans' wrecked sitting room into the night-drenched gravel road separating our houses. Trying to keep things light I joke with my new friends that they would have ample places to sit given the fact that I have 12 metal chairs. I bang on the front door and Eid dutifully rolls it back. He eyes the visitors carefully and allows me to give them the penny tour.

Here's the empty banquet hall. Here's the papaya grove. This? This is the other banquet hall with my 12 metal chairs and here are the empty bedrooms. See? I'm not a threat to yours or anyone else's country. I'm just a weird guy doing weird things and I wouldn't trust me either. But it's cool, you can trust me. Because I'm an idiot.

Abdul, Hassan, and David seem far more interested in drinking my warm beer than discussing anything further. I leave them to their own devices sitting on my metal chairs and show Abdul the roof.

"Good view,' he says looking over light scattered in the distance.

"I can't take credit for it. The place isn't mine. It's Liberland—"

"Right, you told me that before," he says, cutting me off, the coals from our previous conversation igniting again. Below I can see Eid watching us from the yard.

"Doesn't make any sense. How are you making money on this?" He says, taking his gaze off the skyline and leveling his eyes at me. I think about the $7,000 hidden under my mattress.

"I don't. I'm just volunteering."

"Stop," he puts his hand in my face. "You're lying again."

He takes a swig of his beer and looks at me like I would look at one of my students caught cheating. At this moment my patience runs off a cliff. I wish I had another story. I wish that I was a secret agent with limitless resources. I wish I was a corrupt politician getting kick-backs from the Somaliland government. I wish I was one of the looters, con artists, and cowboy capitalists that Abdul has seen over the years. At least then I would have more than a couple hundred dollars in my bank account and I wouldn't live out of a backpack. I'm here. I'm trying to help. I'm sick of feeling like a fraud.

"Call me a liar one more time and I'm going to have my security throw you out of the embassy."

My pulse hammers in my ears. It doesn't matter what he thinks. For right now, I'm an ambassador with a mansion and a man with a gun. He cracks a toothy smile.

"Alright," he says, setting his beer down and clapping me on the shoulder. "Alright, now I believe you. You're just caught up in this."

"Yeah," I say. "I'm just caught up in this."

He laughs. I see Eid slowly return to his guard house. Abdul laughs and leaves me standing on the roof. I'm too young to see the fall of the Berlin Wall. I'm too old to travel through space. For this exact moment I have a beating heart and a willful disregard for my own safety that has taken me to this balcony at this moment. I'm done being called a liar.

The parade of drunks files out of the foyer of the Liberland Embassy leaving only the wreckage of beer bottles and twelve metal chairs. David clings to Hassan's arm, the Ethiopian gin having claimed the better part of his motor skills. Abdul nods at Eid as we pass through the gates. Hassan's phone rings as he loads David into his car. He answers it and looks my way.

"Hey guys, my wife is home. She wants to know if you want to come for dinner," Hassan points out a house on the opposite hill. I think about the can of tuna and half sleeve of Pringles I have to satiate my gin filled stomach. Dinner sounds great.

"I'll drive you," Abdul says to me. I could easily walk to the house but I wonder if the guards will notice that I am illegally drunk. Maybe Abdul's offer is a gesture of good will.

"Okay, we'll meet you guys there," I say, walking with Abdul. I wave at the Chinese ambassador who is smeared across the passenger seat of Hassan's car. They drive off. I hop inside Abdul's car.

This, my friends, was my third mistake.

STRANGER'S CARS

Abdul's 4x4 pulls out onto the dirt road right behind Hassan and David. The inside of his car is impeccably clean, lit neon purple from a custom stereo unit. Abdul follows close behind the other car as I try to make pleasant, very drunk small talk.

"'So, how long have you known Hassan and David?' Abdul cranks the volume of his stereo system until the windows are shuddering with base. I can feel it in my stomach agitating the gin in my belly.

"I don't really know those guys. Just met them today," he says.

He whips the car around the opposite direction. I crane my neck to see Hassan's car rolling off into the dusty night, as I do I notice the rifle tucked under the back of Abdul's seat. A cold boozy sweat coats my neck. I do not know this person. This person knows no one that I know. We are both drunk and he is taking me somewhere in his car.

"Hassan's house is that way," I say.

He steps on the accelerator. I can hear rocks spit up in back of us and the momentum pins me against the passenger seat. He laughs and kicks the music up another notch.

"You like this song?" he asks, staring at me instead of the dirt road in front of us.

"Yeah, it's good," I say, blood in my ears louder than the music. I can't do anything but go where Abdul wants to go.

"They put me in prison for like three years—" He begins unwinding a prison story as we speed faster and faster away from the fortified neighborhood of Masala. We're spit out into the desert foothills. No fenced buildings, just tents on rocky desert hills. With every second of inertia my situation gets more dangerous.

I *don't know how many turns we've taken since leaving my place. Are we a mile away from the embassy right now? Two miles?*

I take a look outside at the rocky ground speeding past. If I jump out I am probably breaking a bone in the middle of a dirt road in Somaliland with no one to help but Abdul. It's not an option.

"—they go wild man. I was on a yacht outside of Vlora—"

He recounts a prostitute-filled yacht party on the Albanian coast as we bore full speed into the night. I look for anything in his car to use to defend myself, but the hospital-clean interior doesn't even have a ball of lint. That's when I get an idea. It would be a shame if someone-

"I've got to puke," I say, clapping a hand over my

mouth and feigning a dry-heave. Abdul takes his foot off of the accelerator and steers us to the side of the road.

"Not in here," he says as I leap out and into the bushes. I pretend to puke into thorny mesquite bushes and scan the area around me. In the distance, I can see the dull glow of the lights on Masala. It must be a mile or two away. I'm alone in the desert with Abdul. I can't get back without him.

I see Abdul checking the passenger side to see if I had made a mess of his leather seats. I try to regain my composure even though my blood is 90 percent gin. I decide that the best way to deal with this is to be selectively honest.

"Wow, I puked a lot," I say because I feel it is a strong beginning to any honest conversation. I stand in Abdul's headlights and lay the cards on the table.

"Look, you're scaring the shit out of me. I thought we were going down the street and now we're in the middle of the desert. I don't know who you think I am, but I'm no one important. I've told you the truth a million times tonight. I'm no one. I feel like shit and I can walk or you can take me back to my place."

Abdul considers this for a long moment as wave after wave of booze surges in my blood.

"Fine, I'll take you back." I hop back into the car.

Mercifully he makes a u-turn and heads back towards Masala. I hang my head out the window at his request. I see my street approaching and again I am once again thinking about hurling myself out of the car. The window begins to roll up as we pass the street. *Shit.*

I slip my head back in the car and again Abdul looks my way and stands on the accelerator. We rocket down into the city taking hairpin turns and drifting through dusty night. We're now entering the downtown area, a no go for any foreigner after sundown.

"Where are we going?" I scream over the music

"Don't worry about it, Mr. Ambassador. We're just—"

BANG.

The car skids and fishtails into the roundabout of Downtown Hargeisa. As we careen towards the center divider, threatening to flip, I think about the twisted wrecks I've seen littering Airport road. I think of Abdulrahman and Faithia. I think of Savannah. I think of all the stupid things I willingly did to put myself in the same car with this maniac. I pray to whichever God is closest.

The car skids to a halt in front of the divider. Once it's stopped, I leap out into the street and catch a glimpse of my savior. A blown tire. I don't have enough time to thank the tire or the terrible infrastructure of Hargeisa because I am running powered by nothing but gin and terror. Broken stone chews my feet through the soles of my boots. My legs heave. My arms pump. I am speed.

I hear Abdul calling after me in the distance but that doesn't matter anymore. Now, the only thing that matters is getting home before the police find out that an illegally drunk foreigner is sprinting through downtown after dark. I leapfrog from shadow to shadow and peel off the street any time lights approach. The terror which blanched the booze from my blood begins to give way and I can feel every drop of gin running roughshod through my body.

I curse myself for all the stupid arrogance that put me right here and right now. I run past khat shacks with their patrons blithely chewing in the shadowy doorways. I curse myself for never being able to settle on any direction and being at the mercy of the situation. I dash past private security guards drinking tea next to their AK-47s. I curse myself for leaving everyone I love to put myself in foolish danger again and again and again.

I run home. I run home. I run home.

A fluorescent light buzzes in the convenience store across from my street. I have no clean water in my place and I know that I will be monumentally hungover soon. My negligence has once again paved my way to a very specific type of hell. The fact that the only convenience store in Hargeisa that is open is on my block is proof of God's mercy.

I stumble through the doors of the convenience store, my shirt soaked through with gin and sweat. I am a looney-tunes caricature of a drunk. I hiccup with each woozy step. I can feel stink lines of booze hovering above my head. I am like a sign sent from Allah to show the family running the convenience store the ill effects of alcohol. I get a large pack of bottled water. The man behind the counter types up my total on his calculator and turns it around to me. I hand over a fist full of moist bills and mumble a pitiful thank you.

Back at the embassy I sit at the foot of my bed in the dark chasing Pringles with large mouthfuls of bottled water. I make a solemn promise to myself.

I will never, under any circumstances, ever, be an ambassador again.

A DIVINE HANGOVER

There is no relevance in this book for me to explain how bad the hangover was. This will not deter me. I want you to imagine that lowest ring of hell that a hangover has taken you to. See if you can feel the stomach tumbling churn, the ice pick headache, and the razors edge nausea. Right about now I bet you want a cool dark room, aspirin, and the ability to fall deep into the shadow realm of sleep until your poor liver has processed your mistakes. However, if you're in Hargeisa you get the opposite of these things.

I lay spread eagle on the bed slowly roasting in the horrific sun while being nibbled on by mosquitos. I would be in the fetal position but it's too hot for that. When I can muster the strength, I tilt a bottle of water into my mouth and sip like it might be my last meal. The idea of ever leaving this room again feels as impossible as walking back to Los Angeles.

Once I can climb to my feet again the sun is beginning to set. I lost this day because last night I allowed myself to be convinced that I had any sort of power and prestige. I let a fake title go to my head and put myself in danger. Of course, I am having these thoughts while standing on the balcony of a mansion overlooking a scatter of nomadic tents below me. I never realized that becoming a politician would make me suck so much.

My phone rings:

"Hello, Mr. Ambassador," says Abdulrahman, his voice far too loud and full of joy. "What are you doing?"

I look around the room that I've been feeling sorry for myself in for the last 18 hours.

"Reading," I say, because it seems like something a person worthy of respect would be doing with their time.

"The food has gone to the desert. Tomorrow, we will go to the village with the security team. You will give the food to the nomads. We make pictures, then we come back. 4 a.m.. Be ready. We go before morning prayers."

Then Abdulrahman hangs up.

I tear the top off a tube of Pringles and find some aspirin.

I will be ready.

SOLDIERS AND PRAYERS

My phone blasts me awake at 3:30 in the morning.I

throw on my button-down shirt and matching socks. I take a water bottle and head out the door. I'm met by Abdulrahman and a young man wearing a New York Yankees hat. Abdulrahman introduces me to his son Cawal. He's in his early twenties and wears sunglasses regardless of the fact that the sun has not risen yet.

"I heard about this and I wanted to come too. Hope that's cool."

Cawal speaks with an American accent which is made all the more surprising given that he tells me he is going to University in Pakistan. I'm glad that he's along for the ride.

"We go to meet the soldiers. Then we pray," says Abdulrahman.

I get in the car. Yes, we need to pray. We all need to pray. We drive to the Vice President's compound where we're met by four soldiers and the Vice President's secretary who will act as my translator. They open the door to one of the Jeeps so I can sit inside while they are praying at the mosque.

I lean my head against the window and shut my eyes. The call to prayer warms the still night. Beyond the gate, I can see the men in fatigues touching their heads to the front of their prayer mats. It's probably a good idea to do the same. I don't like bothering God for things because I think that he probably has more pressing concerns than addressing my litany of woes, but given the number of automatic weapons that I will be traveling with it seems that a prayer would be in order.

I pray that we stay safe. I pray the food makes it to where it is going. I pray for Somaliland and Abdulrahman and the nomads. I pray that Iraqi Kurdistan finds some kind of peace, that Kosovo gains acceptance, and that Transnistria opens to the world. Liberland will be fine. I don't pray for Liberland. They would want it that way.

I pray for Savannah. I pray for both of us to find out where we are going. I pray that the place is somewhere together. I pray for my family and friends all around the world. I thank God for keeping me safe the many times that I could have become a state department statistic. I ask God to make the path forward clear and give me the courage to walk it. I run out of things to talk to God about well before the soldiers are back from the mosque. I drift off to a light effortless sleep.

WADI VROOM

My head smacks into the window jolting me awake. I grab a hold of the handles affixed to the ceiling of the Jeep as the machine chews its way up a rocky hill.

"I thought that'd wake you up!" says Cawal, his sunglasses back on and a broad smile across his face.

The sun is beginning to douse the desert from between the mountains. I look out the rocking window at the endless expanse of Somali desert. The Jeep in front of us climbs over another rocky chasm only to careen down the other side. I brace as we're about to do the same. Our Jeep rattles down into a small canyon sinking us into relatively level sand.

'Wadis!' says Cawal with unrestrained excitement.

These are dry desert riverbeds which serve as a desert super highway. A driver with a keen eye can navigate between wadis and partially exposed roads all the way to Ethiopia. I am beginning to see why Wassim's road is so important. We carve through the wadi only to be shot out onto the scrubland. Bouncing over sand and rock I white knuckle the handle to remain in my seat. A big turn sends my head smacking into the window again. Abdulrahman beams from the front seat.

"How much longer?" I call to Cawal.

"Maybe only like, 6 more hours!" he says, clinging close to me as the jeep takes a dive into the next Wadi.

I should have prayed more.

BUS VERSUS GRAVITY

"I think that bus is in trouble," says Cawal.

He is correct. The bus is on its side. I've seen a bus before and it should be on its wheels. Our caravan comes to a stop in a deep ravine when we find the toppled vehicle surrounded by perplexed people. They're the first human life we have seen in the two hours we've been scrambling through wadis.

The soldier in the lead car gives us a hand signal and our small column comes to a stop. There is a rattle of Somali language, the door locks pop open, and everyone hops out. I stand next to Cawal as the soldiers, Abdulrahman, and the vice president's secretary huddle up.

"What's going on?" I ask Cawal. He takes off his Yankees hat and dabs his brow.

"I don't know. I think we've got to help them," he says.

"How?" I ask.

"Rope probably," he says.

As if on cue, several coils of rope appear in the hands of the soldiers who trot over to the downed bus. Cawal gives me a nudge to follow him and I do as I am nudged. Soldiers lash ropes to the top of the bus and through the open windows. Without instruction the passengers, soldiers, Abdulrahan, Cawal, and I arrange ourselves across from the disabled vehicle with rope wrapped in our fists. Someone says words that sound like *one, two, three*. Then everyone begins shouting. We pull the rope taut, running towards the empty desert.

The bus gives out a metallic groan as it rises from the rocky floor and wheezes back down onto its wheels. We all drop the rope and a cry of victory rises up from the assembled crowd. Then, as soon as we'd arrived, we were back in the Jeeps bumping along the desert.

I lean forward in my seat to talk with Abdulrahman who looks exceptionally pleased with himself.

"What would have happened if we didn't come along?" Abdulrahman doesn't turn to answer me.

"Someone is always coming. In the desert we have to take care of each other," he says.

CAMEL MILK

The jostling of the Jeep lulls me into a hypnotic trance. The alien landscape rolls by, an endless expanse of rocky berms, jagged mountains, and of course, the mesquite bush. A troop of gnarly baboons tumble across our path on their way to do whatever it is baboons are doing in the middle of the desert.

This is a wild place full of dreamlike calcified arabesques and islands of Martian stone. It's like a Dr. Suess illustration that could kill you really quickly.

We pull out of the network of ravines and onto a sandy road. Even though we're still on dirt, the road feels smooth as glass. The horizon becomes a ruler swipe through the sky instead of an endless wall of rock.

Geel! Geel!

The shouting snaps me out of my trance. I know this word means camel due to the fact that I have been treating myself to camel burgers on a biweekly basis. I follow the gaze of Abdulrahman until I see a small speck on the horizon.

A lone camel stands next to a young boy with a jerry can.

The caravan peels off the road dipping back into the rocky desert. I do not know why we are driving towards a boy and his camel, but everyone seems to be very excited about it.

We stop next to the boy and Abdulrahman leans across the lap of the soldier to talk with the shepherd. The conversation goes like this:

Abdulrahman: *Something.*

The boy: *Something regarding the camel and his jerry can.*

Abdulrahman: *Something about the water bottle he is holding up.*

The boy: *General agreement.*

Everyone in the Jeep except me: *General enthusiasm!*

We pile out of the Jeep. Abdulrahman empties out some of the water bottles and hands them to the boy. He then tips his jerry can of camel milk into each of the bottles. Abdulrahman looks like a kid on Christmas.

"You want this?" asks Abdulrahman.

I look to Cawal. He nods his head. I dump out my water bottle and hand it to Abdulrahman. When everyone has a water bottle full of warm camel milk we stand in the blazing desert sun and raise a bottle to the shepherd boy. I take a hearty slug of the viscous fluid.

The milk tastes like pure, unadulterated dusty camel. It begins with a punchy note of earthy funk that shouts CAMEL! As it drapes heavy across the tongue it begs you to wonder, who was this camel?

The flavor hangs in the back of the back of the mouth, ending with notes of beef, hose water, and of course… camel hair. It leaves one wondering. Where am I? Why am I drinking this?

I work my way through a good quarter of my bottle because I am both polite and thirsty. I wonder what digestive fireworks would await me if I finish the bottle.

"You like it?" Abdulrahman asks.

I turn to see my caravan looking at me awaiting my assessment. I utter a close mouthed *mmmmmm,* thinking that if I can't say something diplomatic then I shouldn't say anything at all. Abdulrahman relieves me of my bottle of camel milk and distributes the remainder among my comrades.

"It's okay. You are not Somali yet,"he says.

He is correct, I am not.

ROADSIDE DINER

I am informed that we will stop to eat somewhere. Since we are technically traveling this is permitted during Ramadan. A small cluster of shacks appear on the horizon. As we approach I can see some makeshift tables and chairs carved out of the gnarled trees dotting the desert. We pull up outside of the town to find a thin rope crossing the path. The convoy stops at the rope. A man wearing a dusty tank top emerges from one of the wooden shacks with a rifle dangling from his shoulder.

He speaks with our lead car. The man looks back and catches my eye. I wave. He unhooks the thin rope from a stick across the road and allows the cars to pass his border. I have a lot of questions about this: Who decided where the rope would go? Don't they realize that a car can go right through a rope? What would have happened if he didn't lift the rope for us? Who elected that guy the keeper of the rope? Where did he get the rope?

At this point I realize that all of these questions can easily be applied to any border in the world. It doesn't matter that the line is invisible if we all believe in it. The world is full of important symbols that we effortlessly obey without a second thought. Every border is just a guy with a magic rope and a gun.

There you go.

That's the lesson of this book.

You can stop reading here if you want.

It appears that this town is one of many temporary settlements that the nomads construct as they are on the move according to the changing seasons. Somalis typically eat without utensils so when we are seated at a long wooden table we are given a bowl of water with which to wash our hands. Syrupy tea is served up piping hot even in the sweltering desert sun. Somehow it is comforting and refreshing.

Each of us receives a thick round of bread made of fermented dough. I watch to see what the others do before diving in. Abdulrahman and Cawal use their fingers like a fork to tear the bread into bite-sized chunks and I do the same. I gather a ball of the dough from my metal plate and pop it into my mouth. The bread has a sort of savory tang to it like a sourdough pancake.

"Like this," says Abdulrahman.

He picks up his cup of tea and pours half on the bread making a sort of sticky mush. The clove and cardamom tea mixes with the bread in a sort of East African maple syrup and pancakes. Fortunately, no more camel milk is served. The rope guy eventually comes and joins us for tea.

We're in his country now.

POLITICS OF SAND

A jackknife mountain range gives way to white desert sand. Glimpses of life sparkle in the desert. A camel bounds down the insinuation of a road. Women walking through the desert look otherworldly in their purple and pink headscarves as they stroll between twisted trees and boulders. Shepherds wave teams of skinny goats across the land staring blankly at our passing convoy.

We come to a stop in a small cluster of buildings in various states of disrepair. As I get out of the jeep the humid heat kicks the breath from my lungs. I feel as if my bones are heating me up from the inside in spite of the gray murky sky above us. The food has been laid out in the desert in individual piles. Large bags of rice, flour, salt, and sugar. A yellow jerry can full of oil and some plastic tarpaulin. I notice that aside from the few people we saw in the desert, the entire village is empty except for my group. I find Abdulrahman who is my oracle of all things.

He sits on rattan mats under a tree surrounded by a circle of brambles. Behind his gold rimmed glasses he looks a bit like a Somali Buddha under the Banyan tree, peaceful and contemplative in the swirl of a thousand things. I pass through the opening of the bramble circle and he gestures for me to take a seat next to him.

"Do you like it here, Abdulrahman?" He takes a deep breath and surveys the open desert.

"Yes. Nomadic is a good life," he says.

He goes on to tell me that people in his family often take a year to live in the traditional way. I look at the empty desert under gray clouds knowing that only a few weeks prior the sky opened up and swept a cyclone across this land. To be nomadic is to be at the mercy of everything around you. It is to survive off of everything you take with you, including your community.

"So what happens next?"

"The nomads will come. You meet with the leader. Then we take pictures and they get their food."

"Why haven't they just taken the food already?" I ask

"You were not here to give it to them," says Abdulrahman. It becomes clear to me that even though the food has been in the village for several days the people were unable to get it because of the simple fact that I was not there to take a picture giving it to them. I realize that I have forgotten what the point of my job here is. I am not an aid worker, I am a politician.

This is about power. The only power that matters is the ability to bend reality. This can be done at the end of a gun or it can be done through glad handing aid. The key question that anyone has to ask themselves if they want to accrue power is, how long do they want to keep it? If you build your empire through violence then that is exactly how you will keep it, and everyone loses eventually. That is why we have soft power, this is the kind of reality bending which doesn't happen on the end of a gun, but instead on the end of a diplomat like myself.

Liberland doesn't care about the nomads or the cyclone. They don't care about a future where this self-determined state on the horn of Africa can create conditions for its citizens to thrive. They care about a new line being drawn on a map. They care about joining the street fight of nations for finite resources and never-ending appetites. It's not about the nomads, it's about the power. The realization fills my gut with ash.

"Where is everybody?" I ask.

"Funeral. Some people died of disease. Clean water is hard to find after the cyclone," I nod, too hot and morally conflicted to say anything to Abdulrahman. I sit under this tree thinking that there are so many differences between me and the people out in this desert, but the most important one is that I get a choice. I can choose to leave.

A line of tall slim Somalis walks slowly from the desert. They're all vibrant clothing and solemn gazes. Maybe thirty people arrange themselves near the food to claim each pile for their own. The secretary appears with one of the nomads and I'm informed that he is the leader. I join the men and I speak through the translator expressing my condolences for their loss on behalf of Liberland. I say that Liberland is happy to provide this aid to his people and that he has my personal assurance that I will tell the president about our experience here. I say platitudes on behalf of Liberland while he looks on with red rimmed distant eyes.

After a brief photo op, the people take their supplies back to their dwellings. Some ask to take a picture with me. Some eye me from the distance of the desert. Some go about their day as if I haven't dropped from another dimension into their world. I want to leave these people to their lives, but of course we have to stick around for photos. If you give humanitarian aid and no one is around to take a picture, did you actually give aid at all?

FRAGILE ANIMALS

The leader takes us on a walk into the flat plain of the desert. He points us to a ripple of rock formations rising out of the sand.

As we approach them, I see that they are not rock but dead goats. Windswept, sandblasted, and sunbaked until hardened into white fossils. They're trapped in the position they died; mid frantic gallop away from the driving storm which would take their lives. I can still see the phone number of the shepherd painted on the skin of the goat. The frozen herd of fragile animals.

We continue walking along the desert until we come to a twisted chunk of metal laying in the sand. Squatting down on our haunches, we examine the remnants of pumps which used to bring water to the nomadic waypoint in the desert. My translator tells me that unless they can get the pumps repaired the cholera will continue to spread and there will be more death. I nod and tell him that I will give this news to the president of Liberland. I tell him this knowing full well that nothing will be done. I am not lying, but I wonder if offering even the faint glimmer of hope in a situation like this is worse than outright falsehoods. I'm a politician. I'm a fraud. We walk back towards where the nomads are collecting their food.

I have nothing to say. The crushing heat and soft sand labors each step back to the small camp. Bad things compound into worse things so quickly when there is no way to organize a response to disaster. The cyclone kills shepherds, scatters flocks, and destroys pumps. The remaining population bands together to recover the lost animals and supplies, but since they have no pumps animals and people alike must drink from puddles on the ground. Waste from the remaining animals mixes with water and cholera spreads throughout the small band of people.

Cholera is a diuretic disease where death comes from dehydration. Sufferers can survive it so long as they are kept hydrated. Clean water and food flow to the sick and the injured and the healthy are left wondering if and when they will become sick or injured. Things go from bad to worse rapidly when there is nothing but the desert and the sky around you. There is a thin margin for life and death because there is no way to stop the dominoes from falling once the cyclone has knocked down the first.

A hurricane smacking into the United States is a disaster which usually does not pose an existential threat to an entire country. This is because we have federal and state level warning systems alongside aid, and relief mechanisms. Moreover, we have international relationships which can reinforce our response to tragedy if our internal services fail. Forces of first responders can be bolstered by volunteers, donations can come from around the world with the click of a couple buttons. Human capital and funds flow to the disaster zone like white blood cells to a virus. Ultimately, the invisible apparatus of the state leverages its mighty power to keep itself alive.

Here, there is no state. No one hears about Cyclone Sagar on the news. No celebrity supported fundraising drives raise awareness. No one changes their imagery on social media encouraging their followers to pray for Somaliland. We return to camp and I am told that it is time for lunch. Cawal, Abdulrahman, and the soldiers leave me standing in the desert looking over the dead goats and destroyed pumps.

GOAT BOLOGNESE

I sit with the men on mats in a small dome tent made of dry desert wood. Cawal and Abdulrahman laugh merrily with the rest of the men. Given that I have no idea what anyone is saying I assume it must be hilarious. I'm shocked that a couple of weeks after near certain death and a series of funerals that laughter is physically possible for these men, but I suppose it is probably more necessary now than ever.

I can smell food cooking from the next tent, roasting meat and spice. I hear bubbling pots and the crackle of wood on a fire. I hope that we are not having camel milk.

A woman brings us a bowl of water to wash our hands. I consider passing on the hand washing for a moment given the recent cholera outbreak but it seems rude. If I die then I hope my mother will know that I did so with good manners. When we have all washed up a large metal pot of steaming goat broth is brought to the center of the tent alongside some small limes. We are served steaming mugs of the unctuous gray broth. It's followed by large metal plates of roasted goat meat, and to my great surprise mounds of white macaroni alongside a dish of what appears to be goat bolognese.

Not knowing the decorum of how to eat macaroni and sauce with my hands I wait until the chief dives in before I make my move. He deftly gathers some of the noodles in his hand and then uses them to hold a bed of the sauce, he then tilts his head to the side and allows the mixture to fall into his mouth. I do the same and look to Abdulrahman for approval. He nods at me.

"We like pasta here. From Italian occupation.Pasta stayed, but the Italians left," says Abdulrahman chuckling at his own joke.

In the 1940s, the Italian fascist dictator Benito Moussolini made a play to challenge the British power projected through the Suez Canal. This resulted in a battle for the desert which brought soldiers from Australia, Sudan, Kenya, Britain, Italy, India, Pakistan and France into Somaliland. Bombing runs were flown from the Gulf of Aden to protect the English retreat and after weeks of fighting, thousands of dead, and wounded, the Italian Fascists had taken Somaliland only to lose it again.

Of course, none of that matters now. The sun set on the British Empire beginning in the late 1940s and the age of colonialism came to an end, shrinking European borders to their modern sizes with nothing to show for themselves but the wealth of conquered people and a vague cultural memory of fighting for something somewhere.

That's why we're eating pasta with goat bolognese in the desert.

EMPTY EMBASSY

The caravan rumbles back to Hargeisa. For hours, we chase a falling sun from sand to dry riverbeds to dirt roads. When we finally hit the chunky asphalt of Hargeisa it feels so smooth we might as well be gliding on a cloud. The soldiers drop me off outside of the Embassy and Eid opens the gate for me.

I lie on my bed under a cloud of buzzing mosquitoes looking up at the ceiling and marveling in the anticlimax of this moment. I have spent five weeks in Hargeisa. I have one week left. I have completed two of my three tasks as ambassador to Somaliland. I have established diplomatic connections between the governments of Liberland and Somaliland. I have purchased and delivered aid to the people of Somaliland. And now comes my final task.

BUYING FURNITURE DURING RAMADAN

There are a great many bed frames in Somali furniture stores which feature roaring lions painted in neon. A disconcerting amount of these bed frames light up or glow in the dark. Some have remote controlled LEDs which make the bed appear more like a hovercraft than a place to sleep. None of these beds are suitable for an embassy in my opinion.

Cawal and I have been wandering through furniture stores for the majority of the day and I have yet to find a bedroom or office set which hits the right balance of boring, elegant, and useful. I am tempted to outfit Liberland with the most ostentatious neon furniture that I can find, but I figure it is better to complete my duties to the best of my ability to protect and defend the interests of Liberland in Somaliland. I decide upon several plain

ERIC CZULEGER

bedroom and office sets as well as a banquet table full of whirls and sconces. I hand over a stack of dollars to the furniture guy and Cawal explains where the Embassy is. I am told that the furniture will be delivered that day.

Around one in the morning a truck rumbles up to the Liberland Embassy packed with furniture and about 10 workmen prepared with tools and small bundles of khat. After a full night of hammering, pounding, and sawing the sun rises and the workmen have left a full embassy in their wake.

I walk through the halls of the once empty mansion that I stalked around attempting to protect myself from Al Shabab with my goat's horn. I've finished my last job as an ambassador. I write up a list of my expenses and my contacts to send back to the Liberland brass. To my surprise, I get an email back from President Jedlicka offering me the position full time.

Should I be an ambassador?

At this moment I feel the allure of power and position raising questionable horns on my head. I think how much good I could do for Somaliland and Liberland. After all, I am in this position for a reason, am I not? I made my way from being an English teacher in Iraqi Kurdistan, through Transnistria to Liberland. Clearly I must be qualified to do anything. I steady myself a second as I realize that I've just lost myself in the fantasy of unearned power and prestige. I'm going to think about it. I begin to write a list of my recommendations to Vit.

I recommend returning to help replace the pumps in the desert and aid in the development of their critical infrastructure. I write about Hans and his mission against the mesquite bush as a possible business partnership. I report about Wassim and the politics of dirt. I tell them to beware getting into cars with people that you do not know and how the center of Hargeisa can be quite dangerous for foreigners. I thank them for the offer and say that I will consider it.

I take out the remaining funds and begin earmarking them for final payments. I spent $8,000 on food for the nomads and $4,000 on furniture for the embassy. I spent an additional thousand dollars paying Eid and I tipped the workers who built the furniture an additional $500. I am left with $1500. It is unmarked and unknown in the world. The money sits heavy in my hand.

I lay the crisp hundred dollar bills across my bed. I don't know when I will sell another article. I think about how the money could give me a month or more to breathe if I am careful. I consider how far away I am from anyone who would know if I took the money. It would be so easy to say that I spent the entire treasury in service of Liberland and Somaliland. If I accept the position of ambassador full time this would be a small down payment on my salary. I pick up the bills and let them slide crisp and tempting across my palm as I count them.

I fold the money, deciding whether to put it in an envelope for Liberland or into my pocket. I realize that I am experiencing a condition which is commonly known as *being a politician*. People have treated me with respect that I didn't earn so they could gain favor which was not mine to give. I helped create the illusion of universal and unquestionable good for the sake of a story which benefits the few and the questionable. I never lied but I allowed the truth to be obscured where it made my life and the aims of those above me, easier. Here, now, in this room, with only a couple days left here in Somaliland, I am faced with the same questions faced by so many politicians.

Do I take the money? Do I take the power? Don't I deserve it?

Of course, I do.

BUYING DRUGS

I take some of the money. I take five dollars. I am going to use it to buy myself some khat. I decide that I'm going to chew that khat until I am remarkably high. I also decide that I am not going to be the ambassador from the world's first cryptocurrency based libertarian microstate to the unrecognized northern region of Somalia. I also decide that it's time for me to get a normal quiet job doing normal quiet things. But first, I'm going to jam as many hallucinogenic East African leaves in my mouth as possible.

I turn off Airport Road into a nearby neighborhood, there I see a man in a wooden shack with the word GAFANE printed across it. GAFANE is one of the two brands of khat here in Somaliland, with its competitor being WHITE HORSE. I decide on GAFANE because WHITE HORSE sounds too much like a euphemism for either heroin or colonialism.

When I ask the GAFANE man for some khat and hand over five dollars he looks at me as if I've escaped from a mental hospital. He reaches his arm in and extracts a full bushel of vibrant green leaves. I'm hit with a whiff of rich chlorophyll. I wrap my arms around roughly enough khat to start my own GAFANE shack and stuff it in my backpack. I walk back towards the Ambassador Hotel with my backpack full of rustling branches. I'm going to have a non-alcoholic beer in the garden while I chew my leaves because my goddamn work here is done.

Minutes later I am taking a seat at one of the Ambassador Hotel's finest plastic chairs, sinking into the gravel, and ordering a non-alcoholic beer. I sneak a hand into my backpack and strip a fist full of GAFANE'S finest leaves from one branch. After a swig of apple flavored beer, I slip a leaf into my mouth.

As soon as I crunch down on it my mouth is filled with a neon green blast of bitter chlorophyll and dirt flavor. The saliva in my mouth is sucked away into the fibrous green mash between my teeth. The leaf turns into a salty forest-flavored cud as I work my jaw like a cow until I can choke it down. I take another slug of apple beer and throw another leaf in my mouth. I have to eat about 40 leaves to experience the finer qualities of the plant.

It's not necessarily gross, but it is unpleasant. If you'd like to experience the joy of chewing khat, I encourage you to eat a couple leaves off a bush growing in any major city center. The leaf or the plant does not matter. I am certain that the taste and the experience will be indistinguishable from khat.

After pushing countless leaves down my gullet I experience no changes in my consciousness other than feeling dumb for eating leaves. The only logical answer to this problem is to order another apple beer and cram more leaves in my face.

I came here to get high and that's exactly what I plan to do. As anyone who has ever taken a drug before knows: if it doesn't work immediately, take a lot more and you'll be guaranteed a great time free of consequences.

When my beer arrives, I adopt a new strategy. I reach into my bag and strip another branch of its leaves. I pack all the leaves into a tight ball and put them between my back teeth.

I chew the plug ferociously until I can wash the fleshy mass down my throat with a huge chug of apple beer. I continue this process of *ball, chew, beer, and recover* until I've dispatched maybe 20 branches and three beers.

I feel nothing other than disappointment and full of leaves. I pay my bill and walk back to the embassy.

GETTING HIGH AND DOING LAUNDRY

While sitting on my balcony looking at the mountains on the horizon, I realize two things:

1. I have not stopped chewing leaves off a branch of khat since I returned.

2. My clothes don't know how much I care about them.

This realization about my clothes detonates a small nuclear explosion of gratitude deep inside of me. There is so much that protects and cares for me as I move through the vastness of this world. I love my boots deeply for cradling my feet as I march through cities and across deserts. I am enraptured with my underwear, the unsung hero in the garment pantheon. I take a moment to remember all of the socks that I have loved and lost throughout the years. Wherever they are, I hope they're thriving.

I snap another leaf off of the stalk. Suddenly, I am filled with the need to do laundry. I must show my clothes how much I care for them and everything they have done for me. I strip nude and run into the bathroom with an armload of my tattered clothes and a fresh stalk of khat. I catch my eye in the mirror and stick out my tongue. It is electric green. I work my jaw which has become sore for some reason. The khat clearly has no effect on me. I then strip another couple leaves off my stalk with my teeth and dive into my naked laundry session.

I pour a bottle of water across my laundry and toss in a bar of soap. With each satisfying twist I can feel the dirt and grime from the year flowing out into the murky water. I add more water and more soap and I scrub as I think about my Kurdish students intoning *good morning Mr. Eric.* I whip droplets out of my shirt with the Albanian flag and laugh as I think about the night Savannah and I spent in Svilengrad after being kicked out of Turkey. I squeeze murk from jeans and socks thinking about Astefano, Vladimir, Transnistria Terry, Bitcoin Mike, Abdulrahman, Wassim, Vit, and the hundreds of other people who helped me along my way over the last year and throughout my whole life.

I think about Savannah, so far away in Bulgaria but walking with me at every step of my journey. I think about whizzing through the uncertain night into Erbil and being sat next to one another in the Turkish police station after being interrogated. I think about holding New Years sparklers on her balcony in Bulgaria while burning with fever and eating Easter lunch across from blind men in a Transnistrian Monastery. I think about groceries in curious markets, stolen nights in cheap hotels, games of chess on rusty trains, fights in strange apartments, cocktails we couldn't afford, and a million years of laughter. I think about a summer in France with Savannah. I think about time to mend up the damage that distance has done to us. I think about how even if I can't afford a ticket back to the United States that it doesn't matter. Savannah is home to me.

I hang my laundry on the balcony, now wearing a pair of dusty shorts. I can hear it's gentle dripping as I try to take one last snapshot of the sherbet horizon at sundown. Every one of the thousand things of the world feels small and insignificant while simultaneously containing the entire world. I think about the spinning globe and the people on it dreaming countries into existence. I balance somewhere in the sweetness between laughter and weeping because this year has come and gone.

I have no idea what a country is.

LEAVING HARGEISA

I pack my big red backpack full of clean laundry. I take a last walk through the embassy which now contains three full bedroom sets, two offices, a banquet table, and 12 metal chairs. I say goodbye to Eid who looks surprised to see me go. I thank him as best I can for keeping me as safe as best he could. I hug him because I don't know enough Somali to convey my gratitude. He rolls the metal gate behind me and I crunch down the road towards the Ambassador Hotel.

I wave goodbye to each of the guards and waiters at the hotel as I pass through. I take my last walk down Airport Road toward Wassim's office. This stretch of road that felt so foreign and dangerous to me just a couple of weeks ago now feels like an everyday commute. The end of Ramadan means bustling restaurants, coffee shops full of old men, and busy markets. The world spins forward again after a brief pause to feel hunger and know gratitude.

I don't know if this Ramadan has made me any closer to God, but at least five times a day I have thought about all the things I am grateful for. I've bowed my head in prayer like throwing darts into the sky and hoping they hit a bullseye somewhere behind the clouds. I never felt God speak to me or the urge to attend a megachurch and speak in tongues, but somewhere past my Catholic school upbringing and general California ala carte spirituality I can feel a glimmer of something true, like the glinting of a jewel at the bottom of a dark lake.

God may have been Faithia's sister warning me against going with the men in the alley or in Abdul's exploding tire. He might have been in that first iftar with Yahia or in Eid's flashlight as he checked every room in the embassy for danger. He might have been in Abdulrahman's generosity, or Wassim's intelligence, or the Vice President's security detail. After my first Ramadan I can confidently say that God *might* be there and that he's definitely not nowhere.

I meet Abdulrahman, Cawal, Fathia, and Yahia for one more cup of coffee at Wassim's office. I return the money and receipts to the office safe to be picked up by the next Liberland Ambassador to Somaliland. I give the driver one last hug and hop in Abdulrahman's waiting car. He drives me up the Airport Road in his big black Cadillac. His gold rimmed glasses glint in the early day light as he pulls into the parking lot. He grins at me before opening the door.

"You will come back to Somaliland?" he says.

I can't tell him that I will, in all likelihood, not return to Somaliland and that I will no longer be the ambassador from Liberland. Fortunately, there is a word for times like this.

"Inshallah," I say.

If God wills it.

WE ARE RIGHT HERE

"*Allez les blues!*"

The crowd roars in the small Bar Tabac in Marseille. Savannah and I sit cross legged on the floor watching France battle Croatia for the World Cup. We've spent the summer doing the cheapest possible things in the city which, as it turns out, is an incredible summer in the South of France. We ride bikes to the beach, play chess in cafes, watch public screenings of films. Savannah teaches English online; I write about cryptocurrencies.

"*Bravo! Bravo!*"

"We're going to win Eczu," says Savannah, knocking back a glass of white wine.

We are going to win. The entire bar leans towards the television as if psychically pushing the ball towards the goal. Crackling silence as Kylian Mbappé drives down the pitch towards the Croatian goaltender. We don't care about soccer, we never have, but at this moment, in this tiny bar in Marseille, Savannah and I are cheering with all of France because when a big voice shouts you want to shout with it. *We* are going to win.

"Bravo! Bravo!"

We're surrounded by the Tunisians that run our grocery store and the Afghan refugees who live above us. An Algerian man owns the Bar Tabac. On this humid day, a Paris-born footballer of Cameroonian descent is about to slam home the winning goal. We are all French for just a moment. Mbappe boots the ball down range. The goalkeeper throws himself in the air. The bar lurches towards the screen. The back of a net somewhere in Russia, swishes as a ball hits home.

"Porrrrrrt, Gooooaaaal!"

Savannah and I leap to our feet with everyone else in the bar.

We did it!

We embrace. We embrace everybody else too. The bartender pops a bottle of champagne.

We did it!

Waitresses fill every cup in the place. The doors and windows of every building in the city fling wide open as people pour into the streets and march to party in the port.

We did it.

Savannah and I are taken along by the celebration hugging and high-fiving strangers. The lines between language, nationality and economics are momentarily suspended as *we* are all an *us*. Maybe a country is a place on a map. Maybe it's a memory that we fight to keep alive.

Maybe it's a corrupt business model or a dream of the future. But now, at this moment, the crowd gathers at Vieux Port, people cheer, light fireworks, and dance for nothing and everything all at once. I am not afraid of the world any more. I am uncertain about the future, but in love with its potential because of individuals that make the globe twirl.

Savannah and I link hands and cheer with our momentary countrymen.

I am right here.

The End

Afterword

MAKE STUFF AND DON'T DIE...
THE AFTERWORD

This book was dead until someone tried to kill me. I was hiking outside of Cape Town, South Africa on a public trail. It was a sun-drenched Saturday, and I was having a lovely time tromping along the base of Table Mountain. When I reached the end of the path I doubled back to spend a bit more time picking my way through nature. I didn't realize that I was being watched by the man who would inadvertently help me finish this book.

By this time the manuscript for *You Are Not Here: Travels Through Countries that Don't Exist*, was chucked into the back of a drawer never to be heard from again. After years of wrangling with agents and nearly producing a documentary series based upon the book, all pathways to publication were shut to me. The book was worthless to publishers and I reasoned that it was unwanted by the world. This was a source of great heartache as my year of living stateless became little more than a lengthy bar story.

Then I was attacked.

As I passed under a fallen tree on the hiking trail a voice came from behind me.

Are you alone?

My nerves crackled. I knew something was wrong. A man emerged from the bushes with a surgical mask on his face and a stocking cap pulled low across his brow. I could feel the needle of my limbic system whipping between *fight* or *fly*. I chose to lie. I told the man that I was catching up with friends and tried to move past him.

I saw the flash of a metal as he stepped in close.

CRACK.

Something impacted my skull above my left eye. There is a blank spot in my memory here. It's an indelible black punctuation mark. Then, I heard myself screaming. I didn't recognize my own voice because it sounded distant and animal-like. When my mind caught up with my body I was running down the mountain towards houses in the distance. In back of me was a man with a knife, in front of me was a treacherous rocky incline. This was not a nightmare. I would not wake up from this. My ankle caught a root, sending me tumbling down the mountain.

When I came to a stop I had lost my glasses and torn bloody holes in my clothes. I looked up to see the man with the knife stalking towards me. At this moment I knew that I was going to die. I felt ashamed that after years of tempting fate that my family would find out I'd been stabbed to death on a mountain in South Africa. A singular regret burned neon bright in my chest as I begged whoever was listening for just a little more time. I never published this book and it would die with me.

I had tried to fly, so I decided to fight.

When the man approached me with his knife outstretched, I kicked him in the face sending him to the ground. I mounted my attacker with my forearm pressed across his windpipe and began beating the knife out of his hand. I looked at the man, his eyes were wide and full of fear. His face was covered with blood. It was not his blood but mine which was leaking rapidly from a wound on my head. I had to get off of that mountain. I left my attacker with an injured hand and staggered, mostly blind into the nearby neighborhood in search of aid.

The next day, with my bloody clothes laid out on the floor like a memento mori, I took my manuscript out of the proverbial drawer. That's why this book is in your hands right now. I implore you: Don't wait. Write your book. Paint your masterpiece. Build your company or go on your adventure. The world rewards courage and humbles arrogance. This I know as sure as my fingers are typing now. Whatever bit of unfinished business hangs a bit too heavy on your heart, take this as your sign to release it into the world.

You don't need anyone's permission to fly.

-Eric Czuleger
2023, Tirana, Albania

Acknowledgments

ALL THE PEOPLE THAT DID THIS
WHO WEREN'T ME

Books and countries are not made in isolation. The manuscript that you've just read is the product of an incredible international community that I have been fortunate enough to call friends and colleagues over the years. So, I'd like to take a moment to extend my sincerest gratitude to the following people:

To C.A. Blintzios, Millie Guille, Sam Moore, and Tash Parker who sat me down one Thanksgiving and demanded to know when my book would be finished, here it is, it's done. My dearest friends David Gibson and Deven Simonson, I thank you for your constant support of my bizarre adventures. I can only promise that they will get more bizarre as time goes by. To Joe Hill, a comrade in arms for telling stories on the fringes of the world, one day we will make something really cool together.

I would never have had the opportunity to go on this quest if not for the guidance of incredible teachers and mentors. Peter Moore shepherded me through the first drafts of this work while maintaining a remarkable amount of composure as I did the opposite. Clare Morgan took a chance on allowing me to study Creative Writing at Oxford. Anna

Beer thought my crazy ideas were worthy of exploring and she has my undying gratitude for this. My mentor in geopolitics George Friedman taught me enough to be dangerous and fired so I could pursue my passion. Thank you, George.

Strange though it may be, I'd like to thank the city of Tirana Albania which has been my home for a significant portion of my adult life. If it weren't for being able to sit and type for hours at your coffee shops and bars this book would have never gotten done. With that being said a huge thank you to my Albanian community, Sara Kraja, Azra Kraja, Misuela Shimaj, Albana Meta, and the many others who listened to me complain about this work non-stop for literally years.

I'd like to thank the first people that had eyes on my work and my life in its various stages of disrepair. My mother, Rebecca Forster, is now and always has been my first line of defense against nonsense in writing and life. Also, I apologize for doing all of these things which put me in mortal danger, but thank you for understanding. To my father Stephen Czuleger, thank you for checking my history and instilling a love of travel deep within me. My brother Alex Czuleger has been a remarkable anchor and constant source of inspiration throughout my travels. Thank you all, I'll be home soon.

Will Hamilton has been a remarkable editor and friend throughout the latter portions of this work and I am eternally grateful for his thoughts and encouragement. Lizzie Lewis, one of my oldest friends and greatest supporters, I thank you from the bottom of my heart for your wisdom and humor. I also want to thank all of the people who helped me along my journey especially Astefanos Dalakta, Cawal Naleeye Sahal, Savannah Fortis, Jack Butcher, Leonora Aliu, Eraldin Fazliu, Atdhe Mulla, Era Buza, Sokol Buza, Hans, Tom, Tariq, Vit, and Mike I could have done none of this without you.

Eric Czuleger's fascination with travel, history, and politics began as a Peace Corps Volunteer in Albania. After service, he completed his first circle of the globe. Returning to the U.S. he worked as a barista, yoga instructor, intelligence analyst, journalist, and tech storyteller. Eric spent his year of statelessness while completing his MSt in creative writing at Oxford University. He's lived, worked, and traveled through 47 countries and climbed two of the seven summits. Czuleger is the author of <u>Eternal L.A.</u>, and <u>Immortal L.A.</u> To follow on Twitter and Instagram: Eczuleger